INDIAN SUMMERS

Gideon Haigh is the world's pre-eminent cricket writer. In a career spanning more than forty years he has written in *The Australian, The Times, The Guardian, The Cricketer,* and in more than thirty books including *On Warne, Mystery Spinner* and *The Cricket War.* He now writes and podcasts for *cricketetal.com*

GIDEON HAIGH
INDIAN SUMMERS

AUSTRALIA VERSUS INDIA
CRICKET'S BATTLE OF THE TITANS

ALLEN&UNWIN
SYDNEY · MELBOURNE · AUCKLAND · LONDON

First published in 2024

Grateful acknowledgement is given for permission to reprint p. 140 excerpt
from 'To John Berry Hobbs on his seventieth birthday' by John Arlott, 1952.
Reprinted with the permission of Tim Arlott.

Allen & Unwin
Cammeraygal Country
83 Alexander Street
Crows Nest NSW 2065
Australia
Phone: (61 2) 8425 0100
Email: info@allenandunwin.com
Web: www.allenandunwin.com

*Allen & Unwin acknowledges the Traditional Owners of the Country
on which we live and work. We pay our respects to all Aboriginal and
Torres Strait Islander Elders, past and present.*

 A catalogue record for this
book is available from the
National Library of Australia

ISBN 978 1 76147 213 8

Set in 11/15.5 pt Stone Serif ITC Pro by Midland Typesetters, Australia
Printed and bound in Australia by the Opus Group

10 9 8 7 6 5 4 3 2 1

Contents

CONTENTS

Introduction

Australia and India share a national day, 26 January, and a national game, cricket. Apart from that, maybe not so much: Australia is thinly populated, India densely; while Australia still defers to a foreign head of state, India has sloughed off its colonial masters. But what overlaps goes deep. The cricket votaries of both countries imagine themselves uniquely passionate. Ashis Nandy thought cricket an Indian game accidentally discovered by the English; John Curtin insisted that 'Lord's and its traditions belong to Australia just as much as England'. And few things are so uniting as having been on the receiving end of English condescension.

For all that, the cricket rivalry of Australia and India was a long time maturing to its present intensity. In the twentieth century, the teams spread fifty-seven Tests over fifty-four years, Australia prevailing twenty-eight times and India eleven times; in twenty-three years of the twenty-first century, they have already played fifty Tests, Australia securing seventeen wins and India twenty-one. In nearly a century and a half of Test cricket, Australia have grown used to being top dog. Not since the West

1

Indies at their peak has another team sustained such a lengthy plus record against them, although Australia have also edged India in two World Cup finals separated by twenty years.

This skews their history to recency. Indians and Australians never saw some of the greatest players their rivals had to offer. There were twenty years between the first two Indian tours of Australia, then another decade until the third. Illness cost Vijay Merchant his only opportunity to play here; Sanjay Manjrekar made it, but not his father, Vijay; Polly Umrigar came as a tour manager but not as a player. Donald Bradman famously got no closer to Indians than passing through Kolkata en route to England in June 1953, when an army car had to spirit him away from the thousand well-wishers who breached a police cordon; Greg Chappell and Dennis Lillee coached extensively in India without ever representing Australia against them. On the other hand, Michael Clarke played almost a fifth of his Tests in the Border–Gavaskar Trophy, while Steve Smith has paid India more than a score of visits as an international and franchise cricketer.

Thus, on the eve of the first full-dress five-Test series between India and Australia in more than three decades, in which the former will defend the Border–Gavaskar Trophy they have held since 2017, this collage of my writings about the countries' cricket relations. It's not comprehensive, in that it is unashamedly biased to their red ball rivalry and reflects my intersections with it. But I hope I'll be pardoned: few Australian summers do I recall so nostalgically as 1977–78, for the simple reason that there was cricket on two television channels not one, and because one of those channels was broadcasting Test matches involving a fabulously exotic team of Indians featuring the likes of Bishan Bedi, Sunil Gavaskar, Gundappa Viswanath, Mohinder Amarnath, Bhagwat Chandrasekhar and Syed Kirmani. All of them became favourites; with Kirmani I was thrilled to discover I shared a birthday. Come to think of it, the first piece I submitted about a cricketer to a newspaper was a tribute to Gavaskar that I posted to the *Geelong Advertiser*. They had the kindness not to run it.

If there were any grounds for complaint in those days, it was that India did not come to Australia often enough and that games in India were invisible on Australian television. And when at last we *did* glimpse cricket in India, India were *not playing* – rather were Australia besting England in the 1987 World Cup final. Still, the game *was* at Kolkata's legendary Eden Gardens and Eden Gardens looked *awesome*. No wonder Steve Waugh's Australians hankered to play there in 2001, even if it did not go so well for them.

All of which represents rather a contrast to today when there's almost a risk of the countries wearying of one another, even if their administrators and bankers never will, and when the Australians many Indian fans know best are those who turn out for their Indian Premier League franchises. David Warner probably has more fans in India than Australia – scratch that, he *certainly* does. Still, there is much here to conjure with. In some respects, Australia has replaced Pakistan as India's favourite competitor, while India's stars have in Australia proved at least as alluring as England's. Australians can claim to have watched Virat Kohli grow up, maturing from the enfant terrible of 2011 into the mellow, metrosexual dad of today.

My selection is centred on eminent players, from Bradman and Hazare to Ponting and Tendulkar, and memorable games, from the great Australian moments of the second Tied Test and Pune 2017, to the Indian triumphs of Kolkata 2001 and Brisbane 2021. The first section, covering the first twenty years of touring, when Australians saw India as mainly a hardship posting, is drawn largely from my book *The Summer Game*; the other three sections, chronicling the relationship's growing significance, are composed largely of reports, essays and columns previously published by *Wisden, Cricinfo, The Cricketer, The Australian, The Guardian, The Age, Tortoise, Sports Illustrated India* and my substack *Cricket Et Al*. Last year's World Test Championship and World Cup finals and this year's showdown in the Super Eights of the T20 World Cup bring us up to date, ready for this summer's action. What comes next, who knows? The message from this book is that it will have a lot to live up to.

GIDEON HAIGH
Melbourne 2024

NEW WORLDS TO CONQUER

The first forty years of cricket interchanges between India and Australia began with the visit to India of a private Australian tour organised by the ubiquitous Anglo-Australian cricketer and sporting impresario Frank Tarrant. This section commences with a foreword I contributed to an excellent history of that unlikely venture. Another twenty years would elapse before an official visit, although India had in the meantime been invited to send a cricket team to Australia, around the time of Partition. Travel to the subcontinent involved as much hardship then as it does luxury now. For decades, Australian travellers would return with tales of hostile crowds, crummy umpiring, starvation diets, sub-standard accommodation . . . and also unforgettable experiences.

Frank Tarrant's 1935–36 Australians
PIONEER DAYS (2023)

Before 'Dada', Sourav Ganguly, there was 'Daddy', as Frank Tarrant was known to the Indian cricket community for whom he was an ambassador to the cricket world. Australian-born, England-made, Tarrant was a cultural intermediary before anyone thought in such terms, and, at last, in Megan Ponsford's excellent book, has a literary testament to his greatest coup.

Megan is not only the granddaughter of Bill Ponsford, runmaker extraordinaire, but the great niece of Tom Leather, who played a handful of games for Victoria in the 1930s. An incongruous presence for many years in Tom's modest suburban unit in Melbourne was a tiger skin – a souvenir, it turned out, of the long-forgotten ensemble of Australian cricketers whom Frank Tarrant assembled to tour India in 1935–36. It was the first such tour of its kind, and outside official auspices, disavowed by the authorities and neglected by *Wisden Cricketers' Almanack*.

Captivated by the romantic improbability of the expedition, Megan has spent a decade following its historical traces and recreating its world – the India of the Raj, of the Anglophile

Chamber of Princes, of not just Maharajahs but Maharawats, Nawabs, Yuvrajs and Zamindars. At its centre sits Tarrant, who turned a successful career as a county professional for Middlesex into an even more successful career as a factotum of the Maharajahs of Patiala, Jodhpur and Cooch Behar, ostentatious enthusiasts for cricket and racing. Perhaps by virtue of his Australianness, Tarrant had a knack for moving seamlessly between occident and orient, and Megan's cinematic eye suggests that the whole saga is worthy of *Save Your Legs!* treatment: he was accompanied on the tour by his wife, Eva, a 'bosomy sofa of a woman', and son, Bert, a ne'er-do-well 'ambitiously listed on the Australian electoral role as an "actor"'. There were other Australians flourishing improbably in 1930s India, from the actress Mary Ann Evans (who as Fearless Nadia was a star of Indian cinema), to Sydney Cup–winning jockey Ray Wilson (whose saddle-shaped tombstone I recently encountered in my local cemetery). The peripatetic cricket coach Frank Warne was there also, six decades in advance of his namesake.

Megan has unearthed a wonderful variety of primary sources, so that we hear of the cricketers' experiences, as it were, first-hand. The team featured some cricketers of renown including Charlie Macartney, Jack Ryder, Stork Hendry and Ron Oxenham, albeit somewhat past their prime and maybe a little rough round the edges. They played very well too, despite the distractions, the exoticism and the epicureanism: it is hard not to smile at the story of the team trying to souvenir the gold dinner plates of the royal court of Jamnagar before shamefacedly giving them back. They kept politics at arm's length, declining an invitation to meet Gandhi, but kept faith with egalitarian values, declining invitations to join any club that maintained a colour bar. Like many subsequent teams, they had varying health fortunes: Frank Bryant gained weight; Arthur Allsopp spent ten weeks in hospital. They returned at the end with priceless memories and, like Leather, mementos: Ryder a panther skin, Hendry an alabaster model of the Taj Mahal, Ron Morrisby a portrait of the Maharajah of Patiala that for decades surmounted his dining room fireplace and must have intrigued visitors to his Tasmanian family orchard. Tarrant christened his country property Jodhpur Estate, although it proved harder to act the squire in Victoria than in India.

Tarrant, Megan reminds us, blazed his trail in the face of administrative indifference, if not hostility. Macartney called the Australia Board 'cricket Hitlers', which if not as much of an insult in 1935 as it sounds now was still a pretty strong sentiment. Canny chancer that he was, Daddy was well ahead of the curve, sensing the potential tapped in our generation by the Board of Control for Cricket in India and its T20 cash machine. In the same way Kerry Packer anticipated Lalit Modi, Daddy can perhaps be thought to lead to Dada.

* Foreword to *The Has-Beens and Never-Will-Bes* by Megan Ponsford (Taylor & Francis), 2023.

Bradman and Hazare

THIS LITTLE SUCCESS OF MINE (2024)

The feat of twin hundreds in a Test match is rare – far rarer than two hundreds themselves. More than 200 batters have scored double centuries; only seventy-seven have twice got started, twice pushed on, twice consolidated and twice thrust successfully for three figures. There lies the challenge. One must do everything twice, fighting tiredness and satiety as well as riding chance and luck. Test cricket had been underway more than three decades before the deed was first done; even during the run-soaked 1920s and 1930s it occurred seldom. Then two batters accomplished the feat in consecutive Tests, from the oldest Test nation and the newest. No prize for guessing that Donald Bradman was the thirteenth to the achievement; but it's worth remembering that the fourteenth, Vijay Hazare, was representing a country independent for less than half a year. And while Bradman's accomplishment has tended to be swallowed up in the totality of his records, Hazare's represented, as Mihir Bose puts it, 'the first truly international cricket feat by an Indian'.

Vijay Hazare   Lala Amarnath

India's first cricket summer in Australia, 1947–48, was long, hot and damp. Bad weather dogged the tourists. They were ambushed on wet wickets at the Gabba and the Melbourne Cricket Ground, and washed out of the Test at the Sydney Cricket Ground between times. But the greatest deluge was runs, which poured from Bradman's bat in abundance: over summer he took the tourists for a total of 1081 runs at an average of 135.12, his eight hundreds for the season an Australian record. One of these, for the Australian XI, was his hundredth in first-class cricket; his single innings in Brisbane was then more than India eked from both all-out totals. There was a sense of Bradman mortaring his twenty years of statistical bricks. Hundreds in both innings of a Test match, Irving Rosenwater noted, was the 'one honour that had thus far eluded Don Bradman in his phenomenal Test career'. He ushered in the new year at Melbourne by filling that gap with a chanceless 132 in 197 minutes and

127 not out in 178 minutes, in the process also passing 6000 Test runs and 25,000 first-class runs.

To this stage, the Indians had registered little with the Australian public, and in some ways it was remarkable they had arrived at all, with the Punjab in the process of being bloodily divided during their preparations for departure. Partition cost India the future services of the pace bowler Fazal Mahmood and opening batter Hanif Mohammad, destined to excel for Pakistan. Vijay Merchant, Mushtaq Ali and Rusi Modi were also, for various reasons, not selected, and the team that did go found turf pitches difficult to assimilate after long careers on matting. In Vinoo Mankad and Dattu Phadkar they had tireless all-rounders, but their captain, Lala Amarnath, and their other batting star, Gil Mohammad, had no impact on the Tests despite scoring freely against the states. Then there was Hazare, at thirty-two years of age the so-called 'Bradman of India', albeit in a lower key and at a slower tempo.

When first they met, in the interstate match, Hazare peeled off 95 and Bradman 156. Bradman was 'very impressed by the soundness ... and the correctness of his stroke production', noting only that Hazare's lack of aggression 'prevented him taking advantage of an attack and tearing it to pieces'. Ironically, Hazare in defending his routine circumspection was wont to invoke Bradman. On his first visit to England as part of a Rajputana side in 1938, he had watched Bradman at Trent Bridge and Lord's play with great deliberation, ignoring the catcalls and the critics alike. 'He and other Australians several times drew away from the wicket when loud booing started as the Australian batsmen faced a bowler,' Hazare recalled. 'He just shelved all the attacking strokes and contented himself with playing out time.'

If he had but known it, Bradman had already another impact on Hazare's career, by being party to Clarrie Grimmett's exclusion from that Australian team – one of history's most controversial omissions, described by Bill O'Reilly as a 'dereliction of selection responsibilities' that left him 'heartbroken'. Rather than languish at home, Grimmett had accepted a lucrative invitation to coach in India from the Rajah of Jath, and in doing so made the acquaintance of the studious Hazare, shortly to break every record during the wartime Quadrangulars and Pentangulars. Hazare became the most devoted of disciples and never forgot the debt he owed his 'guru', writing to Grimmett during his highly successful Indian tour of England in 1946:

> Let me note here that this little success of mine in the cricket
> sphere is entirely due to your valuable instructions which
> I will never forget, at least in this life. I will also be thankful
> to you if you will in future, as in the past, kindly help me by
> giving necessary instructions.

The relationship between players and their coaches in India is, and remains, uniquely deferential. Sachin Tendulkar's mentor, Ramakant Achrekar, is shortly to be the subject of a biopic; Virat Kohli gave his instructor, Rajkumar Sharma, a car. But the relationship between Hazare and Grimmett remains particularly fascinating for its transnational nature and its ardency. For Grimmett championed Hazare: he let everyone know how good the young man was, quite openly barracked for him. Which didn't always make life easy. Hazare was earnest, stoical, never happier than when oiling his bat, applying lime to his pads or polishing his boots. The back cover of his autobiography, *Cricket Replayed*, features neither blurb nor action photo, but a simple nostrum: 'A true cricketer submits to fate without complaint'. But he approached the Test in Grimmett's home city of Adelaide with a tincture of dread: 'I had another worry.

My cricketing GURU, Clarrie Grimmett, was all the while singing my praises and told them of my doings at home.'

Hazare had first to survive two days in the field, prolonged by Amarnath dropping Bradman at slip on 2, which in five hours he inflated to 201. Hazare finally bowled Bradman with his pawky seamers, as he had in Sydney, but India went into the sabbath rest day on two for 6 chasing 674. They were five for 133 before Hazare was able to rally resistance, finding a sound partner in the all-rounder Dattu Phadkar, and the 105-degree day drew the sting from Australia's attack. Hazare reached three figures ten minutes from stumps, his eventual 116 taking four and a half hours, and the sixth wicket raising 188.

India's innings of 381 had both failed to reach to follow-on and to satisfy Hazare. 'He [Grimmett] was watching me throughout the Test,' he recalled. 'I had the uncomfortable feeling of a schoolboy appearing for a practical examination before stern examiners. I had to vindicate my GURU.' When Bradman threw Indian straight back in, the opportunity was quickly upon him, Mankad and Amarnath falling in the first over. But Hazare saw off those other stern examiners Ray Lindwall and Keith Miller by standing up to them, hooking consecutive bouncers from the latter to the fence. When Bradman would not give him another leg-side catcher, in fact, Miller refused to bowl anything other than off-breaks. Hazare took advantage and reached his second hundred in the last over of the fourth day with an on-drive to the fence off Sid Barnes. He was last out for 145 in 313 minutes as Australia completed another innings victory.

For some, summer was all a bit too pitiless. 'Bradman has played this series of Tests in a very austere fashion,' wrote Victor Richardson in Kolkata's *Illustrated News*, 'and the Indian team has been given no quarter or privilege of any kind and has battled against a team eager to win by as big a margin as possible on every occasion.' But Hazare had no complaints: after the match he was gifted a gold cigarette case by India's high commissioner which he carried the rest of his life – empty, he being a non-smoker. Nor did his guru. Dining with his disciple after the Test at Dundula, in suburban Firle, Grimmett glowed with satisfaction. 'Vijay,' he said, 'I am a very proud man today.'

In light of his achievements, Hazare was excused India's next fixture, in Mildura against Victorian Country. But it was in that unlikely setting that the Indians learned the stunning news of the loss of their own national guru. On the way to a late-afternoon prayer meeting in Delhi, Mahatma Gandhi had been shot by a Hindu extremist, Nathuram Godse. The cricket team's manager, Pankaj Gupta, described it as a 'national catastrophe', and reported his players as grief stricken: 'We have been stunned. None of us could get any sleep last night. We just sat around sadly listening to the All-India radio. Some of us wept at the news.' It is hard to see Hazare as one of these. His devotions were Catholicism and cricket; as Vijay Merchant put it: 'Net practice was a matter of religion to him.' All the same, the team were so shaken that there was thought of calling off the tour. In the event, the Fifth Test in Melbourne was preluded by a minute's silence for the Mahatma – perhaps the first time that the death of a non-British leader had been so honoured in Australia. 'The Indian players seemed to lose heart in the final game,' thought Bradman – perhaps it is no wonder.

Bradman himself had by then clarified his own future. The night before the Test, he had announced his availability for the forthcoming tour of England. 'I have today advised my co-selectors that I am available for the Australian tour of England,' he told journalists, reading from a statement. 'At the same time I wish to say that the game against India will be my last first-class match in Australia, as I shall retire from cricket at the conclusion of the English tour.' Invincibility beckoned.

Of the summer past he was content to observe: 'One is not ungenerous to say the Indians were not quite equal to the task.'

The scoreboard, showing 0–4 Australia's way, would tend to support his argument. Bose goes further, arguing that Hazare's hundreds provided Indians with too much solace: 'The whole tour became just a case of Hazare scoring a hundred in each innings. In years to come it set a precedent. Indians would come back from a wretched overseas tour blocking any memory of defeat and the humiliations by concentrating on the odd moments of individual glory.' Still, by hinting that Indians could stand comparison with the most exalted company, Hazare provided a glimmer of the future: seventy years later, India would begin their first successful series campaign in Australia with victory at Adelaide Oval.

Australian Tours of India 1956-57 and 1959-60

BENAUD'S MISSION (1996)

As the 1958–59 Ashes series wound to its conclusion, players could not help thinking of their next international engagement. For those who'd been on the brief stopover three years earlier, the prospect of eight Tests in Pakistan and India made them uneasy. Johnson's Australians had arrived in Karachi from Rome in October 1956 after a fortnight break in Europe, and been horror-struck by conditions. Everything was weirdly alien: the heat, the dust, the low-bouncing matting surface on which they lost the Karachi Test, the tendentious umpiring, the untrustworthy food.

Everyone had fallen ill, especially Gil Langley (hepatitis) and Benaud (dengue fever) in Madras. Jim Burke was so adamant he'd not return now that he retired, and others thought about absenting themselves. But think about it was all they did after a report from Alan Davidson during the Fourth Test at Adelaide Oval. Davidson was returning from the nets when he saw Bradman and thought he'd head over for a chat. After exchanging pleasantries, he popped the question: 'Don, is it compulsory to go to India and Pakistan?'

'You've retired, have you?' Bradman replied, quick as a flash. Davidson gulped, 'Err, no, Don. I haven't.'

'That's good to hear,' the Don continued genially. 'And, when you get back to the rooms, you might tell them what I've just told you.'

When Benaud's side was named on 10 March 1959, the captain at once set to work. However players regarded it, the journey would be a huge challenge: Pakistan, notably, was unbeaten on home soil.

Benaud was a fastidious planner. In the hiatus between the England and India legs of the 1956 tour, for instance, he'd asked BBC Light Entertainment boss Tom Sloan if he could take a three-week television production course. While teammates cruised the continent, Benaud spent thirteen hours a day observing drama, comedy and sport go to air, culminating in a day at Newbury watching the peerless race-caller Peter O'Sullevan. Not that Benaud intended going into television: it just 'might be handy to know something about it in later years'. For Pakistan and India, Benaud thought, health would be paramount. He recommended that the Australian board advertise for a medical officer, and Colin McDonald's elder brother Ian was chosen from a short-list. Some political fore-knowledge would also be useful, and Benaud wrote to Menzies:

I have no doubt that, in addition to cricket on this tour there will be a certain amount of diplomatic importance attached to the 14 weeks we are abroad. I know that you are an extremely busy man and the matter probably comes under Mr Casey's department [external affairs] in any case. However, if possible, I would appreciate a few lines of briefing perhaps from Mr Casey or someone in the department on particular aspects of relations between India, Pakistan and our own country.

Menzies did better: four weeks before departure, Benaud received a formal briefing from an assistant secretary in the Department of External Affairs, Peter Heydon, who had just returned from four years as Australian high commissioner in India. Most critical, however, were the pitches Australia would play on. Three years before at Karachi, the coir mats had nullified Lindwall and Miller, but proved ideal for the brilliant Pakistani medium-pacers Fazal Mahmood and Khan Mohammed. The Pakistan board was now promising turf pitches, but Benaud was wary. As the team gathered in Brisbane on 29 October 1959 for a preliminary match marking Queensland cricket's centenary, Benaud ordered four consecutive early morning practices on mats. If his team failed, it wouldn't be for want of preparation.

At the Gabba, Benaud met his manager: erstwhile Test all-rounder and now honourable member for Prahran, Sam Loxton. His had been an unexpected choice: he was the first manager since the war who was not a member of the Australian board. But then, the subcontinent had a reputation among administrators almost as fearful as its reputation among players. 'I got the job mainly because I'd been there with the Commonwealth XI in 1953–54,' Loxton recalls. 'And also because, what board member would be silly enough to go there? They called for nominations and I'm not sure they got any apart from me.'

Thoughts of such a gruff, soldierly man acting the diplomat had caused great ribaldry. At the Prime Minister's XI match dinner, Hassett had told the audience: 'I would advise Mr Menzies to have army and navy standing by. A week after Sam gets to India, war is bound to break out between the two countries.' But Loxton had also approached his task methodically. He'd written to Menzies himself, requesting customs clearance for 400 dozen cans of beer: they were forwarded to Ray Gullick, senior trade commissioner in Delhi. And he'd digested strict instructions from the Australian board's treasurer, Bill Dowling:

19

he should not allow any Test to proceed until presented with a receipt for the telegraphic transfer of £6500.

'No dough, no play?' Loxton asked.

'That's what I'm saying, Sam,' Dowling said. 'You are also under no circumstances to hold out any hope of an invitation to Pakistan from Australia.'

'What you're saying is that we can't afford to have them here,' replied Loxton. 'Understood.'

India would be trying. After Australia won the First Test at Delhi in a canter, the Board of Control for Cricket in India became difficult to deal with. When they were late delivering their telegraphic receipt for the Second Test match guarantee at Kanpur on 19 December, Loxton honoured his promise to Dowling and confronted the BCCI's assistant secretary.

The Indian was evasive: 'Do not let us spoil a beautiful friendship over money.'

'Try me,' Loxton barked. 'I want it please. I have instructed Richie that no player is to get togged until I have the money.'

'But what about the game?' queried the official.

'That's not my problem,' Loxton replied. 'You know the rules.'

Loxton's receipt arrived just in time for the match to commence, but most of the Australians wished it hadn't. Davidson (12/124) bowled incisively on a crumbling pitch, but Jasu Patel, a thirty-five-year-old Gujarati off-spinner with a suspiciously cocked elbow, swept India to its first victory against Australia with 14/124.

It was, players agreed, the harshest cricket environment they'd encountered. The umpiring had to be borne philosophically. The heat was stifling. Davidson, bowling fifty overs a Test, was in the process of losing 26 pounds (12 kilograms): 'At the end of the day I'd be a bloody zombie. I just kept telling myself: "Back foot front arm."' The noise never abated, whether it was the explosion of crackers or the clunk of the bottles that flew at the faintest provocation. The relentless press of the crowds, the spartan accommodation and incipient paranoia about the food gnawed nerves.

Christmas was spent pleasantly enough at Kanpur's Kumula Retreat, a rambling estate owned by Sir Padampat Singhania, whose precincts were roamed by monkeys, green kingfishers and peacocks, but few fancied the food. 'I had two Jatz crackers with peanut butter and a can of Foster's,' remembers Burge. 'And I didn't normally drink. I'd just got sick of Coca-Cola.'

While the Australians played their next match at Ahmedabad against a Universities XI, their lodgings were a hostelry called the Hotel Ritz: a reconditioned prison whose foyer featured an unlikely endorsement from the Duke of Edinburgh. Says Jarman: 'Gavin Stevens and I were taken to what they called "the stable wing". And that's what it was: a stable. There was a dirt floor with a mat on it, no glass on the windows, just bars, two old wooden beds. We said: "No thanks." We carried the beds to the foyer, which was this cement floor painted green, and slept there with Wally Pugh [Australian Associated Press] and Michael Charlton [ABC].'

In some degree, it was character-forming. 'You couldn't help but be shaken,' says Ian Meckiff. 'The huge extremes of poverty to wealth, the number of people when you walked down the street. I think I learned more about life in three months on the subcontinent than I have in all the rest of my days.' Gordon Rorke agrees: 'There's no doubt I came back a different person. Living in Australia, we just had no idea. I came back with a huge appreciation of how lucky we were.' But it could also be deeply unsettling. In Bangalore, Doc McDonald, Gavin Stevens and Charlton visited a birth-control clinic. Stevens recalls: 'The guy who picked us up drove past this body by the side of the road.

21

We all asked whether he shouldn't stop, but he didn't take any notice. When we were coming back, the same body was lying there, and we were a bit more insistent. But he said: "No. He is all right." All right with the Lord, I think.'

Charlton, a perceptive, eloquent man, was intrigued by the cricketers' struggles to assimilate their environment:

> There could have been no greater contrast than that between the Australians with their muscular, rather strident culture, their breadth and uncomplication, and the extraordinarily intricate geology of hierarchies, huge and minute, in India. The Australians were inclined to do things like put their arm round a bearer and call him mate, then not understand why this was thought unusual.

But Charlton had problems too. He was striving to arrange an interview with Indian Prime Minister Jawaharlal Nehru. They'd made provisional arrangements at the Test in Delhi, but finalising matters using Benaud's Bombay room phone proved frustrating. Benaud recalls:

> Michael was as unflappable as they come, but at the end of half an hour explaining that 'no his name was Charlton, not Nehru, and he was in Bombay, not Delhi', he snapped and started shouting and threw the telephone across the room against the concrete wall with a run of expletives I never imagined could come from a true blue ABC and BBC man.

When Charlton finally pinned his subject down, it afforded an insight into cricket's primacy in the subcontinent: 'We went and filmed an interview at his home there on very short magazines of very bad film. To my shame, I'd not realised just how much he loved cricket. On his desk, surrounded by huge piles of paper, was a colour photo of him opening the batting for Harrow.' In India, all roads led to cricket.

Then came the illness Benaud had always feared. First victim was the tall, raw-boned Rorke, who had found the diet of dry toast, bananas and fried fish especially gruelling. His mother had sent him a Christmas cake at Delhi but, once reclaimed from customs and cut into twenty pieces, it had vanished quickly. One day at Delhi, Rorke turned to Kline and said miserably: 'Spinner, I'm hungry.'

'Steady on, Gordon,' Kline replied. 'You know what the Doc says. We're not allowed to eat any of the salads.'

Kline looked away momentarily and, when he turned back, found Rorke heedlessly tucking in. The paceman bowled but two overs on the first day of the ensuing Kanpur Test, left the field, and was obviously not up to more. He cabbed to the ground and volunteered to bat when Australia was collapsing in its second innings, but Benaud insisted: 'Don't even think about it.'

And that evening, Rorke could think of nothing but the toilet. 'I must have been forty times,' he remembers. 'My room-mate Burgey couldn't believe it, and we almost had a fight about it. Not that, at the time, I could have lifted a pin.' Rorke was admitted to an Ahmedabad military hospital for a blood and stool test which diagnosed hepatitis, then was taken in by a Salvation Army doctor and his pregnant wife. 'I had no idea what was going on,' Rorke recalls. 'Beyond the fact that I felt incredibly weak and my eyes were bright yellow. I moved into this beautiful old Indian house and they put me in a bedroom upstairs.' It was a remarkable act of kindness, as Rorke discovered when the doctor knocked on the door after a couple of days and asked: 'Gordon, I have to ask you a favour. Can you move downstairs? My wife is about to have a baby.'

In ten days' convalescence while the manager organised his home passage Rorke shed three stone (20 kilograms). When Rorke's BOAC Comet landed in Sydney, Mosman cricket official Keith Johnson barely recognised him. He told Rorke's mother and girlfriend: 'Brace yourselves. You'll get a shock when you see him.' Rorke languished six months in bed and the disappointment hit him hard: 'I'd put so much work into that tour. I'd gone to the gym, I'd done miles, I'd built myself right up. And it all disappeared in three days.' He'd played his last Test.

Staying at Brabourne Stadium for the Third Test, Loxton and McDonald had another responsibility foisted on them. It began comically. Loxton recalls:

I had all the booze and the soft drink in my room in a big tub with ice, and my door was always open. Nothing'd wake me up. The idea was that, if anybody got thirsty during the night, they could come into my room and get what they wanted. This particular night at the end of the day's play, the boys were sitting on my bed having some Foster's, and I said finally: 'Right, that's it. Off my bloody bed! You lot can do what you like, but I'm for sleepy-byes.' Then, about 4.00 am, there was a loud banging on my door, so I jumped out of bed . . . and I must have knocked over a pyramid of cans three or four feet tall, every single bloody can. The din was incredible: these bloody tin cans banging and rolling round on the concrete floor. That bloody Grout. Anyway, I went and opened the door and who should it be but Arthur Mailey? I'm standing there flabbergasted and all he says is: 'I see now why we lost at Kanpur.'

Seventy-four-year-old Mailey had been despatched by the *Daily Telegraph* to discover how Australia had lost its first Test to India.

But Doc McDonald was appalled: 'My heart sank. Arthur was a lovely man, but over seventy, and I thought: "This is no place for him." Sure enough, within a couple of days, he was very ill. I took him to the hospital and we organised a flight home. Poor Arthur. He saw no cricket at all on that trip.'

A week later in Madras, the night before the Fourth Test, it was the turn of twenty-seven-year-old South Australian opener Gavin Stevens. He recalls: 'The boys were all going to the cinema that night, but I suddenly felt a bit sick so I said to the Doc: "Look, I'm not too well. I think I'll go home." Pretty soon, I was throwing up, and crawling across the room to the toilet.'

Roommate Jarman discovered him and bolted for Doc McDonald, shouting: 'Hurry up, Doc! I think he's gonna die.' Stevens had acute hepatitis. Next morning, Benaud, Harvey and Colin McDonald came to see him. Stevens heard one of them say matter-of-factly: 'Well, he can't play.' Stevens was confined to bed for ten days. He was too weak to leave for Calcutta with the team and implored Wally Pugh not to write anything home about his condition that might upset his wife – Pugh refrained.

Eventually, Stevens persuaded reluctant medical staff to book him a flight, and he was the one white face on a Vickers Viscount that left Madras the next day. By the time he rejoined the team, another player had gone. Kline had been invalided home with hepatitis – to the surprise of his wife, Stella, who read of his repatriation in the newspaper and hurried to collect him from Essendon Airport.

Indeed, Stevens watched one morning as the Australians took the field with ten men. He hastily called the hotel: Meckiff, who relied on Kline as his alarm clock, had overslept. 'They've just gone out on the field and realised that you weren't there,' Stevens said. 'You better get down here sharpish.' Meckiff recalls: 'Yes, I was a big hit in Calcutta. I think Rich gave me a few extra overs that day to make sure I didn't do it again.'

Stevens' ambition of leaving India with his mates was hard won: 'By the time I got to Sydney I was wrecked, in really bad shape. Les Favell's parents were there, fortunately, so I stayed with them for a while. I can't even remember getting back to Adelaide and seeing my wife again.' Stevens played no further first-class cricket. When he saw Harvey again twenty-five years later, Harvey said: 'You were unlucky, Gav. You could've been the most famous man in the history of cricket.'

'Yeah?' said Stevens. 'How come?'

Harvey answered: 'You could've been the first man to die on tour.'

Despite it all, Australia prevailed. O'Neill, Harvey, Favell and Grout guaranteed the better of draws at Brabourne and at Eden Gardens, while Benaud's 8/86 underwrote an innings victory at Corporation Stadium. Benaud also received high marks for diplomacy and sportsmanship. Australia's high commissioner in Delhi, Walter Crocker, informed Menzies that the team had been 'a magnificent advertisement . . . putting us more firmly on the map than all our other efforts rolled into one'. It had again been a triumph of team spirit. Friendships formed were lasting. When Favell's first son was born three months after his return, he named him Alan for his roommate Davidson. When Jarman's arrived twelve months later, he named him Gavin after his roommate Stevens. Jarman also sponsored the immigration to Australia of Pakistan's young Anglo-Indian batsman Duncan Sharpe.

Nonetheless, it was probably fortunate that the tour ended when it did. By the Fifth Test in Calcutta on 23 January 1960, the longest fuses had burned short. Harvey recalls: 'Col and Ian McDonald had been giving us lectures all through the tour: "Come on, fellas, be nice to these people. We're all diplomats on this tour." But even Col got fed up at Calcutta. We had this bloke lbw twice, plumb, and he was given not out. We were all still fuming when Davo bowls him neck and crop, off stump, and Col runs all the way from the fine leg boundary and kicks the remaining stumps over and says: "That must have been bloody close."'

Australians in India 1964

X VERSUS XIII (1996)

After two weeks' motoring on the continent, the Australians converged on Rome's Ciampino Airport for the flight to Bombay on 30 September 1964. And they were not long on the subcontinent before the usual grievances emerged. After the luxuries of English hotels, accommodation seemed squalid. After the gentility of English audiences, the combustible Indian crowds had to be treated with great care. At one practice before thousands of locals, Jarman referred to Ian Redpath by his nickname of 'Gandhi'. Hundreds of heads swivelled: Redpath was 'Redders' for the rest of the trip. In contrast to the uniform excellence of English umpiring, too, Indian arbiters seemed at best incompetent, at worst partisan. Even the committed Christian Brian Booth found it hard to bear when he was given out stumped for 74 off Bapu Nadkarni at Brabourne Stadium: 'I came down and missed it, and I was ready to keep walking. But the ball had jumped and it bounced off the keeper's chest back down the wicket, so I thought: "You beauty." Then, as I was walking back into my crease, the keeper whipped the bails off with his glove and appealed. Out.'

After a workmanlike 139-run victory in the First Test at Madras underpinned by Graham McKenzie's 10/91, this Second Test at Bombay against the Nawab of Pataudi's side was a travail. As Bob Simpson and Bill Lawry were padding up to open on the first morning, Norm O'Neill keeled over clutching his midriff. No-one took much notice at first – O'Neill was known for his nervous vomiting before an innings – but eventually a doctor was fetched and O'Neill sent to hospital. The first the captain knew of this drama was when he saw Booth walking out at the fall of the first wicket.

'Where the hell's Normie?' he asked.

'He's in hospital,' Booth replied airily and continued on his way.

As the Test unfolded, it seemed like ten men were pitted against thirteen. One inexplicable decision followed another. One could only laugh. As they walked into the Brabourne dressing room at tea on the third day, Burge asked Booth: 'How do you think Pataudi batted today, Sam?'

Booth replied: 'I thought his third innings was the best.'

As they sat in their room at Brabourne that evening, Booth recalls:

It had been one of those days. Incredibly hot, terrible umpiring, everyone had diarrhoea, Norm was crook, Johnny Martin had sunstroke, the cockroaches were running across the floor, the mattresses were a couple of inches thick and you couldn't sleep. And we just started laughing at the hopelessness of it, couldn't stop, laughed until we were almost sick.

Simpson and a few teammates went in search of their comrade O'Neill, with only a doctor's address as a guide. When they knocked furtively at the appropriate door, it was opened by a short, swarthy man who looked nothing like a doctor and who issued the mysterious greeting: 'Would you like to see my pet?' When the doctor seemed very insistent about his animal companion, they finally agreed, and leapt back a few feet when he revealed a domesticated household python.

For all that, India was a far better side than that encountered four years before. Nadkarni and Bhagwat Chandrasekhar spun the Australian second innings from 3/246 to all out for 274 and, when India prevailed by two wickets on 15 October 1964, the tourists had to bear local jubilation philosophically. Officials at the airport advised: 'We're sorry, but we can't take you to the waiting area. You'd be trampled to death.' The Australians traipsed to a designated open area off the runway whose main feature was an abundance of aeroplane wreckage. Their Vickers Viscount twice aborted take-off before leaving for Calcutta.

Australia in India 1969–70

A LOT OF HARD YAKKA (1996)

The Australians' first impressions of India echoed those of Benaud's team ten years before: dirty, poor and slightly scary. As a coach took them from Madras Airport to the Connemara Hotel, Keith Stackpole studied the reactions of teammates and his own:

> You could see the mouths of the blokes drop. You could see them thinking: 'What's happening here?' It was close to midnight, there was hardly any light, and it was pelting with rain. Yet I could see people sleeping in the street. 'Hey, look at that bloke.' We got to this old-style, high-ceilinged place, a little bit cold, and suddenly we realised we were in a country where, even at the hotel, everyone was coloured. We were virtually frightened to leave our mates and go to our rooms.

After a warm-up match against West Zone at Poona, thousands greeted the Australians' arrival for the First Test in Bombay. Thousands more watched the Australians practise. The players thought the local habit of garlanding them with jasmine and

31

marigolds rather charming, until they realised that they also invited a penumbra of flies and mosquitoes. They also thought the idea of staying in the digs at Brabourne Stadium pretty nifty, until they studied the dormitory. The beds were three-inch kapok mattresses on wooden bases, the air-conditioning almost unusable. 'You couldn't sleep with it on because it was as noisy as a diesel truck,' says Paul Sheahan. 'Then you couldn't sleep because it was so damned hot.'

The clincher was the food. They'd listened to medical warnings with mounting alarm, but now found that it under-stated the situation. Ian Chappell recalls:

> One evening, some of the players were looking for toasted sandwiches at the stadium. They were told that the cook had gone but that there was some bread in the kitchen. Brian Taber went downstairs and came back with a loaf under his arm. 'If you want to eat another meal in this place, don't go down and look at the kitchen,' he said. Being curious, a couple of us went to investigate and we found cats in the refrigerator, rats running over the uncovered food, green slime on the floor, barred windows with no glass, and a rubbish tip with an unbelievable stench outside the window.

Test cricket in India, the team also discovered, could be excru-ciating. Outfields for the First Test were shorn to a stubble, the pitch was of reddish soil laid on bricks, and the hard Indian cricket balls hit the bat like armour-piercing bullets. India's pawky off-spinner Erapalli Prasanna frequently employed seven leg-side fielders, and batting any length of time was like walking through Death Valley in the noonday sun.

Replying to India's laborious 271 in half as many overs, Stackpole spent almost five hours over a hundred gripped by cramps and dehydration. Redpath felt the after-effects of his glandular fever as he made 77: 'The first few runs I took in India almost killed me. I was panting and puffing even when I was running singles. I thought I'd never see out the tour.' Doug Walters, who helped him add 118 in three hours, found the mirrors that the crowd flashed in his eyes a sore distraction: 'The mirrors worried us a bit, especially when we were batting, but we soon found that the best idea wasn't to complain, because if we made complaints to the umpire it only incited the crowd to do it more.'

But the Australians sensed their grip on the match tighten as they secured a 74-run first-innings lead on the fourth morning. They clustered round the bat, appealing insistently, and hastened through their overs. When umpires Sambhu Pan and I. Gopalakrishnan denied him another over before lunch, Lawry remonstrated by throwing his cap to the ground. After the break, the Indian innings began to expire. Alan Connolly bowled economically, Johnny Gleeson enigmatically, and twenty-four-year-old off-spinner Ashley Mallett savoured his first taste of Indian conditions.

Born in Sydney and raised in Perth, Mallett had forged a path to Test cricket by heading for Adelaide in the winter of 1967 with his leg-spinning pal Terry Jenner to take a job in the local hospitals department and take advantage of counsel from the sapient Clarrie Grimmett. The effect had been immediate: a tour berth to England in 1968, a cap in the Fifth Test at The Oval, and Colin Cowdrey's wicket with his fifth delivery. A tall, myopic figure, more reminiscent of a bookkeeper than a bowler, Mallett was known for long silences and an occasionally spectacular lack of co-ordination. At the Poona Turf Club the week before, for instance, he had started a frame of billiards, taken careful aim with his cue . . . and torn an agonising zigzag straight through the felt.

Yet, with his height, Mallett used the breeze like a weather-vane, and now bowled maiden after teasing maiden as India declined rapidly to 7/89. The Australians finally struck resistance when left-hander Ajit Wadekar was joined by tailender Srinivasaraghavan Venkataraghavan. The crowd, which had been incensed by the fragility of India's batting, settled for fifty minutes to encourage them.

At length Venkat executed a crude cut at Connolly that travelled through to the keeper missing the bat by a foot. To the bemusement of Taber and first slip Chappell, Stackpole hollered an appeal from gully. To their further bemusement, umpire Pan raised his finger. Taber laughed to Chappell: 'Bit of a roughie, eh!' Venkat, a little disconcerted, went on his way. In the Australians' celebratory huddle, Taber cheerfully chided Stackpole: 'You only appealed 'cos you're a Victorian.'

'I thought I heard something,' said Stackpole.

'Well, it wasn't his bat,' Taber replied. 'He missed it by a foot.'

What they weren't to know was that the spectators' disappointment was being turned to disenchantment. Ears pressed to their transistors round Brabourne, listeners heard the judgement of commentator Devraj Puri that the bat had not even approached the ball. As the Australians returned to their positions, bottles began to litter the outfield. Outfielders Walters and McKenzie moved in to stay out of range. As Connolly continued to Prasanna, the demonstration worsened: hessian round the tennis courts behind Brabourne's East Stand was ignited. Smashed chairs and awning covers were incinerated in the North and Bombay Cricket Association Stands.

Although smoke had begun blowing across the arena, Lawry told umpires Pan and Gopalakrishnan he wanted to go on, for his side was close to a handsome victory. Connolly agreed. 'I reckon I can clean up the tail with this smoke,' he said. 'They won't be able to see the ball.'

Others were less keen. From the press box at square leg traipsed the septuagenarian scorer Jehangir Irani and *Indian Express* reporter Ghulam Menon, who protested that they could no longer see the game through the haze. The umpires and Lawry turned them back. But there were shortly other intruders to worry about. Mallett pointed out a mob hurling their collective weight against a mesh barrier in front of the smoking East Stand. Lawry ignored them. As riot police attended to the displaced spectators huddled round the sightscreen, he again insisted that play continue. Even when his deputy Chappell suggested that the dressing room might be a safer option, all the captain would say was: 'Hell, we need a wicket badly.'

Five minutes before stumps, the Australians got one: Mallett bowled Prasanna to leave India 9/125. But, after another over, stumps were drawn: by the Australians rather than the umpires just in case their withdrawal was impeded. Walters, arriving late, secured a bail. 'I'll try and poke someone's eye out with it,' he explained drily.

The local police chief advised the Australians to remain on the ground while insurgents in the Members' Stand were removed, and it was another twenty minutes before riot police began escorting them through a hail of missiles to their Brabourne quarters. Gleeson was hit a stunning blow on the back of the head by a flying bottle, while Lawry was narrowly missed by a wicker chair. The mob's most persistent members then laid siege to the dressing room and broke every window, encouraging further retreat to the toilet block. Finally – having given all interlopers five minutes to leave the ground – the police chief ordered a lathi charge across the arena to evict the last troublemakers. The official casualty list numbered fifty injured.

The Australians were advised not to leave Brabourne that evening, not that anyone was planning a night on the town.

An eight-wicket victory was completed next morning. No-one felt much like celebrating.

Following riots during Tests at Calcutta in January 1967 and Hyderabad just a month before, the insurrection at Brabourne caused deep local self-examination. KN Prabhu of the *Times of India* lamented: 'It is a novel and sad state of affairs that the violence latent in our public life should spring to the surface on our cricket fields.'

Henceforward, the Australians would be chaperoned everywhere by a contingent of police and armoured cars. The threat of violence, however, was not nearly so confronting as the quotidian experiences of touring life. Lawry bemoaned the absence of Australian journalists to tell the team's side of the story: remarkably, not one Australian media organisation had sent a correspondent. Although the drawn Second Test at Green Park passed without incident, tempers frayed again as the team went to the Kanpur Terminus to catch the 8 p.m. train to Jullundur for their game against North Zone. There seemed to be thousands of people there, both well-wishers and itinerants looking for shelter, and the Australians had to cart their cricket cases and luggage over four tracks and through hundreds of beggars in order to reach the platform. Lawry and Bennett had requested a hot meal for the team on the train but, when porters freighted the platters aboard, they revealed only cold chicken and cold vegetables: neither of which the Australians could eat. Lawry grabbed the local liaison officer, seething: 'We can't eat this food! Take it away!'

Ian Chappell kept a level head. Leading Australia for the first time at North Zone, he belted 164 in three hours including 24 in an over from Ashok Gandotra. And four days later he stood tall amid a jerry-built Australian total of 296 in the Third Test at Delhi's Feroz Shah Kotla, making 138 in four and a half hours. It wasn't enough to stem the tide of Prasanna and Bishan Bedi. Before an increasingly frenzied crowd, they spun Australia to a seven-wicket defeat. The not-out pair of Wadekar and Gundappa Viswanath performed a lap of honour with their captain, the Nawab of Pataudi, while the Australians traipsed from the field with the sound of firecrackers ringing in their ears.

It was the Australians' lowest ebb. They slunk away to Gauhati for a game against East Zone, where they were picked up from the airport by a truck for the 30-mile (50-kilometre) drive to another festering hotel. Half a dozen players were ill to varying degrees. Stackpole woke at 6 a.m. on the morning of the match feeling queasy and, crawling to the toilet, vomited violently all over the bathroom floor. His roommate, Sheahan, had Bennett fetch a doctor, but hotel staff didn't clean the mess for another twelve hours. Fred Bennett gave a speech to the local dignitaries oozing diplomatic unction: 'And may I say that Australia genuinely looks forward to playing a Test match in Gauhati.' Fifteen cricketers quietly but audibly chorused: 'Bullshit!'

The Australians' next stop, Calcutta, was in social and political turmoil. Hundreds of thousands of refugees had poured into Bengal after floods in East Pakistan, exacerbating its usual overcrowding, while the city had been racked by the indiscriminate violence of Maoist extremists called the Naxalites. The Australians soon learned, in fact, why Calcutta was known as 'the city of dreadful night'. At 6.30 p.m. on the day of their arrival, the Great Eastern Hotel was ringed by 3000 demonstrators, with placards protesting the presence of former national serviceman Doug Walters: they believed, mistakenly, that he had served in Vietnam. Every window in the hostelry was systematically smashed.

Practice at Eden Gardens then proved impossible. The team was virtually overrun by a crowd of 20,000, whom not even the baton-wielding paramilitaries of the Eastern Frontier Rifles could repel. Yet it wasn't India at whom the players directed their discontent. Touring such a country, in fact, could be fascinating, and not without its humour. Connolly, McKenzie and Stackpole once boarded a cab which lurched away, evidently on the power of only one cylinder. 'Jeez, mate,' said Connolly. 'What's wrong with your car?' The taxi driver responded philosophically: 'Mister, there is nothing wrong with my car except that it was made in India.' The Australians' real beef was with their board. It was hard not to believe that the authorities had deliberately stinted on costs. Several players who would align with Kerry Packer's breakaway World Series Cricket eight years later – Chappell, Walters, Mallett, McKenzie, Stackpole and Lawry – look back on the trip as a watershed. Stackpole says:

> India was a fabulous place to tour. Everyone was really friendly and mad about their cricket. But I reckon the seeds were sown then of the WSC revolution. The conditions we toured under were appalling. Some of the hotels were so pathetic you wouldn't have had a pig in them. And we all started to wonder: was it the board trying to save money?

Such recalcitrant thoughts were checked by the beginning of the Fourth Test, where the Australians moved inexorably into a winning position over the first three days. Complemented by Mallett, McKenzie bowled skilfully in the heavy, misty air. Then Chappell, adding a cubit to his stature with every innings, batted four and a half hours for a poised 99. Finally, last man Connolly hoisted four sixes in a quarter of an hour, using a bat he'd bought in Bombay from former Test spinner Bapu Nadkarni. With a 123-run first innings lead, Lawry scented victory. But in India, nothing was so straightforward.

The strife of Tuesday, 16 December 1969 began as the Australians were poking gingerly at their breakfasts. With only 8000 tickets available, queues of 20,000 outside Eden Gardens quickly became a stampede. Police waded in with lathis and tear gas, leaving six dead and 100 injured. The tourists were stunned. Lawry and Bennett drew up a message of sympathy. But the tone had been set for an unruly day. There was a palpable tension in the ground when play began and, as Connolly and Eric Freeman barged through the Indian middle order, the atmosphere grew uglier.

The butt of the spectators' anger became Pataudi, who continued a wretched run with the bat by pulling injudiciously at Mallett. His exit was followed by a volley of missiles from the Ranji Stand and, after four deliveries had been bowled in Australia's second innings chase of 39, all hell broke loose. Spectators from the stand, discomforted by bottles and rocks thrown from above, spilled onto the field. Two thousand police were unable to contain the bombardment, and play ceased. Lawry and Stackpole stood guard over the stumps. As the Ranji Stand's refugees were steered across the ground to a less populated quarter, a dozen photographers rushed to the centre of the ground. One, Miren Adhikary of the Bengali daily *Basumati*, advanced on the Australian openers shouting: 'Riot! Riot! Photos!'

'Get off the wicket!' Lawry shouted back. 'Go on, get off it.' He chased Adhikary off the pitch and gave him a shove to indicate he wanted no-one on the ground. The photographer went down like a poleaxed prizefighter. Adhikary's colleagues delightedly captured the tableau, which did not flatter Australia's captain. Order was restored after twenty minutes and, with the complicity of an apprehensive Pataudi, the arrears was cleared in another half hour.

With the scores tied, Lawry advised Stackpole quietly: 'Pat's just told [Subroto] Guha to bowl you a full toss. Just push it away for one.' 'Gee,' thought Stackpole. 'That's the first time anyone's ever told me he's going to bowl a full toss. I'll have a go at it.' With some relish, Stackpole pulled it for four. 'You bastard!' Lawry laughed as they made for the dressing room.

'Bill,' Stackpole replied, 'you woulda done exactly the same thing!'

'Hang on, Stacky,' said Lawry as they neared the pavilion. 'This could get ugly. We'd better protect Pat.'

He called to Pataudi: 'Hey Pat! Follow us!' They flanked the Indian captain as he walked through a hail of abuse, spit and wicker chairs on the way to the dressing room.

But it wasn't over yet. Back at the Great Eastern Hotel, Lawry and Bennett decided to throw a small team celebration. To their amazement, twenty Indian journalists turned up in expectation of joining in. A harassed Bennett had to explain that the function was private. Under protest, the reporters repaired to the hotel's Permit Room, where guests and visitors equipped with a permit could buy liquor. Dinner broke up around 9.00 p.m. and a few players went out: Lawry and Bennett to the movies; Connolly and Ray Jordon to see Geoff Lewis, a British jockey racing in India for the English winter. Most, though, retired to their rooms. And later in the evening a whole posse of reporters huddled outside the door to the room occupied by Freeman and Mallett. Freeman recalls:

A few of us were sitting around having a few drinks with not much on, when there was this knock at the door. It's this photographer wanting to take our pictures. Well, I told him to piss off. Then he starts knocking again, so I tell him to go away a second time. Third time, he just opens the door, goes flash bang, and runs off down the stairs. Well, that was it. We'd really had enough. I set off after him, and I ran down

three flights of stairs. When I caught up, I grabbed his shirt,
but it just came off in my hand, so he got away.

By the time Connolly and Jordon returned at midnight, the
hotel was in uproar. 'We had a helluva job getting back into
the hotel,' Connolly said. 'It was all boarded up and we spent
ages trying to convince these guards that we were Australian
cricketers.' Having won a Test, the Australians had inadvertently lost a public. The next day's newspapers were full of Lawry
apparently coshing Adhikary, and the story that 'McKenzie and
Redpath' had set upon other innocent members of the photo-
graphic profession calling them 'bloody Indian dogs'.

Calcutta's English-language daily *The Statesman* belied its
masthead in a report of Adhikary's 'disgraceful' treatment:
'Lawry ... could not keep his temper in check and knocked
over the poor photographer and struck him with his bat. It
was a horrible sight, and one was led to wonder what Lawry
thought himself to be. Would he have done the same in
England or South Africa?' Bennett, meanwhile, was wearily
drafting a statement explaining the true circumstances of the
hotel fracas. It was futile.

As the Australians set off to Dum Dum Airport for their
flight to Bangalore, their bus ran a 200-yard gauntlet of stone-
throwing demonstrators while it ascended a hill just outside
the city centre. Lawry was stunned:

Before we had time to collect ourselves, rocks the size of
half house bricks were smashing into both sides of the bus,
shattering nearly all the windows ... The driver tried to
accelerate up the hill while all members of the team flung
themselves on the floor wondering whether they would be
dragged out and stoned to death if the bus stalled.

One rock flying through an open window just missed Freeman's head. 'I felt it as it went past,' he said. 'If it had hit me I would have been history.' With unusual presence of mind, he collected the projectile as a souvenir, joking that he would give it to Sir Donald Bradman as a Christmas present. The tour was becoming farcical. As the Australians prepared to play South Zone, they heard that the Press Photographers' Association secretary Shyamal Bose was threatening a strike. In the event, photographers covered the match wearing black armbands.

Lawry was wondering what he could do wrong next and found out on the last day when, as he and Gleeson saved the game, he tried to waste some time by claiming that a woman in a bright sari by the sightscreen was distracting him. Repercussions followed when the Australians left the next day:

> On the flight from Bangalore to Madras I asked the beautifully gowned Indian air hostess for a cup of tea. She replied politely, but with a trace of feeling, that she wasn't sure whether I would be getting a cup of tea. When I asked why, she produced a newspaper which suggested that, when I had objected to the woman in the sari standing in front of the sightscreen at Bangalore, I had insulted India's national dress and Indian womanhood . . . Denied my cup of tea, I should have realised by then that this was not going to be my tour.

From a cricketing perspective, the tour was a triumph for Lawry. When Australia won the Fifth Test in Madras by 77 runs over Christmas 1969, thanks to a hundred from Walters and 10/144 from Mallett, it completed a notable 3–1 victory. Australia had not won an away series so conclusively for a decade. Yet the trip had been a public relations disaster. Where the approachable and animated Benaud had commanded a rapt Indian following in 1959–60, the remote and ruthless Lawry had been followed everywhere by catcalls and jeering. Some spectators at Madras had even dangled him in effigy from a noose. Detractors looked back on Lawry's attitude at Bombay as having set the tone of the whole series. The Indian Wadekar wrote: 'With a little graciousness, the unfortunate episode at the Brabourne Stadium could have been avoided. We had only one wicket left and there was a whole day to go. Yet, with a pall of smoke blowing across the field and the umpires unable to communicate with the scorers, Lawry insisted on continuing the game. The riotous incidents of the last half hour left their mark on the rest of the series.' In hindsight, Lawry agrees:

> I think any criticism I got in India was probably right.
> Normally I take those sort of things in my stride, but I think
> I had an attitude that had been ingrained in me by Peter
> Burge and Col McDonald, who'd told me about their tours
> there. So I was a bit outspoken when I shouldn't have been,
> because I was really on edge to make sure that the food was
> adequate and the hygiene was all right. Which it wasn't.
> It was disgraceful really and I think we were badly let down.
> It was probably all right if you were a drinker on that tour
> because at least you could write yourself off. But the Redpaths
> and Lawrys and Stackpoles and Sheahans, who weren't big
> drinkers, who were just trying to be dedicated sportsmen,
> found it hard. Relaxing was nearly impossible.

Nor was there scope to relax now. Though the Australians cheered lustily as they left Bombay for Nairobi on New Year's Eve, they still had another dozen first-class matches including four Tests against South Africa ahead, and did not realise how depleted conditions in India had left them. All the team were underweight, sick or both: Graham McKenzie had shed a stone

43

(6.5 kilograms) and felt woefully lethargic; Alan Connolly had come down with bronchial pneumonia after ill-advisedly choosing fish at the team's Christmas dinner. The ABC's Alan McGilvray was shocked when he met the team's BOAC VC-10 at Johannesburg's Jan Smuts Airport on 2 January 1970: 'They looked haggard. Their eyes seemed to be standing out of their heads and some of them looked positively yellow.'

THE TIE THAT BINDS

In the twenty years from 1977, India and Australia created the form, if not quite the substance, of a significant cricket rivalry: the two outstanding batters of the period, Allan Border and Sunil Gavaskar, went on to bless the trophy that still bears their names. India actually had chances to polish Australia off in 1977–78 and 1985–86, and failed to seize them; the World Cup, in 1983, proved easier, its impact on Indian cricket being felt to this day. Nothing in this period rivalled the tie, Test cricket's second, that Australia and India succeeded in playing over five days of high scores and low farce at Chepauk – indeed, the rivals may not have played a greater Test match at all. Dean Jones was arguably the first Australian whose career was defined by his performances against India; he wouldn't be the last.

Bishan Bedi

LEFT-ARM HETERODOX (2023)

There is a certain genus of cricketers – an elite of the elite – who are not only supreme at their skill but somehow seem to embody it altogether. Shane Warne wasn't just leg spin's greatest exponent; to bowling, he somehow brought the full force of his vibrant personality. Wasim Akram wasn't merely the left-arm pace bowler supreme, but an encyclopedist of the craft, the master of all its aspects and dimensions.

Bishan Bedi formed part of this club. He *was* left-arm slow bowling. He was its greatest champion and its most joyous ambassador. He bowled it on the field; he bowled it in his head; he bowled it into eternity. Once you saw him, he became the benchmark, the reference point for all other practitioners. He wakened you to its possibilities, and once wakened you never forgot them. More than forty years have elapsed since he bowled, but he led me on to other favourites like Ravi Shastri, Daniel Vettori and Rangana Herath, and I fancy I still see him when I watch Ravi Jadeja, or Mitchell Santner. He also brought a unique spirit to cricket – an expansiveness and chivalry. He bowled to deceive but, frank and big-hearted, was the least deceptive of men. To face him must have been like having your pocket picked then given your wallet back.

Three times did Bishan tour Australia: as a young man in 1967–68, as a colourful guest in the Rest of the World XI in 1971–72, and as captain and guru in 1977–78. On that last trip, India brought their fabled four spinners, as complete an ensemble as has equipped any team: not just their skipper but gnomic Prasanna, crafty Venkataraghaven, and Chandrasekhar, *sui generis*.

We tend to remember that Chandra took twelve on a dark, pebbly pitch at the MCG, but Bishan also took ten . . . in Perth . . . at the WACA. Can you credit it? The world's slowest bowler on the world's fastest pitch in the world's breeziest ground. To a boy, as I was, this was a kind of revelation: how much subtlety and variety could be wrung from a physique that testified to an enjoyment of earthy pleasures, an approach so seemingly artless, and an arc like an angler's cast. It was intensified by Bishan's seeming indifference to the rest of cricket. He hoicked earthily; he treated fielding as a bit of a chore. But in an over of Bishan's, he made the world stand still, almost on tip-toe. The ball took so long in its path, time enough for thoughts to rush through a batter's head; yet it was almost always a cardinal error to commit too soon.

Beaten in two squeakers, India just lost that series – imagine had they pulled it off, more than forty years before Virat Kohli's men of 2018–19. Remarkably, perhaps, I suspect that few Australians would have begrudged them. More powerful teams have visited our shores, but none so completely charming: valiant Mohinder, soulful Viswanath, suave Vengsarkar, loveable Kirmani. It is incredible to think how long they stayed, all summer, and how far they travelled, from Port Lincoln and Hastings to Griffith and Nambour. They came to my home town, a white-bread industrial city called Geelong, where they trussed up the local XI. They felt like part of us, fascinating house guests, whom you'd have been happy to have stay forever. Who of us in Australia had ever seen a patka before, such as those Bishan coiled around his head? Mind you, he could have bowled in a trilby and been just as entrancing.

It's no fluke, I think, that Bishan is the subject of some of cricket's best photographs. There was a feeling of a mystery to be unlocked, if you could just stop time long enough to study closely. There's Ken Kelly's vivid close-up, with the signature detail of Bishan imparting to the ball with his right thumb a last unconscious nudge into his left hand. There's Adrian Murrell's study of him warming up, only the whites of his eyes visible, as though lost in tantric contemplation. There's Patrick Eagar's side-on snap at Lord's which captures Bedi connected to the ground only by the outside of the toe of his left boot, like a hot air balloon straining at its moorings. Seeing an Eagar sequence of Bedi in a copy of *MCC Masterclass* so inspired another young Sikh, Monty Panesar, that he committed to a lifetime in the same genre.

Something about the very memory of Bishan pricks you about directions the game has taken. Can you conceive of him in an auction? He was not to be bought and sold. Can you imagine the fatuity of putting a number and his name on the back of his shirt? It would have been like an explanatory caption on the *Mona Lisa*. He also belonged to a now-forgotten species of cricketers – those rebel souls of the 1970s who were often at loggerheads with their administrative classes. Bishan was the Indian counterpart of Ian Chappell and Dennis Lillee in Australia and John Snow and Tony Greig in England. Today's cricketers, memorable and exciting as they may be, are in the main pampered yes-men, who never speak out of turn, lest they upset a brand, roil social media. They are represented by agents and unions, firewalled by entourages. Imagine the courage it once took to resist cricket's overlords, its self-constituting national monopolies, not least the stern and reproving Board of Control for Cricket in India – to be one-out against leviathan, usually running the gauntlet of the press, and in doing so courting the suspicion of the public.

Suresh Menon's wonderful biography, *Bishan: Portrait of a Cricketer*, collates a host of confrontations with the BCCI. During one Nagpur Test, for instance, the BCCI stuck Bishan's team not in a hotel but in an MLA Hostel in which only he and the team manager had running water. Bishan remonstrated so fiercely with the local official that he was arraigned to appear before a BCCI disciplinary committee – sitting, by the way, in a five-star hotel in Mumbai. Having been reprimanded, Bishan learned that the BCCI had not booked his return tickets to Chandigarh, and there were no seats on the train. So it was that the captain of India travelled to a Duleep Trophy game bunked in a luggage rack for 1400 kilometres, then took a bus the last 250 kilometres.

I've called him Bishan here advisedly, because I did have the good fortune to know him, just a little, although with him it always felt like more. Such was his immediate warmth; it was like being wrapped in an instant hug. 'You and Ray Robinson!' he said when we were first introduced in England fifteen years ago. 'My favourite Australian writers!' And much as I liked being recognised, I was the more chuffed by his reference to Ray Robbie, likewise my favourite, and something of a personal hero. Bishan had a capacity for immediate, easy intimacy, and a fund of opinions expressed with an absolute unguardedness, whether about his reverence for the Nawab of Pataudi Jnr, his ambivalent relations with Sunil Gavaskar, or his utter contempt for administrators generally. No coaching sinecure or commentator's blazer for Bishan. He was absolutely his own man, proudly Indian, utterly cosmopolitan. Had the

Australian Arthur Mailey not said already said it, after being criticised for advising the Englishman Ian Peebles in 1930, the remark could have come from Bishan: 'Spin bowling is an art, and art is international.'

How dearly beloved he was too. I once had a night out with him at the Delhi Golf Club, where he received a non-stop stream of well-wishers and petitioners as though they were personal friends – only to quietly confide that he had only the vaguest idea who half of them were. When we came out, I thought that my driver was going to faint with excitement. 'Naveen, I'm so sorry to have kept you so late,' I said as we returned to the city. 'Sir!' he said. 'It was *Bishan Bedi*.' I had to pinch myself too. Good heavens, it was.

Bhagwat Chandrasekhar

HAND OF FATE (2023)

Lightning proverbially never strikes twice in the same place. The Boxing Day Test of 1977 is an exception. Leading 2–0 in the series, Australia were two for 122 on the second afternoon chasing India's 256, only to barely take the game into a fifth day, thanks to cricket as scintillating as it was symmetrical. Bhagwat Chandrasekhar was already an Indian matchwinner, having bewildered England away and the West Indies at home. Here his 34.1 eight-ball overs resulted in analyses of six for 52 and six for 52; a wretched batter, he was also dismissed by each of the two balls he faced in the match. There have perhaps been more remarkable all-round performances, but none so uniform.

Nothing about the ins and outs was predictable. Chandra's first wicket fell to a long-hop, the second to a full toss. There were other lapses in length, assistances from variable bounce. But nobody expected otherwise from Chandra, because what singled him out in India's sweetly various slow-bowling cartel was his capacity for producing that delivery of which nobody else was capable – a capacity that made Viv Richards describe him as his most awkward opponent. The special in that spell in Melbourne was the wire-guided missile that trapped Bob Simpson in the second innings – it hit his front pad while the bat was still in the process of being taken back.

Nobody has bowled like Chandra; nobody has had to. Born in Mysore, he was five years old when one day he noticed he could not lift his right arm. The diagnosis was polio, the treatment plaster and cod liver oil: over the next two years, the boy recovered sensation, but suffered such a withered arm that he had to tackle table tennis and badminton left-handed, and to play cricket as a wicketkeeper. When finally Chandra had a bowl for Bangalore's City Cricketers he lacked the strength to pause and tweak the ball; all he could purvey, by cocking his wrist, holding the smooth side of the ball with his long, sensitive fingers, and whizzing his arm over, were fast, flat leg-breaks, top-spinners and googlies. He hardly compared to his idol Richie Benaud, but he had a rare bond with his captain on debut in January 1964: the Nawab of Pataudi Jnr played with the handicap of one eye, having been blinded in the other in an automobile accident.

The Nawab's suitably Nelsonian disposition made him a great advocate for Chandra after the bowler took a match-winning eight wickets against Australia later in the year. Chandra returned the regard: 'He had charisma. He had glamour.' And if Chandra had neither, he had mystique, born of uniqueness, which not even *Wisden* could quite comprehend. 'The belief is that the thinness of his arm gives it the flexibility of whipcord, enabling him to produce the extra bite in his top-spinner,' speculated the almanack, unable to achieve complete certainty in these days before all-seeing cameras and super slow-motion replays were available to decrypt the outwardly mysterious. To describe 'Chandrasekhar the Destroyer', Ramachandra Guha reached for the mythological: 'Unlike Siva nothing caught fire at the mere blink of an eyelid but the right wrist could wreak destruction with an almost equal rapidity.' Its capacities were focused on victory: in fourteen Indian wins under Pataudi, Ajit Wadekar and Bishan Bedi, he claimed 98 wickets at 19.27 at a strike rate down to 45.4. Rajan Bala's biography was entitled *The Winning Hand*.

Then there were the shortcomings of India's fielders, never reliable, and the caprices of India's selectors, never predictable. Chairman Vijay Merchant never reposed great faith in one so unique. Administrators were standoffish. Managers were wary. Ten years before his coup at the MCG, he picked up a slight ankle injury at the same ground. It went untreated and even unacknowledged until Chandra learned he would be flying home. When he arrived in Bangalore, he was greeted by a wheelchair and accused in the report of the manager Ghulam Ahmed of hiding a pre-existing sprain. Then he missed two years of cricket after his debut with injuries, including a badly broken jaw, sustained in a scooter accident while commuting to work. In fighting his way back, Chandra had only himself to rely on. In forming his combination with Bedi, Erapalli Prasanna and Srinivasaraghavan Venkataraghavan, he then proved that lighting can strike four times in the same team.

Sunil Gavaskar and Gundappa Viswanath

THE LITTLE MASTER(S) (2024)

For more than a decade, Sunil Gavaskar and Gundappa Viswanath were Indian batsmanship front and back – captains, professionals, brothers in arms, brothers-in-law, small men with great reputations defying an age growing bigger, taller and faster. They were the nearest India have come to an axis like Hutton and Compton, great contemporaries of contrasting methods, except that they were never in their own eyes rivals – which did not prevent admirers calibrating their allegiances with a certain fineness.

Gavaskar was day-in, day-out the best opening batter of his era, which was a very fine one. Gordon Greenidge and Desmond Haynes might have been more explosive but were lucky to be spared facing their own bowlers; Barry Richards and Glenn Turner had excellent credentials but played too few Tests to judge; Geoff Boycott came and went rather too wilfully. Gavaskar played 125 of the 129 Tests that India played during his career, coming in first in all but eleven of his 214 innings, in seventy-nine of which he passed 50. In twenty Tests against Australia he averaged 52; in twenty-seven against the West Indies he averaged 65. Cricket should never be reduced to mere accountancy, but Gavaskar was batting's chancellor of the exchequer – a byword for prudent husbandry, balanced budgets.

Gavaskar, it needs to be granted, was a fine sight. His defence had a pristine quality, and he enjoyed full mastery of all the offensive shots. But with him, it was primarily about the how many, rather than, as it was with Viswanath, the how. Where Gavaskar exuded a columnar orthodoxy, Viswanath was all rasping cuts and pulls, exotic flourishes and flicks. With Gavaskar, you were always conscious of the acquisition of runs. With Viswanath, you hardly cared how many he was – you just hoped for a little longer to watch. You wanted Viswanath, just for once, to be a little greedier: the trouble was that, as Frank Keating thought, his batting combined 'utter grandeur' with 'almost sheepish modesty'.

Where Gavaskar was so fierce in defence of his wicket that he once held a Melbourne Test to ransom in protest against what he claimed was a mistaken decision, Viswanath made an exquisite touch hundred in the same innings on a heinous pitch. He was also one of international cricket's very last 'walkers', for reasons he could not quite put his finger on. 'I don't know why I do it,' he said. 'It all happens on the spur of the moment. I don't like to stay in the middle when I am out.' He didn't like the opposite either: as captain in the Golden Jubilee Test, he recalled a batsman, England's Bob Taylor, given out in error.

In other words, where Gavaskar was a personality readily admired from a distance, Viswanath was a personality to engage the sympathy – 'the best-loved cricketer', as Ramachandra Guha put it. Comparison was inevitable, especially in an era where the primacy of Test cricket and the continuity to seasons simplified head-to-head evaluation. Yet the pair took the edge off it by their companionable regard. This didn't arise simply because Viswanath married Gavaskar's sister Kavita. Perhaps each saw in the other something they themselves lacked a little of: the value of Gavaskar's wicket cost his batting some freedom; the generosity of Viswanath's spirit may have cost him some runs. Certainly they never failed to speak of one another with admiration and affection. In March 1982, Gavaskar even called Viswanath 'the best batsman in the world', at a time when there were a few pretty damn good candidates; Viswanath disclaimed the title, pointing out his colleague's enormous challenges as an opener in an era rich in new ball talent. By outlasting the slightly older Viswanath by four years, Gavaskar probably came to hold the palm. But on a shared pedestal they looked comfortable cohabitants.

Kapil Dev
FIRST ACTION HERO (2009)

In 1982 Scyld Berry, the very excellent cricket correspondent of the *Observer* who has lately become the editor of *Wisden*, published a fine book on England's recent tour of the subcontinent, entitled *Cricket Wallah*. No English writer to that point had studied India with such clarity, sympathy, or indeed rosy prophecy, for he far-sightedly concluded that the country would become 'the capital of cricket': demography, he believed, was destiny.

In one judgement alone was *Cricket Wallah* amiss. On the basis of the tour's two one-day internationals, Berry thought that limited-overs cricket held 'no great attraction' in India. Batsmen were still technically correct, and spin bowling endured, 'integral, not an adjunct' to the game, for it 'suited the rhythms of Indian life'. In fact, he had just watched the cricketer who, more than any other, would challenge both those appealing preconceptions.

Two hundred and seventeen of Kapil Dev's 432 Test wickets were taken in the heat and dust of India by uncompromising toil; he brought a gaiety to batting in a team that sometimes seemed unaware that Tests were no longer timeless. Above all, by leading India to the World Cup of 1983, he turned his country's cricket priorities on their head – and all this from most inauspicious beginnings.

'There are no fast bowlers in India,' fifteen-year-old Kapil was told when he complained about the short rations at lunch at a training camp at Brabourne Stadium in 1974. The judgement was hurtful, but not unfounded. In India's most recent home Test, the new ball had been taken by Eknath Solkar (two overs) and Sunil Gavaskar (one over), then surrendered to the slow-bowling wiles of Bedi, Chandra and Prasanna. It had not, however, been ever thus. Peer back to pre-war, pre-Partition India, and the country's opening attack was probably superior to Australia's. The likes of Tim Wall and Ernie McCormick had nothing to teach Mohammad Nissar and Amar Singh, except that Nissar's best years were swallowed by World War II, while Amar succumbed to pneumonia aged thirty.

A 'feeling of loss' pervaded Indian cricket in their wake, according to its historian Mihir Bose, which intensified over the next forty years whenever the country's batsmen crossed paths with bowling of real pace. Ray Lindwall and Keith Miller made them suffer in Australia, Fred Trueman lorded it over them in England, and Charlie Griffiths nearly killed Nari Contractor in Barbados. Most ignominiously, Clive Lloyd's pacemen set about Bedi's batsmen like sadistic thugs in a dark alley at Sabina Park in April 1976.

By that stage Kapil had been a first-class cricketer for one season, without much encouragement. In his second game for Haryana, versus Delhi, he played against Bedi, who was selling one of his Gray-Nicolls bats, and had set a reserve on it of Rs 500. With help from his friend Ashok Malhotra, Kapil scraped together Rs 475, but there were no discounts, and no gimmes either: his first tour, to Pakistan, was played on pitches apparently prepared for the diplomatic parity of drawn Tests.

From the first, nonetheless, Kapil upset cricket's prior balances of power. In *Spin and Other Turns*, Ramachandra Guha describes the first morning of Kapil's Test career, how in his second over the teenager sent a bouncer past the pentangle on Sadiq Mohammad's cap, 'very likely the fastest delivery from an Indian bowler since independence'. Sadiq's summons of a helmet was so unforeseen that it took some overs to arrive; as Guha notes: 'It is a wonder there was one at the ground at all.' When the West Indies toured India soon after, they dished it out, as was their wont, but Kapil was no less hostile. Normally above the fray, *Wisden* described the Chepauk Test as 'a bumper war' in which India 'for once gave as good as they got'. Bose believes it a hinge point in Indian cricket history.

Kapil altered also the Indian team's internal dynamics. The dominant presence in the country's cricket to that time had been Gavaskar, batting's classical sculptor: patient, implacable, self-sufficient, self-involved, peppery temper beneath a surface urbanity. Kapil, ebullient and sanguine, provided a rival to national affection, and a new source of national self-definition. Gavaskar, great as he was, could never rival the epic grandeur of a Viv Richards. Kapil, in an era of the international game uncommonly blessed with fast-bowling all-rounders, more than held his own against them. Remember? Botham, Imran, Hadlee: all fierce rivals. You could imagine them in a western saloon. Botham would be the one chesting open the swing doors and shouting the bar, Imran the one comfortably encircled by comely belles in crinoline, Hadlee the one staring fixedly at his ice water. But that Kapil – he held aloof. He had the liveliest and least imitable action of all, a skipping, bounding run of gathering energy, and a delivery stride perfectly side-on but exploding at all angles, wrists uncoiling, arms elasticising, eyes afire. Which was part of his significance. No fast bowlers in India? Kapil could have hailed from no other country.

All that stood in the way of Kapil's bowling was his batting, full of generous arcs and fearful cleaves, signed with an exuberant pull shot that featured a chorus-line kick from his crossed front leg. At first, teammates took Kapil's run-making more seriously than he did himself: he reached the first of eight Test hundreds in Delhi thirty years ago only because Syed Kirmani sacrificed himself, a cacophony of calls sending them to the same end. He retained a sense of play and adventure into which even opponents sometimes entered. At the Gabba in December 1980, he launched Jeremy Coney over the roof of the Clem Jones Stand and into Stanley Street during an innings of 75 off 51 balls; the puckish New Zealander waved his white handkerchief like a flag of surrender.

Selectors were sterner, benching Kapil after the Delhi Test of December 1984 when he hit his second ball for six and his third down long-off's throat as India stumbled to defeat against England. But Kapil, for all that he accomplished, never really repented. He won the Lord's Test of June 1986 with three fours and a six off Phil Edmonds; he saved the follow-on there four years later with four consecutive sixes off Eddie Hemmings. Lord's was the venue, too, of that storied World Cup final after which Kapil could have retreated to an ashram but remained one of the most significant players who ever lived – all because of one catch. It came from the top edge of the bat of Viv Richards, then on course to be matchwinner for the third consecutive World Cup final, and it looked suspiciously like providence.

Kapil had deposed Gavaskar as captain in one of those Indian intrigues that outsiders find unintelligible, and led his country with expected spirit and unexpected smarts. Gavaskar, never a one-day natural, had had a wretched tournament, and been first to fall that day in India's ramshackle 183. The West

Indies in reply had charged to 1/50. Now Madan Lal bowled a bouncer – a bouncer to *Richards*. What's Hindi for chutzpah? The crowd on the mid-wicket boundary began shrinking back; even Father Time ducked. In the event Richards miscued, but the ball would have fallen safe had any other fielder been stationed near the drop zone. As it was, Kapil Dev turned, ran back with the flight of the ball, loose stride eating up the distance, cast a split-second glance over his shoulder, and collected the descending ball in his fingertips – making even this look deliberate. Has a more difficult catch been made to seem easier at a more critical moment in the annals of the game?

India had won one game in two previous World Cups, against East Africa; now they won what remained their only global trophy until the Twenty20 World Championship in 2007. Both wins similarly tilted the cricket world off its axis. One-day cricket went forth and multiplied in the subcontinent, to the extent that the next Cup was held there four years later, just as Twenty20 did twenty-four years later, making India its social, cultural and financial fastness.

Kapil was part of that shift, too, shoulder to shoulder with Subhash Chandra's Indian Cricket League, while Gavaskar was firmly in the camp of the official Indian Premier League. Much else had transpired between times, but it was almost as though their unspoken rivalry had never quite ended. The ICL has floundered and the IPL prospered, so Gavaskar might consider his the last word; yet today's stylish, aggressive Indian stars, like MS Dhoni, Virender Sehwag, Ishant Sharma and Zaheer Khan, are more obviously Kapil's spiritual heirs.

Mohinder Amarnath

IN EXTREMIS (2003)

To play sixty-nine Tests for one's country is an enormous honour. To miss sixty-four in that same period is to have endured some of the gravest disappointments cricket can inflict. The record of India's Mohinder Amarnath is unlike any other; it strangely befits a player whose career was of almost unique extremes.

He was known, universally, and in appreciation of his affable and equable temperament, as 'Jimmy'. If he did not loom among countrymen like contemporaries Gavaskar, Vishwanath and Kapil Dev, he was a cricketer's cricketer: contributors to a 1996 book of tributes, *Grit & Grace*, laud his decency (Viv Richards calls him 'one of the nicest men to have ever played the game') and his determination ('Concede didn't seem to be in his vocabulary,' says David Boon).

He needed both. He was the last chosen in every reconstitution of India's Test team, the first excluded in every purge. At his peak in the early 1980s, he was freely described as the world's best batsman; he then suffered a loss of form so abject and ruinous that it seemed almost ghoulish to look.

Much of Jimmy's career is explained by his father, one of India's most eminent batsmen and eristic personalities. Lala Amarnath was a cricketer of gallantry and elan. Recalling the blue handkerchief that protruded from his great contemporary's trouser pocket, Vijay Hazare thought that Lala displayed 'showmanship that would have been the envy of an advertising expert'. Also a fearsome martinet, Lala forbade his three boys from playing any sport but cricket, prohibited their using anything softer than a cricket ball, and orchestrated games in his garden where pots stood in for fielders in order to develop skills of placement. In Indian cricket, meanwhile, the name Amarnath invited reverence or revulsion: the sins of the father were regularly to be visited on the son.

Jimmy made himself a still greater target. He batted, as his father demanded, with a flagrant disregard for danger. In an era replete with fast bowling and unrestricted in use of the bouncer, he never stopped hooking – despite many incentives to do so. He suffered a hairline fracture of the skull from Richard Hadlee, was knocked unconscious by Imran Khan, had teeth knocked out by Malcolm Marshall and was hit in the jaw so painfully by Jeff Thomson in Perth that he could only eat ice-cream for lunch. 'What separated Jimmy from the others,' Michael Holding said of him, 'was his great ability to withstand pain ... A fast bowler knows when a batsman is in pain. But Jimmy would stand up and continue.'

It was as a combatant of fast bowling that Jimmy enjoyed his finest hour. He spent three years by the wayside after being maimed by Hadlee in 1979, but re-emerged with a helmet, a two-eyed stance and 1182 runs at 70 including five hundreds in consecutive away series against Pakistan (Imran and Sarfraz) and the West Indies (Holding, Marshall, Garner) during the first half of 1983.

Tall, slim, apparently impervious to fear, he advertised his resolution with a red handkerchief that always protruded from his pocket – à la Steve Waugh. I have some grainy video footage of Amarnath batting in the West Indies that is nonetheless absolutely stirring, the crowd noise drowning the commentators' voices as he hooks and pulls off the front foot. When he had to retire for stitches to a head wound at Bridgetown, he washed the bloodstains from his shirt while waiting to resume, and on doing so hooked his first ball from Holding for six. When India won the 1983 World Cup, he was man of the match in both the semi-final and final.

Then, a few months later in India, came a reversal of fortune as complete as any in history. Jimmy made 11 in two hits against Pakistan, and 1 run in six tortured innings against the West Indies. I followed international cricket closely in those days, had been thrilled by Amarnath's comeback, and can still recall my incredulity as the daily papers reported his steady accretion of failures – many years later, it still tweaks my curiosity like few sport stories.

What happened? Who knows? Yet every cricketer has had an experience like Amarnath's, that sensation of being the butt of a giant joke. Reality television has recently wakened viewers to the compelling nature of humiliation. Lovers of cricket have subtly acknowledged this for years – their game contains greater scope for humiliation than perhaps any other, in the defeated trudge of the batsman bowled for nought, the wounded air of the bowler hit for six, the shame of the errant fielder.

Here, again, Jimmy was the cricketer's cricketer. Having scaled Olympian heights, he shrank to the level of the most inept park bumbler. Yet there was, remarkably, another comeback in him; a year later, having recalibrated his technique again on more orthodox lines, he saved India with a gritty hundred in Lahore, followed it with three more, and was not displaced until the advent of Sachin Tendulkar – a player to whom, for all his greatness, I find it harder to warm. Tendulkar makes cricket seem inevitable; Jimmy Amarnath's career reminded you instead of its true evitability.

Dilip Doshi
A MAN APART (2006)

Anyone who grew into their cricket in the 1970s will remember how crisply the world then divided. From Australia came moustachioed bandidos in baggy greens. In the West Indies originated towering, raw-boned fast bowlers. England provided the dour professionals and resourceful defenders. And India? India was the home of spin – apparently, in fact, its last bastion, in an era besotted with pace supported by a crescent of slips.

Everyone knew the chief quartet: Prasanna, Bedi, Chandra and Venkat, so original and so different from one another. Then there were others, who had to make the best of limited opportunities: left-arm slow bowlers as good as Rajinder Goel, Rajinder Hans and Padmakar Shivalkar, and the excellent off-spinner Shivlal Yadav. *Primus inter pares* in that group, though, was Dilip Doshi.

Doshi was thirty-two by the time he found a niche in Tests, and already steeped in the traditions of which he was part. He was a negligible batsman, and with his unathletic physique, baggy creams and thick square spectacles reminded Alan Ross of a French semiotician, a Barthes or a Lévi-Strauss. It was a subtle analogy, for Doshi's bowling was full of double-meanings and hidden depths, both inviting and aggressive, patient and probing.

In Australia in 1980–81, Doshi was a revelation. It's often said that Australians favour visiting players who seem to reflect, and thus endorse, their own mores – Botham and Flintoff have, in their days, been typed 'almost Australian'. Yet touring cricketers have also become popular here for the opposite reason, that they savour of distant places and different ways of life. Patsy Hendren, Maurice Tate, Freddie Brown and Ken Barrington were quintessential Englishmen; Garry Sobers and Wes Hall were archetypal West Indians; Imran Khan was no version of Australia Lite. Doshi cut an unlikely figure, but his love of cricket was abundant and obvious, and he was incurably game; though he might be slow across the outfield, he never gave up a chase; even in adversity, his smile was never far away. He was brave, too, bowling seventy-four overs in the Melbourne Test with a fractured toe.

With a ball in his hand, Doshi was never other than poised, setting the field like a finicky host setting the table. He had one of those approaches you could watch all day: a dainty run that turned him exquisitely side on, followed by a delivery stride where his bespectacled eyes would be just visible over his high right arm. His body would pivot into a follow through that brought his left hand below knee level.

Although Doshi could turn the ball an appreciable distance in responsive conditions, what left the strongest impression was how long he could make it hang in the air, as though suspended in a cobweb. Greg Chappell collared him in Sydney, but Doshi came back by dismissing him twice in Adelaide, sweeping at a ball that bounced too much in the first innings, then beaten in the air coming down the wicket in the second. Chappell turned on his heel without trying to remake his ground, bowed his head penitently, and stripped off his gloves in his few strides for the pavilion. 'Too good,' he seemed to say, 'too good.'

Australian spin bowling was then in a parlous state, and Doshi was a tonic to palates jaded by the monotonies of medium pace. 'Doshi taught us by example,' wrote Bill O'Reilly. 'Refined, thoughtful and brilliantly executed spin can offer the game an exciting future.' O'Reilly would live just long enough to see Shane Warne fulfil the prophecy he'd made watching this improbable visitor.

Yet while Doshi took 114 Test wickets at averages and strike rates in Bedi's class, he came and went quickly, not so much for reasons of form as because he was out of tune with the mores. The early days of the proliferation of limited-overs cricket were characterised by formulaic thinking, including the idea that spin was de trop. Doshi gave up fewer than four runs an over in his fifteen one-day internationals but could not keep his place; he took a fabled 8–7–1–1 in a Sunday League match for Notts against Northants and was left out of the county's next game. Even his pedantic way with field placings was held against him. Didn't he realise that spin bowlers were there to speed up the over rate and kill a few hours while the fast men got their breath back?

His autobiography also makes it clear that Doshi harboured his own objections to the game's trajectory. Most players are broadly in favour of commercialisation; certainly, they would no sooner object to it than fluoride in the water supply. In *Spin Punch* (1991), Doshi is almost entirely antagonistic to 'professionalism and money-mindedness'. The Indian team, he says, had a 'one-track obsession' with money that he found 'quite disgusting'. The Board of Control for Cricket in India, meanwhile, was 'a government within a government, almost totally not accountable to anyone'.

Doshi was, in his own account, a man apart. He reports that he declined the opportunity to write a newspaper column because it would 'bring out into the open what were essentially confidences'; he thought throughout his career that advertising and endorsements were 'totally out of hand'. He even recalls a team meeting before the first ODI in India where the conversation was entirely devoted to sponsorship, prize money, logo royalties and match fees: 'Cricket was discussed only as an afterthought.'

Hovering over the book is the figure of Sunil Gavaskar, now so gushing about the honour of representing India, but whom Doshi depicts darkly as a petty tyrant 'bogged down in personal likes and dislikes', and 'either evasive or flippant' when challenged – as, for instance, when he instructed Doshi to take more time over his overs against England in 1981–82, then left the bowler to bear the brunt of criticism for India's abysmal over rate.

Such selfishness, in Doshi's view, was contagious. In one vivid anecdote, Doshi recalls apprentice paceman Randhir Singh taking the ball on a green-top in a tour match at Canterbury. In a trice, three catches were dropped by the 'stalwarts who stood in the slips apparently for no more than a pleasant chat amongst themselves'. Not only was no apology tendered, but no-one took any notice. This, said Doshi, was the 'crudest and ugliest face of Indian cricket'. If his own face did not ultimately fit, perhaps it is a testament to him.

The Second Tied Test

THEIR FINEST HOUR (2015)

The odds on a Test match finishing in a tie are incalculable, but clearly astronomical. Nearly 500 Tests had to be played for it to happen once, when Australia and the West Indies split 1474 runs and forty wickets right down the middle at the Gabba in December 1960. More than 500 further had to transpire before the event reoccurred, as the shadows lengthened towards the end of a stupendous Test involving India and Australia at Madras, where first 1392 runs had been interspersed with only twenty-seven wickets, then seven fell for 94. Even then, at the denouement, with just a ball remaining, the scoreboards at Chidambaram Stadium disagreed by a run, as though themselves disbelieving. Confusion reigned before euphoria broke.

In a modern era so dedicated to scaling cricket down, too, the dimensions of the match seem almost inconceivable. The longest individual innings lasted eight hours, twenty-two minutes. The heaviest individual bowling effort involved 407 deliveries, and five players bowled more than forty-five overs apiece. The final day started at 9.30 a.m. and climaxed at

5.19 p.m., accommodating 347 runs and ten wickets. Nobody knows how many attended, but claims must be close to those of the first Tied Test – a proverbially huge number. It was in a way a coming of age for both teams: for India against Australia, and Australia in the subcontinent, each captain striving to win, each country curiously fascinated by the other.

Both XIs were defined by axes – one established, one new. In India's case the polarities were those of mercurial all-rounder Kapil Dev and master batsman Sunil Gavaskar, their alternations as captain an invitation to comparison and critique. After Gavaskar's three-year reign had been ended by a torrid tour of Pakistan, Kapil Dev's tenure had built rapidly towards a defining triumph in the World Cup. Gavaskar won the top job back after a disappointing home series against the West Indies, and Kapil had even been omitted from the team for what was deemed an irresponsible shot in the Delhi Test against England in December 1984. But India's defeat in that series led to Kapil's restoration as captain, and he had come clean about his feelings for Gavaskar in an autobiography in June 1986, claiming that the batting star had 'never given me the same kind of support playing under me that I gave him when I was playing under him', and 'played under my captaincy on sufferance'.

The pair, of course, were as individually different as their skills and their statures: Gavaskar the peerless technician, the rationalist supreme; Kapil the creature of inspiration and energy, Indian cricket's *élan vital*. Their public rupture was healed over with what in hindsight seems remarkable ease – Kapil walked back from his own autobiography, claiming he had been misrepresented by his co-author; Gavaskar kept his own counsel, and contributed usefully as India got the better of England in England for the first time. The effect, however, was to invest any event involving the two with a murmurous undertone, and Gavaskar's exclusion from the first two one-day internationals against the visiting Australians was popularly viewed as a continuance of various agendas: 'Kapil takes his revenge' read *Mid-Day*'s unambiguous headline. None was assuaged when chairman of selectors Chandu Borde insisted that Gavaskar had merely been 'rested'; he was bombarded with threats and abusive telephone calls. As if sensitive to the potential for ruction, the Board of Control for Cricket in India asked the Vedanta guru Swami Parthasarathy to address the team before the match. Gestures of inclusion ensued: before Kapil walked out for the toss, Tamil Nadu's governor Sundar Lal Khurana presented Gavaskar with a silver salver in token of his hundredth consecutive Test match.

The new axis in the Australian team was between that of its hard-bitten captain Allan Border, with eighty-one Tests behind him, and its hard-headed coach Bob Simpson, with three decades of uncompromising perfectionism to draw on. Border had been grappling uneasily with leadership for more than eighteen months as the outstanding player in a callow team: the next most experienced of his touring party were vice-captain David Boon, left-arm spinner Ray Bright and middle-order batsman Greg Ritchie with sixty-one caps between them; the rest shared fifty-eight Tests in toto. At home against India, they had very nearly come to grief: only rain on top of Border's resilience had saved the hosts from the ignominy of a Boxing Day Test defeat. Australians had traditionally shied from the notion of the national team needing a 'coach': to their minds, elite players should need no nursemaiding. But since the simultaneous retirements of Greg Chappell, Dennis Lillee and Rod Marsh, and the defections of fifteen other players to South Africa, they had been compelled to reconsider – the concession to their reservations was that Simpson was referred to as 'cricket manager', as though an adjunct to 'team manager'

Alan Crompton. Nobody mistook Simpson's very hands-on purpose, least of all himself: he determined to rebuild the team from the ground up, beginning with fielding, where he led drills of furious endeavour. The team trained in such infernal heat at Baroda that they were rewarded at the end with a spraying by the local fire brigade.

In India, however, there was heat, and there was *heat*. As the Australians descended their airliner's gangway in Madras, near midnight on Monday 15 September 1986, they noticed the strong odour of sweltering tarmac, the oppressive humidity that quickly soaked their clothes, and the general torpor of the city's 'second summer'. Awaiting the relief of the north-eastern monsoon, Madras would be the third player of the First Test. Chepauk's Chidambaram Stadium, the unbroken circle of its stands excluding such breezes as there were, was just about the city's least habitable quarter, suffused with the reek of the filthy, cloacal stream of the Buckingham Canal. Simpson was a hard taskmaster, but not a foolish one. He granted his charges a day off ahead of the Test at Fisherman's Cove, a resort on the Bay of Biscay, then kept their trainings light, with lots of time at their Taj Coromandel digs. It was here, in fact, that Border hinted at something of a new composure in his role, summoning to his suite the twenty-five-year-old Victorian Dean Jones. Jones had made 67 runs in his only four Test innings more than two years earlier, before being distracted by injury, indifferent form, and the inducements of South African agents. He had come on tour with no certainty about his role – indeed, he and his West Australian roommate Mike Veletta suspected that they were vying for the same place. Border more or less confirmed it: 'I want you to be my number three for the next few years. Do you want it?' Jones stammered a thrilled acceptance. From Border, who had always seen himself as a caretaker, and who had flirted with resignation more than once, this was itself a maturing step. Border's faith and Jones's alacrity strengthened both of them.

Few contributions Border would make to the First Test would be greater than the simplest: his calling correctly when Kapil tossed the coin on Thursday. It was a relief to certain individuals in particular: Ray Bright had suffered an overnight case of food poisoning and was slumped on the dressing room couch. But it was mostly a general lift: India's batting unit, even without an injured Dilip Vengsarkar, was replete with quality, having piled up 520, 445 and 4/600 during the recent series in Australia. In an exploratory opening spell of three overs, Kapil found no swing; twenty-year-old Chetan Sharma, despite pounding the ball in, found little bounce; spinners Shivlal Yadav, Maninder Singh and Ravi Shastri were soon bracing for long spells. Boon and his opening partner Geoff Marsh were little troubled through the first hour, save by the climate, quickly shedding helmets for sun hats.

The Australians were surprised to find that the heat vexed the Indians just as much. Jones had been in only a short time after the fall of Marsh when he crossed paths with local boy Krishnamachari Srikkanth. 'Oh Deano, terrible hot isn't it?' he confided. Jones was puzzled: 'Hang on a minute. It's hot for me but you live here for heaven's sake. Surely you can take it?' Srikkanth shook his head: 'When it's this hot I don't stay in Madras; I go and live in Bombay . . . This humidity is killing me.' With the thermometer nudging 40 degrees Celsius, the hygrometer hovering at 80 per cent, the concrete of the stands was hot to touch and the fumes from the canal thick enough to cut. Boon worked on changing his gloves about every eight overs: fortunately he had brought a dozen pairs to India. Jones started to hear the squelch from his shoes, as sweat sloshed out of their eyelets. The pitch was so hard underneath it felt like running on concrete. Consolation for the batsmen was that the bowlers had it worse, the margin for error tiny, with Boon favouring his back foot and cutting adeptly, Jones quick to advance on anything offering the scope. Neither threatened to break away, but nor was the dull roar of the crowd enlivened by appeals.

The most animated sections of the day involved umpire Dara Dotiwalla, who began to fret about Jones's footwork to the slow bowlers, and how his spikes might scuff the featureless surface. This flushed Simpson from the stands, remonstrating that Dotiwalla was overstepping his authority. Rather than stand on his rights, Jones made the change voluntarily. The Indians were not fussed. They had nothing to do but bake. After lunch, Jones and Srikkanth passed one another again. 'I knew we were in for trouble when I was coming to the ground this morning and I saw the rats running away,' Srikkanth now quipped.

Boon's would be the first century of a run-rich Test. He reached the landmark, for the third time in four Tests, courtesy of a misfield at cover from Kapil's bowling after tea. His celebration was weary. Jones thought he was looking off colour, and tried farming the strike for a time in a fashion the Australians had discussed: between times Jones reached his own maiden Test fifty, in three and three quarter hours with just two boundaries. As the close approached, the Australians prepared for the second new ball, Border rousing the queasy Bright to act as nightwatchman – a wise precaution as Boon exhaustedly nicked off in the day's penultimate over. But 2/211 was everything Simpson had hoped for, and Jones's 56 from 171 balls precisely what Border had mandated. The batsman could not sleep with excitement, shrugging off his bed clothes at the Taj at 3 a.m., looking out over the city lights, and forward towards his destiny.

The heat and humidity of each day of the Test was a little worse than the last. Bright hung around eighty minutes on Friday in spite of himself, sweeping a six as he gasped for breath, before returning to the dressing room with eyes streaming tears. Jones's hard grind of the day before now paid off; wearing superlight pads lent him by Steve Waugh, he felt unassailable through the morning, treating the left-handed Maninder roughly, leaving the crease before ball's release and revelling in his sense of control. 'How do you like them apples?' he would ask, as each boundary pealed from his bat. 'How do you like them apples?' If the idiom was a mystery to Maninder, the alpha maleness was clear. An on-driven boundary from Shastri took him to a maiden hundred. But even Jones was beginning to suffer. He felt pins and needles in his extremities; he bent over and started to vomit; then he feigned vomiting in order to urinate. Teammates swarmed around him at lunch, when he was 131, like a pit crew around a racing car, stripping, showering, refreshing, redressing and re-equipping him for the afternoon, even if he could stomach no more than a banana, and he resumed batting with neither thigh pad nor protector. By now, Jones was not noticing much. If he could not hit a four, he and his captain walked a single. His solicitous opponents came over with suggestions for tonics: 'It looked at one stage as though they were more worried about me than they were about the match,' Jones recalled. His captain was more gruff. 'That's fine,' said Border, when Jones, approaching the ninth hour of his innings, confided that he might have to retire hurt. 'We'll get someone tough out here – a Queenslander.' Jones did not miss the reference to Ritchie, and seethed about it, pushing on until, on the brink of tea, he nicked Srikkanth wide of slip to become the first Australian double-centurion in India. An exhausted slog cost him his wicket fifteen minutes after the resumption, concluding the match's highest partnership, 178.

The drama was not over yet. While Border plunged on, Jones plunged into an ice bath prepared by physiotherapist

Errol Alcott, which nonetheless felt strangely lukewarm. Waugh thought him like a 'walking corpse', and pretty soon he was not walking either, having suffered a syncopal attack as teammates attempted to rehydrate him – their dutiful baggage man Govind Bawji Vadolikar hastily summoned an ambulance from the Apollo Hospital. When Border re-entered the dressing room after scoring his own hundred and was told of Jones's collapse, he felt culpable: 'My God, I've killed him.' In fact, connected to a saline drip and ministered to by half a dozen starstruck doctors, he bounced back quickly, even if he was not to regain the 8 kilograms he lost over those two days for another eighteen months.

The Australians pressed on for thirty-seven further minutes on Saturday morning, and struck after an hour of the reply, removing an indiscreet Gavaskar, then Amarnath and Srikkanth in consecutive balls after lunch to reduce India to 3/65, still more than 500 runs in arrears. Again the slow bowlers bore the brunt of the labour, Bright's left-armers in harness with Greg Matthews' off-breaks. But with two days' fielding in their legs, the batsmen were hard-pressed too: Mohammad Azharuddin, Ravi Shastri and Vengsarkar's locum Chandrakant Pandit played with a freedom that was almost light-headed. At 7/245 late on the third day, India looked doomed to follow on. Had Dotiwalla upheld Waugh's lbw appeal against Kapil (8), they assuredly would have. As it was, two years since he had been disciplined for a similar misdeed, India's captain harangued his players at stumps for essaying one-day shots in a Test match.

It was to be a case of do as I say, not as I do: his first three balls of Sunday, Kapil hit for four, and kept going from there, while Sharma and Yadav maintained a vigil at the other end. Tall and straight as a pillar topped out with a white helmet or sun hat, he was severe on every bowler, cutting Reid, hooking McDermott, defying Bright's spin by hitting over mid-wicket and Matthews' by stroking inside out. To attack or defend? Border thought simply to wait, but had to concede the follow-on, and eventually a virile hundred, Kapil's fourth, studded with twenty-one boundaries. Speeding up the match, India's skipper had put the ball in his rival's court: how prepared was the Australian to lose in order to win?

The answer, at least at first, was not very. India's slow bowlers now slowed the tempo adeptly, and the Australians struggled to challenge them, tempers fraying in the enervating heat. Shastri enjoyed his hundredth Test wicket, bowling Marsh; when Maninder dismissed Jones, he ran 30 metres to shout the unintelligible idiom: 'How do you like them apples?' Australia's scoring rate over forty-nine overs never passed 3.5. It looked a little as though the Test had given its all and would end in stalemate, like eight of the preceding dozen Tests between the countries, and four of the last six Tests at Chepauk. Back at the Taj, however, Australia's captain and coach compared notes. While batting, Border had seen deliveries from Maninder and Shastri turn sharply from the rough. While India had an enviable fourth-innings record, Simpson worked out that no country had scored as many as 348 on a final day to win a Test. What a shame, they agreed, if a Test so good so far should peter out. Border decided to sleep on it, and woke refreshed and resolved. 'You can have another bat,' he told Kapil when they met at 9 a.m. 'We will be going for a win,' Kapil advised his charges on returning to the dressing room. The public of Madras were caught faintly unawares: only 5000 were in attendance as Gavaskar and Srikkanth began the Indian chase on Monday, but word of their obvious ambition spread through the city so that the ground filled steadily towards capacity.

With a minimum of eighty-seven overs to be bowled, requiring a scoring rate of 4 an over, Border's declaration was a beckoning invitation. The openers soon made it look nearly foolhardy. Srikkanth swished six swift boundaries before being caught on the run at long-on. Gavaskar, supported by Amarnath, followed with unaccustomed flamboyance, punching straight, driving on the up, looming large. When his back knee touched the ground as he stroked McDermott through the covers, Border felt an anxious pang: while Gavaskar always exuded control, this was command. Jones and Waugh, batting purists, were perversely enthralled. It was Gavaskar joining the batting pageant – even, at the scene of his record-breaking thirtieth Test hundred, outdoing it.

Border was hemmed in. Two of his four specialist bowlers, the pacemen Reid and McDermott, were impotent; a third, Bright, was still unwell, coming and going from the field. There had been no rest day, conditions were at their worst, and the canal stench was so overpowering that some fielders wore handkerchiefs over their mouths. Australia had one trump, Matthews, who had taken his first five-for in the first innings, and was toiling towards a second with eccentric determination. When not whirling away over after over, he was on the boundary edge either bantering with the crowd or taking advantage of a small stool they offered. At one point, he called for a jumper, then a second, explaining that he had seen a documentary about livestock herders in a desert country who wore woollen overcoats to 'keep the cool air in' – it seemed more like a proclamation of Australian resilience, a demand that the weather do its worst. Dotiwalla denied him a bat-pad appeal at silly point against Amarnath, then half an hour later granted one at short leg to leave India 2/158.

Either side of tea, Matthews and Bright worked to slow India's scoring, to keep Gavaskar off strike, and Azharuddin pinned down on leg stump. Each batsmen hit a six, but between times were becalmed. With the hosts needing 144, Gavaskar drove prematurely at Bright, and Jones timed his leap at extra cover perfectly, thinking as the great batsman departed: 'I wish the little bugger had got out for a duck but I admired every minute of his innings.'

Border kept thinking that, sooner or later, India would settle for a draw, allowing him to bring catchers in. But as the final score of overs approached, the chase surged again. Pandit swung about him robustly and there was an explosion of approbation as India came within two figures of their target with seven wickets remaining. Then, suddenly, a break: Azharuddin and Kapil holed out in consecutive overs. Again, though, remission was temporary. For a studious player, Shastri could swing a bat in generous arcs: just over eighteen months earlier, he had joined Garry Sobers in hitting six sixes in an over in a first-class match, all down the ground off a left-arm spinner. As he hit Matthews into the crowd, Border skewed his field to leg. 'Christ,' he thought. 'There's no justice here. We score 570, declare twice to make a game of it, and we're going to lose.' The need was down to 57 when Pandit, pulling back to make room, dragged on.

Still the Indians continued their headlong pursuit. No sooner had Border drawn his field in than Shastri hit again into the stands, rousing the fans further by the tamasha gestures of clapping his bat on his gloved hand. Lengthy adjustments ensued, drawing the ever officious Dotiwalla into the fray, who began to remonstrate about the over rate. Border barked back. Dotiwalla gestured towards the pavilion, as though expelling the Australian captain. 'He can't send me off, Babsie, can he?' Border asked Boon. Boon shrugged his shoulders. Somehow the match continued, but when Tim Zoehrer appeared to stump Chetan Sharma soon after the aggrieved umpire shook his head, the Australians shook theirs. Batsman and keeper had a colourful contretemps; Sharma followed up with clumping strokes; the target shrank to less than 18 from five overs, with four wickets in hand.

Bright came back, queasily but willingly, and struck with consecutive deliveries. Sharma aimed down the ground, and miscued to mid-on; More aimed to leg and was trapped, Dotiwalla pausing dubiously before raising his finger. Number ten was Yadav, with a solid defence and a strong bottom hand. If he was to hit, Shastri counselled, Yadav should aim with the spin. He duly hoisted Matthews over the fence, almost swinging himself off his feet in the process. But in the penultimate over, with four runs required from nine deliveries, Yadav was bowled trying to repeat the stroke off Bright. When last man Maninder Singh defended the next two deliveries, the toils of 2400 previous deliveries depended on what occurred in the last half dozen. By now the ground was reverberating, the heat, humidity and stench forgotten. The press box was electrified. Calcutta journalist Debasish Datta had never smoked before, but when a lit cigarette was passed to him he began puffing. Kapil and his team looked on Shastri as their saviour. The Australian enclosure eyed number eleven Maninder confidently. 'How nervous do you reckon this bloke would be?' Simpson asked manager Crompton.

Matthews took the ball for his fortieth over of the day out of eighty-seven, his baggy green rank with sweat, his dirty creams clinging to his flanks. After coolly defending the first ball, Shastri tugged the second behind square, where the ball took a bad bounce as it approached Waugh, and the batsmen scurried back on the misfield; pushed in front of square, the third ball yielded a single that tied the scores. It was playing safe *and* taking a chance: India now could not lose, but depended on a batsman with a Test average of 4.7 to drag them to victory. Border's fear had been victory by a bold blow from Shastri; now the likelihood was a scurried single for which he could plan. At last he drew his field in, standing at silly point himself, placing Marsh at short leg, and enjoining Matthews to bowl straight at the stumps. Maninder fended away the over's fourth ball, but missed the fifth, and umpire Venkat Raju, over-shadowed throughout the match by his voluble partner, had his arm aloft almost before the appeal had commenced. Border never actually appealed: he was too busy scrambling after the ball. Waugh was typically cool: he swooped on the striker's stumps, souveniring two.

Was there an inside edge? Maninder entreated Raju to change his mind; Shastri was so convinced that he ignored Raju altogether, and was at first bemused at the Australian celebrations; Raju was equally adamant otherwise, even if he suspected the decision played a part in his never umpiring another Test. There is a theory, ventured by some, that criticisms of Indian umpiring from overseas had led to their indulging visiting teams; yet the Australians could easily point to the counterexample of Dotiwalla, who seemed to do them no favours. Waugh put it most simply: 'Like us, he [Raju] wanted to be part of history.' Whatever the case, the scorebook is unambiguous: lbw Matthews 0, match tied. Also tied was the man-of-the-match award, between Jones and Kapil, although the Australians so esteemed Matthews' 10/249 that Border gave him the ball and Waugh a stump. But there could be, as Tiger Pataudi noted, no doubt of the fitness of the result: 'It was a match India did not deserve to win nor did Australia deserve to lose. A draw would have been a satisfactory outcome, but a tie took the game into the realms of fantasy where there were no losers and the greatest gainer was Test match cricket itself.'

The participants, fleetingly antagonists if closer to co-religionists, benefited also. A year later, India hosted its first World Cup and Australia won, both drawing on confidence forged in that cricket crucible at Chepauk. The players? The glory does not fade; if anything, the events of Monday

INDIAN SUMMERS

22 September 1986 grow more remarkable for each passing day. The running total of Test matches has more than doubled in the ensuing thirty years, and there have been no further ties – except, perhaps, those that bind.

Tendulkar in Perth 1992

THE LITTLE MASTER ARRIVES (2009)

A t the time, there was nothing much about the Australian summer of 1991–92 to arrest its easy slide into cricket past, the home team winning Test and one-day series easily, India and the West Indies slipping out of the country to the sound of their own feet. Only in hindsight has more been detected to it – so very much more.

For Australian fans in particular, it was a summer of four fascinating premonitions. They enjoyed their first glimpses of Shane Warne, of Brian Lara, of Sourav Ganguly and of Sachin Tendulkar – of the last, a baby-faced nineteen-year-old who blasted more than 1000 international runs in that few months, the impression was nigh unforgettable. In a triumph, it would have been special; in a badly beaten side, it bordered on uncanny. By summer's end, Allan Miller was writing in *Allan's Australian Cricket Annual*: 'Bow, bowlers, to the great and mighty Tendulkar!'

Think back to international cricket circa 1991–92. It seems an eternity ago. There were seven full Test nations. There were only two umpires per Test, and the standing officials of that

Australian season were all locals – with all the possibility of martyred grievance when eight lbws befell India in Adelaide, and only two were upheld against Australians.

India had not visited Australia for six years, had played one Test in the preceding fifteen months, and it showed. In match after match, batsmen shambled across their stumps, fended at balls they should have left, ducked balls they should have played. Captain Mohammad Azharuddin struggled with his mantle, and a much-vaunted line-up steadily ran out of vaunts: Sanjay Manjrekar seemed incapable of an attacking stroke, Kris Srikkanth of a defensive stroke, Dilip Vengsarkar of any stroke at all.

Vaunts of Tendulkar, meanwhile, steadily became a chorus, especially after he became the youngest player to score a Test century in Australia, taking particular toll on the callow Warne. In the crowd at a one-day match in Sydney soon after was seen a banner: 'Oh, what a feeling . . . Tendulkar!' The invocation alluded to a popular television advertisement for Toyota: the tyro was being added to the common culture.

The innings that really quickened the pulse was played on the other side of the continent, in conditions quite opposite, and also quite alien to those in which Tendulkar had been trained. Perth's WACA Ground in those days was a little like a lonely, windswept pass in the wild west, where ambuscades awaited unwary travellers. The bounce was almost vertical, the carry far and fizzing. Not even Australian teams liked it much: the arena was known for sparse, parochial crowds mainly interested in watching fellow Westralians.

On their first visit to the WACA that summer, in November 1991, India had been bundled out by Western Australia for 64, a prelude of their future problems with the rising delivery. In pursuit of Australia's 346 in the Fifth Test three months later, they looked shaky at once. Srikkanth was hit a glancing blow on the helmet by Craig McDermott, and turned to watch it bang into the sightscreen after a few bounces, rolling his eyes expressively. By stumps on the second day, the tourists were a punch-drunk 5/135, and lost their nightwatchman without addition next morning.

By this stage, Tendulkar was poised to counterattack, and did so thrillingly. New cap Paul Reiffel thought the Indians looked 'jaded' during the Test, as well they might have, trailing 0–3. For Tendulkar, though, there was the familiar challenge of Australia but also the new assignment of number four: he welcomed it, his tiny figure crossing the crease to square cut at the top of the bounce, easing into line to drive down the ground, swaying from harm at the inevitable short stuff.

The people of Perth had, as was their wont in those days, stayed away in droves: there were fewer than 5000 spectators, and the Channel Nine cameras could not avoid panning across empty terraces. When Tendulkar stood on his toes to slash McDermott, Reiffel, Merv Hughes and Mike Whitney, the crack from his bat seemed to echo round the stands like the report of a Lee-Enfield. Tendulkar cut, in fact, more often than seemed wise, and at balls closer to his body than a purist probably would have liked; it was the cricket of a batsman trusting his nerve, following instinct rather than instruction. Every ball looked likely to get him out until it came near him, when it was subdued, controlled, countered.

In truth, it was a race against time, with the innings expiring at the other end, a race into which Tendulkar hurled himself with 81 between commencement and lunch, racing from 50 to 100 in fifty-five deliveries, and putting on 81 in ninety-one minutes with Kiran More: an Indian ninth wicket record against Australia. Nor had the cares of cricket quite taken their toll on Tendulkar. When he drove McDermott through mid-on for four to reach his hundred, he removed his helmet to show a brief, boyish smile, unselfconsciously reminding onlookers that he was only just old enough to vote, and barely looked old enough to shave.

When Tendulkar skewered Whitney to backward point to finish on 114 from 161 balls with sixteen fours soon after, the Perth crowd did their best to honour him: 5000 had a reasonable stab at sounding like 50,000. More, inspired, prolonged the innings another 32 runs and thirty-three minutes, limiting India's arrears to 74 if only slightly narrowing its eventual defeat margin of 300 runs: it would be some time before India abroad were a fraction as formidable as the team they were at home.

Nonetheless, against the evidence of the results, there was something to Sunil Gavaskar's remarks after the series: 'India got a lot from this tour.' What might have been a rout at Perth was really only a defeat: Australia would lose the corresponding Test of the following summer in just over two days, by which time India would be utterly annihilating England. A year after that, Tendulkar, who had arrived in Australia with a Test average less than 40, had a Test average greater than 50, and there was no looking back – until, perhaps, now.

WORLD CHAMPIONSHIP WRESTLING

Who Will Be The World Champion? *was the title of an Indian television programme that aired during the 2001 Border–Gavaskar Trophy. Never mind that there was no actual cricket world championship, or stake, or prior arrangement at all: Australia was simply the benchmark that India needed to aim for. Which, celebratedly, they did: after losing at Delhi, they struck back from the brink of disaster at Kolkata, and pushed the visitors over their brink in Chennai. That Test at Eden Gardens, then, was the making of an epoch: dealt with in detail here, it marked the beginning of the notion that India, with its star-studded batting line-up of Tendulkar, Dravid, Laxman and Sehwag, was a potential match for Australia in particular and everyone in general. The fiasco of the 2008 Sydney Test then underlined the political and financial stakes, which have only continued to grow.*

Kolkata Test 2001

A CRICKET ODYSSEY (2016)

The note left with the concierge of Kolkata's Taj Bengal Hotel on the night of Monday 12 March 2001 bore the signatures of 'Vinay', 'Mahmud' and 'Sanchayita', and was addressed to 'our cricket team'. When it was duly conveyed to him, coach John Wright felt a mix of admiration and chagrin. 'You guys can still win this match,' read the message. 'We believe in you.' Indian fans, eh? Who could doubt their faith? But their logic – well, reflected Wright, there was none in evidence here.

As the match stood after two days, India were 8/128 chasing Australia's 445, seemingly en route to a consecutive three-day defeat which would cost them a series, a trophy and respect. If only his players displayed such conviction, Wright reflected, before slipping into a restless sleep, helped by four cans of Heineken and five cigarettes. India's first foreign-born coach wondered if his tenure might already be over.

For it was not just the Test the note seemed to defy, but the whole tilt of cricket. Since the World Cup of 1999 had concluded in damp misery, the Indian game had been in upheaval. A captain and his deputy, Mohammad Azharuddin and Ajay Jadeja, had been enswirled in the fug of corruption. Anointed as successor, Sachin Tendulkar had been unable to provide other than his usual solo excellence. He had been succeeded by Sourav Ganguly, symbolising the steady rise of the game in Bengal since the administrative ascendancy of the local potentate Jagmohan Dalmiya. But a shoulder injury had then incapacitated the linchpin of India's attack, Anil Kumble, while no wicketkeeper had made himself a fixture since Kiran More.

Then there had been the role of coach, held for an unhappy year by Kapil Dev. The appointment of the low-key Wright reflected the desire for a clean break. While coaching Kent in England's County Championship, he had made the acquaintance of Ganguly and his deputy Rahul Dravid. They warmed to his easy-going ways, and their say-so had helped sway an appointment panel. But he found a team that while replete with talent was hidebound in its practices, unfit, unfocused and without the most basic equipment: the kit consisted of three stumps, three baseball mitts and thirty cones. Administration and selection were politicised, intrigue routine.

The visit of the Australians set pulses racing. They had bossed Test cricket for six years, secured the World Cup, virtually owned the Ashes, and overwhelmed India three times at the countries' last encounter, part of a victory streak that on their arrival extended fifteen Test matches. There was an asterisk against their status: thanks partly to relatively infrequent visits, they had not won a Test series in India since 1969. But they meant business. Their captain, Steve Waugh, who unlike predecessors was stimulated by the challenges of the subcontinent, had taken to calling the country 'the Final Frontier'. When Wright dropped in on their training sessions at Brabourne Stadium, he was awed by its vigour and purpose. He drove his own players harder – as hard as some had been driven. They responded well, but deficiencies were hardly difficult to spot.

The media, seldom less than excited about a cricket visitor, were strung up to concert pitch. A new twenty-four-hour news channel called Aaj Tak (Till Today), the first of its kind, was to pioneer a new approach to cricket, covering it almost as current affairs. Aaj Tak's news cycle was punctuated with cricket updates and reviews, plus a text graphic of the live score at all times, while its nightly show *Who Will Become the World Champion?* positioned the Tests as a battle for world supremacy.

The cricket struggled to match such billing. In the First Test at Mumbai, India looked not so much a frontier as a vulnerable principality ripe for annexation. After Waugh sent India in, the taut control of Glenn McGrath, Shane Warne and Jason Gillespie, reinforced by hundreds from Matthew Hayden then Adam Gilchrist, overwhelmed their hosts by ten wickets in less than 250 overs. The team's dashing young batsman Ricky Ponting atoned for failure by compiling a brace of unbeaten hundreds in the ensuing tour game in Delhi, before the team arrived in Kolkata in time for Holi. So confident were the visitors that Waugh and opener Michael Slater came equipped for celebrations, Waugh with a bottle of Southern Comfort, Slater with a big cigar – although they and four others who had been on the losing side of a Test at Eden Gardens three years earlier took superstitious care not to occupy the same places in their dressing room.

Wright and Ganguly had a great deal more to contemplate. By now their best fast bowler, Javagal Srinath, had joined Kumble by the wayside. And two of their specialist batsmen arrived below par, Rahul Dravid so stricken with fever that he could not practise, VVS Laxman so in pain from his lower back he needed constant ministrations from physiotherapist Andrew Leipus. Ganguly himself was out of sorts with the bat, and the team's tail was long and vulnerable. The mantle of number one slow bowler, moreover, now fell on Harbhajan Singh, a combustible Sikh from Jalandhar who had been expelled for misbehaviour from Bangalore's National Cricket Academy but recalled to the colours on Kumble's recommendation. Since his father Sardev had died the year before, Harbhajan's skinny twenty-year-old shoulders had been bearing a heavy load, including control of the family ball bearing factory and the care of five sisters. He had been challenged by the Australians in Mumbai, broken through early then been collared. Now in his tenth Test he would have to fill both stock and shock roles – and, when Waugh called correctly, on a first day to boot.

Evidence to tea was that the toss had been a decidedly useful one to win, on a pitch finely latticed with cracks but hard as a dancefloor underfoot. The opening partnership of Hayden and Slater was not broken until after lunch, and Hayden's huge stride and scything sweep menaced the close-in fielders as they had in Mumbai. He had arrived in India with a spotty Test record; having schooled himself in batting on specially desiccated surfaces at Brisbane's Allan Border Field in preparation for the tour, he seemed almost to have already played the Tests in his mind. But nothing about this Test was to prove remotely foreordained. Four balls after the interval, Hayden picked out deep backward square leg, falling three runs short of a second consecutive Test century. Approaching the crease in a whirl of long-sleeved arms, relying on overspin and mixing in the occasional seamer, Harbhajan began exerting a measure of control. And when Zaheer Khan had Justin Langer caught at the wicket, the pitch and the environs grew abruptly more hostile.

Steve Waugh would describe Eden Gardens as 'the Lord's of India', such was its heritage and theatre. When it reverberated, it was like listening to the crowd noise amplified through headphones – total, inescapable. As Australia's captain looked on from the non-striker's end, Harbhajan now struck four times in the space of four overs, the roar from 75,000 throats never abating. The last three wickets composed India's first Test hat-trick, even if the umpiring decisions were of a certainty hard to justify. Ponting was pinned on the crease right enough, but the possibility of an inside edge from Gilchrist and a bump ball from Warne went unentertained by SK Bansal and Sameer Bandekar (the third umpire) respectively. Not that this disturbed the jubilant pile-on of fielders, or the captain, who was inspired to take the ball up himself and win an lbw verdict against Michael Kasprowicz.

It had been a while since Australia had found themselves eight down for as few as 269 anywhere, although they responded with the resourcefulness of a champion team. Waugh, never rushed, as laconic with his strokes as his words, was born for such scenarios. He bunkered coolly down with stiff-armed and soft-handed Gillespie to see the evening out and they resumed next morning as if performing a toilsome but necessary chore. Bansal evened up his earlier interventions by keeping his finger down when Gillespie nicked Prasad early, but there were no further alarms: their 133-run partnership, Australia's biggest for the ninth wicket in more than a century, emerged at the jogging pace of three an over, before a final flourish of 43 in forty-nine balls involving Waugh and Glenn McGrath bulked Australia's total to 445. After spending five chanceless hours over his first Test century in India, Waugh presented Harbhajan with a seventh wicket by falling to a sweep shot. It would prove the last cause for Indian celebration for more than a day.

With not quite an hour until tea, India were desperate not to lose a wicket: they lost both openers. Two boundaries from Tendulkar stirred the crowd to frenzy; a successful lbw appeal by McGrath stunned them to silence. Having acclima-tised painstakingly, Ganguly and Dravid fell four balls apart, beginning a phase of five wickets in twelve overs. Highest scorer was Laxman on 26 not out. He came in at the close for further maintenance from Leipus; at eight for 128, India seemed beyond treatment. Wright's night in room 214 was 'one of the loneliest, most desolate nights of my life' – that bedraggled exhortation by the three fans was the only note of hope. Otherwise, he could hardly believe the gap that had opened between the sides: 'The Aussies were an exceptional team, but we were playing as if we didn't think we belonged on the same park.'

Once his charges are in the field, of course, the impact a coach can have is necessarily limited. But the following morning, Wright had a brainwave that may have changed Indian cricket history. He was fortunate to have the time to make it. At 9/140, Venkatesh Prasad was struck on the full, and India seemed to have been rounded up more than 300 runs in arrears. But Bansal turned the lbw appeal down, and Laxman was able to push on from 37 to 59 with strokes of some panache, confounding Warne by driving him through and over the off side from outside leg stump. Like someone trying to remember the drift of an old song, Wright recalled something he had once read by Ian Chappell, which recommended the number three role in a batting line-up be held by a strokemaker, to take advantage of attacking fields and dispose of loose deliveries. It was not even half a theory – really just a view. But for want of some other inspiration, and faced with a batting line-up out for 176, 219 and 171 so far in the series, he put the proposition to Ganguly. Dravid's 73 runs in those innings had taken him almost seven hours. Ganguly agreed that Laxman might be the better bet at first wicket down, and Dravid acquiesced.

Waugh and his coach John Buchanan had their own decision to make. Waugh's predecessor Mark Taylor had been a reluctant enforcer of the follow-on, after being thwarted by Pakistan at Rawalpindi, preferring to maximise Warne's fourth innings opportunities; Waugh was less reticent, confident in his attack's all-round capacities. India, he now reasoned, was toppling. It was time to administer the coup de grace. Word had reached India's dressing room by the time Laxman re-entered it. 'Keep your pads on, Lax,' Wright said. 'We want you to bat at number three.' The tall twenty-six-year-old Hyderabadi felt disarmingly confident. India had struggled previously to find a role for him. At number six, he had seemed almost an afterthought; at number one, he had felt a little sacrificial. Number three was where he had batted for much of his first-class career, including where he'd piled up 353 for Hyderabad against Karnataka in the Ranji Trophy semi-final a year earlier. Openers Sadagoppan Ramesh and SS Das now negotiated the dozen overs through to lunch while Leipus continued his task of keeping Laxman supple and pain free.

Eden Gardens was now officially hot, which the Australians had expected, their hair cut military short, but which constrained their captain from allocating spells too long. The crowd, all those Vinays, Mahmuds and Sanchayitas, somehow never seemed to tire, the atmosphere as unanimous and celebratory as a religious festival. Hearts soared as Laxman took guard after lunch and drove his first ball from McGrath down the ground for four. The roar echoed again when Das worked Gillespie to fine leg and returned for a second, only to have Gilchrist point out a fallen bail, disturbed by a heel. But somehow the waves of acclamation kept coming, surviving even the disappointment of Tendulkar's second cheap dismissal in the game just before tea, carrying along the Indians and crashing over the Australians like the breakers on a shore. Every so often Laxman produced a shot that seemed totally out of keeping with the seriousness of negotiating a follow-on: pull shots from the pace bowlers when they attacked him from round the wicket; a cover-drive and an off-drive on the up from Kasprowicz, and finally a nonchalant on-drive from the same bowler that took him to his second half-century of the third day in ninety-three easeful deliveries.

At length, the local boy Ganguly settled in, redoubling the acclaim, winnowing the arrears away to double figures. But the duel of the day, perhaps of the match, was Laxman against Warne. The leg-spinner was not quite at his best. He had missed much of his home summer with a broken finger; he found Kolkata's heat and airlessness enervating. But he kept whirling away from all angles, probing away at a leg stump rough that occasionally offered extravagant deviation. It would prove a kind of trap. Laxman was undaunted by deviation; on the contrary, it provided room to manoeuvre, long legs and quick feet extending his sphere of influence. There were on-drives, off-drives, cover-drives, all hit as if from a stationary tee. When Warne then flattened his arc, Laxman laid back and pulled. Although he was within sight of his century when his captain nicked off, Dravid was on hand to help consummate the landmark, calling Laxman through for a quick single from Warne: at 166 balls with seventeen fours, the hundred had been a virtual scamper.

Stumps brought helpings of reality. The deficit had been reduced to 20 runs, but India held precious little batting in reserve, and the Australian juggernaut had after sixteen Tests a certain inevitability about it. 'It'll be over tomorrow,' commentator Tony Greig said airily. 'More time on the golf course.' The Australians were of the same mind. Waugh eyed his Southern Comfort thirstily. Slater, who had nursed some reservations about the follow-on, playfully drew his cigar under his nose. 'This result is so close I can smell it,' he said, to the amusement of Gilchrist, who had not in his eighteen months as a Test cricketer known defeat.

The Australians bowled that morning as though drawn on by that odour. With a second new ball, McGrath and

Kasprowicz hit the deck hard; Gillespie punctured the defences of both Laxman and Dravid, inside edges streaking away for lucky boundaries. Then when the ball started reversing, Waugh opportunistically turned to Ponting, who wobbled deliveries around at a zesty medium pace – an lbw reprieve granted Dravid caused Australian expressions to darken. But Waugh's attacking fields ensured that the supply of boundaries was never quite cut off, and with India in credit each had a context as runs the visitors would have to get themselves. On the stroke of lunch, Dravid reached his first half-century of the series, extending the partnership to 144.

Batsmen, bowlers and fielders were now up against the limits of their endurance. Laxman's back and Dravid's fever were taking their toll. Teammates cut towels into strips for ice-filled neckerchiefs, which reserve players Hemang Badani and Sarandeep Singh would run out in relays the rest the day. But after by now more than 160 overs in the field, with only one wicket in the last seventy overs, and four specialist bowlers, it was the Australians running shortest of options. In the afternoon, Waugh had to turn to his brother's occasional off-spin, and the seldom-used varieties of Hayden, Slater and Langer, hoping to bring back a key bowler if a wicket fell. None did. Minds were even beginning to wander. Keeper Gilchrist and first slip Warne idled the day listing their ten favourite movies, songs and supermodels. Back in the dressing room, twelfth man Damien Fleming got a glancing view of himself in a mirror and jested ruefully: 'Good one to miss, Flem. Good one to miss.'

Both batsmen hit boundaries early in the afternoon session to reassert themselves, and Dravid for the first time took the lead. His pride had been slightly piqued by his demotion, and the Australians had known it. 'Three to six,' they had chirped at him on his coming in the night before. 'Six to out of the side.' He was not about to forget it. Warne had dismissed him seven times in Tests already; now Dravid was playing him with ever greater ease, using his feet, then sitting back to enjoy the errors of length. As a cut to the boundary streaked away, Warne bent low from the waist, out of exasperation but as if in supplication. It was one thing for Tendulkar to be his master; now a whole country seemed ranged against him.

Just after drinks, Dravid passed 86, his previous highest against Australia. There was a new menace now. Although cooled by a fresh neckerchief, he was experiencing painful cramps. Dravid abandoned all thought of the match, the session, even the over. 'Let me get through this one ball,' he repeated to himself. 'Let me get through this one ball.' But as Leipus came out with a tablet, it was the Australians who looked in greater need of relief: they sat or lay down, squatted and stretched.

Now the milestones were looming ahead. A Dravid flick through mid-wicket raised the double-century stand; a Laxman cover-drive raised his personal double-century. 'It really has been a masterpiece from VVS Laxman,' assented Ian Chappell, never one to bestow such tributes lightly, in the commentary box. On 97, Dravid faced Warne, who theatrically adjusted his field, beckoning and despatching like a dramaturge. Four times Dravid took his stance only to be kept waiting. At last he came down the pitch and on-drove his 205th delivery for his thirteenth four to attain his ninth Test century. He waved his bat in circles, then jabbed it meaningfully at the press box – a departure from his usual equanimity that told of the passion of his engagement. By tea his sangfroid had returned: he walked off a deferential step behind Laxman, while the Australians appreciatively applauded.

With India 200 runs ahead, the scoreboard bore a further message: the Cricket Association of Bengal, fiefdom of Jagmohan Dalmiya, announced a substantial cash reward for Laxman, to be enhanced as he scored more. He was entering uncharted statistical territory too. When he whipped Hayden into the deep for a long single after tea, he became the maker of India's highest Test score, surpassing Gavaskar's undefeated 236 at Chennai in December 1983 – a thrill for both partners, if a cause of reminiscent headshakes among older press box colleagues.

The partnership had outgrown efforts to save the game – against all odds, it was offering a winning strategy. Laxman considered hitting out with an eye on the possibility of a triple-century by stumps, but thought better of it: better just to keep grinding. 'Well played, Jam,' he counselled his partner, still fighting cramps. 'Hang in, Jam.' Dravid could by now hardly lift his arms, but felt the relief of a slight breeze.

A détente emerged. As the batsmen knuckled down, intent on depriving the Australians of even a consolation wicket, Waugh set more defensive fields. In thirty-two overs after tea, 98 runs were added, and the conclusion was muted, even in the Indian dressing room, accoutred as a triage unit: Laxman went to Leipus's treatment table and Dravid to the luncheon table for intravenous drips. At dinner that evening at Ganguly's palatial home, which was thronged by Vinays, Mahmuds and Sanchayitas, the Indians tried to absorb the implications of their new ascendancy. Their lead had stretched to 315 – no team in India had chased so many for victory. Winning was the only way to keep the series alive. Winning was the way to claim half a million rupees staked by the Cricket Association of Bengal. Yet Ganguly was circumspect. To lose having worked so hard to save would be devastating. Wright made a different argument. Waugh's team had written the book on winning – their relentless pursuit of victory was why they had enforced the follow-on. Why not challenge them to draw a game? The consensus formed: to bat on, until the innings had lasted so long that India could not lose and Australia could not win.

And so, the following morning, in front of what looked like the greatest crowd yet, Laxman and Dravid resumed. McGrath, having taken India's fourth wicket on Tuesday, took their fifth and sixth on Thursday. Laxman's 281 ended after ten and a half hours and forty-four boundaries from 452 balls when he picked point out with a tired drive; Dravid's 180 concluded after seven and a half hours and twenty boundaries from 353 balls, when he was too bone weary to turn back from an aborted single. Ganguly stood inscrutably on the balcony as Zaheer Khan and Harbhajan threw the bat until, at the end of the day's thirteenth over and the innings' 178th, he beckoned his batsmen in with a hesitant wave, having set the visitors a distant target of 384, and challenged his bowlers to winkle out ten wickets in seventy-five overs. This essentially meant Harbhajan, who alone among bowlers in the match had found conditions congenial, obtaining bounce from his overspin, menacing pads and inside edges with his wicket-to-wicket line. Ganguly threw him the ball for the innings' eighth over, and Hayden at once drove a chance to mid-off, which Prasad inexpertly spilt – the first luck Australia had enjoyed in days.

It did not lift their spirits. At the long interval, the equation required 360 runs from Australia at nearly a run a ball. It was a gauntlet they might have picked up in a one-day scenario, but after sixteen hot sessions of Test cricket they were heavy-legged and -hearted. The pitch was playing tricks at last: a ball from Harbhajan took off from the rough and broke keeper Nayan Mongia's nose, forcing Dravid to fill in. Such inconsistencies added to Australian foreboding, not least because they had condemned themselves to batting last. Before play, Waugh had enjoined his teammates to price their wickets highly: 'If we're forced to fight for a draw, let's do everything we can to achieve it.' He wondered later if he should have reiterated his message: he had the sense that, as Wright had foreseen, players without the incentive of victory could not quite agree on an approach. Confusion certainly enveloped Gilchrist, the matchwinner of Mumbai, averaging 60 in his brief but gilded Test career, who found himself on a king pair. Suddenly it was all he could think of: another zero, first ball. Whatever happened, he must, must not sweep – on this surface, in these circumstances, it was too dangerous.

Australia's innings flattered to deceive, coasting past 100 at a run-a-minute with just one wicket down, Langer hinting at a chase by slog-sweeping two sixes from Harbhajan. But they were hectic, febrile strokes, and Langer quickly top-edged a lap shot to backward square before Mark Waugh played fatally back to a skidder, filling Eden Gardens with celebrations that sent further tremors through the Australian dressing room. Hayden and Steve Waugh found themselves flocked by dusty, animated close-in fielders near enough to shake hands with, even if the din was so great that greetings would have been inaudible. When they traipsed off at tea, India and Australia had 223 runs and seven wickets to play with respectively. Wright's sense was that 'something had to give'. In five tumultuous overs it was Australia.

Harbhajan's accomplice, improbably, was Tendulkar, an inconspicuous presence for four and a half days, shrewdly thrown the ball by Ganguly for a few of his hard-spun legbreaks. Harbhajan caused Waugh to fend to short fine leg, Ponting to bunt to short leg. Then Tendulkar tossed up to the befuddled Gilchrist, drawn to play the stroke he had determined to abjure, hit lethally on the back leg, and 'as lost and lonely as I have ever felt in my life' as he walked off.

It was not for want of company. Crowds at Eden Gardens have never been truly estimable, its capacity overwhelming logistics, so it might have hosted larger attendances; what seems sure is it never *felt* as full as on 15 March 2001, stands heaving with motion, without a speck of empty terrace to be seen. As Tendulkar continued, Hayden played around a full delivery and Warne misread a wrong 'un, and the finger of SK Bansal shot aloft. Australia had lost eight wickets in 100 runs; the last two would have to survive twenty-five overs to save the game.

This was a proud team, and it kept its green and gold colours fluttering for nearly twenty more overs as shadows lengthened across the field and smoke billowed from burning newspapers, relieved by light pouring through the gaps in the stands. Failed by their batsmen, Australia's bowlers were undismayed, obdurate. At last, in the innings' sixty-ninth over, and Harbhajan's thirty-first, McGrath plunged a pad down the line of the stumps and was adjudged the fifth Australian lbw. In more than 1500 previous Test matches, only twice had a team come back to win after following on, and circumspect captains have not let it happen since. As Wright has put it: 'It's as if Laxman and Dravid are looking over their shoulders.'

The Australians were bamboozled. Waugh had his Southern Comfort for company as he drowned his sorrows, Gilchrist playfully broke Slater's cigar over his knee. They were to have to sit on the tarmac at Dum Dum Airport for hours that evening as they awaited the Indian team still celebrating at Eden Gardens. But, as their captain said, they could hardly begrudge the victors, having tasted so much victory themselves: they had also played one of history's most astonishing Test matches, which in the end probably did them as little harm as it did their opponents good. 'Thanks for saving my job,' Wright quipped to Laxman afterwards, only half in jest. Victory probably also prolonged Ganguly's captaincy and the life of a squad that would go on to be one of the country's finest. And as that group took a slow circle of the outfield to commune with all those faithful Vinays, Mahmuds and Sanchayitas out there, they enjoyed a heady sense of in whose name it was all for.

Kolkata Recalled

RETURN TO EDEN (2021)

This time two decades ago, Australia had reached a cricket zenith unexampled in history. Steve Waugh's team of talents held every trophy available, from the Ashes to the World Cup; they had just won their sixteenth consecutive Test, having left behind the long-standing streak of eleven set by the West Indies in the 1980s.

Nor was the supremacy solely about its storied names: Waugh, Warne, McGrath, Gilchrist, Langer, Hayden, Slater, Gillespie et al. Everything about the Australian system, from the robust Sheffield Shield to the fecund Academy, excited envy. Perhaps you remember the attitudes then prevalent, with their undertone of hubris: 'If only someone would give us a game!' And then, India did.

We're approaching twenty-year anniversaries of this landmark 2001 Border–Gavaskar Trophy series. Next Thursday marks twenty years since the start of the Kolkata Test, which India won after following on – only the third team in history to do so. The decider in Chennai finished on 22 March with India winning by two wickets, taking the rubber 2–1.

The series also seems to mark the onset of a gradual Indian edge on Australia in Test cricket. Australia had the satisfaction of winning their next series in India, and winning at a canter at home in 2011–12. But even with this, the arc of history since Kolkata has been bending towards India, by nineteen wins to fourteen.

On taking over as Australia's coach in May 2018, Justin Langer spoke of winning in India the way Steve Waugh used to, as an 'ultimate test' of prowess and character. He has couched ambition for renewal of his contract in terms of taking Australia there next year.

For India, meanwhile, Australia has succeeded Pakistan as the most satisfying foe. Sans the political, religious and historic subtexts, it offers in many ways a more wholesome, less fraught rivalry than with its neighbour.

So 2001 seems ripe for reconsideration, for a ranking in historical significance comparable to, say, the 1960–61 series between a very white Australia and an entrancingly dark West Indies – the series that inspired the Frank Worrell Trophy and myriad retellings of the first Tied Test.

One looks back twenty years and finds a very different world that was in some ways closer to 1960–61 than today. The calendar was crammed but not constipated; 2001 contained no International Cricket Council event. There was neither Elite Umpire Panel nor Decision Review System (DRS). There was no T20, let alone an Indian Premier League or Big Bash League. There were no Test rankings, let alone a Test Championship – not that we needed either, so imperial was this green and golden age.

Six months after the Sydney Olympics, Australians were confident of our place at the centre of the sporting world. Richie Benaud, 1960–61's captain, was the suave and ageless face of 'the cricket' on Channel Nine, although only in summer; the network was indifferent to Tests abroad. There was no free-to-air coverage of the series in India. At the time the Kolkata Test reached its climax, Melbourne's Nine viewers were watching *The Footy Show*.

In India, by contrast, broadcast media was on the brink of radical change. In his book *India on Television* (2008), Nalin Mehta calls 2001 a hinge point in the coverage of cricket in that country, led by the new Hindi news network Aaj Tak, which turned the three Tests into 'news' at every opportunity, to the extent of running an all-day ticker with the score and cutting away to studio chats at lunch, tea and drinks.

Daily programming kicked off with cricket previews, and climaxed each evening with a talk show entitled *Who Will Be The World Champion?* – on the principle, as its news director explained to Mehta, 'that if somebody was to go and beat Mike Tyson, the guy would be considered world heavyweight champion, so why should we not apply the same rule to cricket, regardless of whether the format of ICC allowed that or not?'

Aaj Tak had picked its moment perfectly: the heavyweight nature of the series has been defined by the mighty 376-run partnership of VVS Laxman and Rahul Dravid in Kolkata which first thwarted the relentless Australian advance. Harbhajan Singh, who might not even have played had Anil Kumble been fit, then effectively won the series with 13/196 at Eden Gardens and 15/217 at Chidambaram Stadium, despite Matthew Hayden's 549 runs and Glenn McGrath's seventeen wickets in a losing cause.

What can be lost sight of is these feats' contexts: that, for example, Harbhajan's wickets in the series cost 17, while seven other spinners paid 52 each for theirs, and McGrath's cost 15, while seven other seamers paid 44 each for theirs; that coming into the series Laxman had averaged 27 and Hayden 24, but that the pair in five weeks piled up 1646 international runs.

In the next few weeks, the media loving anniversaries, you can count on recapitulations of the events of twenty years ago. But as it settles so smoothly into history, let's not forget a few counterfactuals. Going into the Kolkata Test with his team 0–1 down, for example, Sourav Ganguly, who had led India in only four Tests, looked to *The Age*'s Peter Roebuck like a captain with 'his head on the chopping block', one who 'might lack the maturity to survive'. After three days, the paper's front page saw Waugh's men 'cruising confidently to a remarkable 17th straight Test victory'.

Though Ganguly did not make a half-century in the series, 2001 became the talisman of a tenure that lasted another forty-five Test matches in which he became India's most successful Test captain to that point. '[We] were able to change the face of Indian cricket,' he said on retiring. 'The team wouldn't take any crap from any opposition.'

Today, Dada is president of the Board of Control for Cricket in India. Despatches from India last week suggest that a political career is his for the asking. Twenty years ago, who would have imagined that possible?

Adelaide Test 2003, Day 5

FROM A LADDER TO A SNAKE (2003)

Steve Waugh's all-conquering XI have made a habit of doing things for the first time. But becoming the first Australian team to concede a series lead to India at home has involved unfamiliar sensations indeed.

This is the team, after all, that score faster, bowl quicker, throw further, catch better, write more tour diaries and produce more limited-edition memorabilia than any in history. Their apologists will need to unearth some convincing rationalisations for defeat in Adelaide, for it was surrendered in most original fashion.

Shortly after tea on the second day India were 4/85 in apparently fruitless pursuit of Australia's 556, a scenario with a not unfamiliar ring in recent summers. In those summers, however, there have been Glenn McGrath, Shane Warne and Brett Lee to clean up opponents as if by force of personality. Now a second-choice attack could not widen the breach and India's batsmen steadily narrowed their arrears to 33.

What followed will truly smart. Australia gave up their second innings in a listless four hours. Ricky Ponting, a majestic first-innings 242 behind him, was kept scoreless for sixteen deliveries and slashed his seventeenth carelessly to backward point. Matthew Hayden, Damien Martyn and even the captain all drove casually. Simon Katich fetched a short ball wide of off stump and eased it politely down long leg's throat. The tail turned itself in without a whimper of protest.

Deprived of their standard first-innings buffer, Waugh's batsmen seemed incapable of readjusting to the needs of the moment. Australia's scoring rate has been accelerating for three years, through 2001 (3.8 an over), 2002 (4) and 2003 (4.1). Very exciting it has been too. But here it was as though the Australians, having grown accustomed to life in fast forward, had forgotten how simply to play and, if need be, pause.

Supporters can protest, not without justification, that this merry-making is jollying up sleepy old Test cricket. But this is not an entirely new Australian problem. The failures of Plan A at Calcutta and Headingley in 2001, for instance, also seemed to generate some confusion about the exact nature of Plan B. And in Adelaide the hosts tripped themselves with their own headlong progress. It is only because Australia accumulated their first innings at 4.4 an over that India needed to score at less than 2.2 to reach their eventual target of 230.

Rahul Dravid never seems to hurry anything. He is probably even fastidious in signing his autograph and makes a little elephant out of the capital R. He was on the field for twenty-seven hours during this Test, batting for fourteen of them, asserting his defiance by reaching his first century with a hooked six but otherwise exhibiting all the aplomb Australia lacked.

In his favour were a pitch that Neville Cardus would have thought fit to be watered by a bowler's tears and what at the moment is not so much an attack as a defence. When England seemed about to bring Ray Illingworth out of retirement a year ago to cover its myriad indispositions, Australia's bowlers looked like bionic men. Now McGrath and Lee are surmounting injuries; Jason Gillespie and Brad Williams have just sustained their own; if Stuart MacGill has not, then he has some explaining to do, so liberally has he been scattering long hops and full tosses.

For one Australian at least Adelaide is not a complete bad news story, with the odds on a stirring Shane Warne comeback shortened sharply. With a touch of theatre, not to mention rather a lot of television, he chose Adelaide as the venue for his first semi-official bowl since his dramatic World Cup exit in February. As Ian Healy squatted behind the stumps and Warne's mentor Terry Jenner looked on sagely, it was just like the good old days.

The good old days, however, will not be returning just like that. A fortnight or so ago this series looked like an unseemly distraction from Waugh's curtain calls. Now it may be part of a more significant climacteric. Australia had no Warne and McGrath in Adelaide but neither did India have Zaheer Khan and Harbhajan Singh, and they relied only minimally on Sachin Tendulkar. The hosts were simply outplayed.

Sourav Ganguly was suitably ebullient during the post-match rites. 'We know Australia will come hard at us in the next two Tests. But we will be ready for them,' he said. 'We know, and they know, that we can beat them.' For Australia that is another new sensation.

Melbourne Test 2003, Day 1

VIRU STAKES HIS CLAIM (2003)

A lavish Boxing Day's entertainment here in the Third Test between Australia and India was enjoyed largely by visiting fans and those who savour the capricious ways that the cricket gods apportion good fortune.

India's combustible Virender Sehwag produced an innings of 195 that Australian bowlers and fielders might have cut short half a dozen times in its first hour – and his generation's finest batsman, Sachin Tendulkar, continued a barren stretch by succumbing lucklessly to his first ball.

With India 4/329, Steve Waugh has the consolation that first-day supremacy counted for little at Brisbane and Adelaide: the teams that scored 2/211 and 5/400 in those instances ended up with a draw and a defeat, respectively. Unfortunately for Waugh, that team in both instances was Australia. Another day or two like this and the space cleared for the Border–Gavaskar Trophy in the Cricket Australia cabinet will have to be filled with one of those tasteful one-day trophies.

Before the first ball odds on an India victory were quoted at 8-1: generous indeed in a two-horse race but explained by a plunge on an Australian win by pessimistic Indian punters. Their pessimism did not seem ill-founded during Brett Lee's first five overs, when the crack of willow on leather was less evident than the clang of leather on headgear. On a pitch offering more vertical movement than horizontal, Lee hit Akash Chopra's helmet once, Sehwag's twice and 150 km/h a few times more.

With a cooler head and a better relay throw to Adam Gilchrist, Lee might have run Sehwag out, but the cricket gods winked and the keeper fumbled. More incriminating video evidence and the third umpire Parry might also have upheld a stumping appeal an hour later but again the batsman rode his luck.

None of this bothered Sehwag. After the first hour he counter-punched precociously. Stuart MacGill's second ball, which landed perhaps six inches outside leg stump, and to which most would have offered a pad, met instead a flurry of feet and a glint of bat as it was launched over cover for six. No batsman radiates such an air of relaxation at the crease as Sehwag. He exhibits all the concentration of a man channel surfing late-night television.

Chopra kept Sehwag strait-laced company, spending an hour and a quarter over his first six runs before warily opening out. But their opening partnership, worth 141 in forty-three overs, was as valuable for what it withstood early as for what it ran to later. The loss with an hour to go of Rahul Dravid and Tendulkar, whose leg glance was too fine to elude Gilchrist, offered the Australians a re-entry point into the game. Sehwag then hit high in the direction of mid-wicket, ending an innings with 100 in fours, 30 in sixes, and perhaps half a summer's luck.

Waugh would have been satisfied with the day had Lee in his follow through caught an apprehensive bunt from Sourav Ganguly with seven overs left. But Lee snatched, stumbled and fell. Proceedings were watched over, for the last time, by the

INDIAN SUMMERS

MCG's seventy-five-year-old pavilion, unoccupied and awaiting demolition ahead of redevelopment for the Commonwealth Games. Resembling a huge haunted house, it was a melancholy shadow of its former glory. Waugh's Australians have four days to demonstrate the same cannot be said for them.

Border–Gavaskar Trophy 2004

SLO-MO REPLAY (2024)

One of the great paradoxes concerns what occurs when an irresistible force meets an immovable object. Australia's tour of India in 2004 offered a cricket resolution. The visitors were at the time irresistible: a team of talents featuring Ricky Ponting, Adam Gilchrist, Shane Warne, Glenn McGrath, Jason Gillespie, Matthew Hayden and Justin Langer at peak proficiency. But India, having beaten them back at the last start and dropped only a single home Test in seven years, had pretensions to local immovability also. Were you to pick an all-time team of India, in fact, 2004 might be your nearest thing to a rough draft. Sourav Ganguly, Rahul Dravid, Virender Sehwag, VVS Laxman, Anil Kumble, Harbhajan Singh and Zaheer Khan were more than a paper tiger.

In the event, Ponting sustained an incapacitating broken hand, leaving Gilchrist as locum. But as great teams do, the Australians turned a vacancy into an occupancy: into the XI, just ahead of the perennially unlucky Victorian Brad Hodge, they welcomed coltish twenty-three-year-old New South Welshman Michael Clarke. Australia were 4/149 on the first day at Bangalore when he took guard. Local hero Kumble was seeking his 400th Test wicket. He might have gained it had his first delivery, which struck Clarke in front, not been a no ball. Clarke did not look back: he was 76 by stumps, all dancing feet and nerveless defence, then eighth out for 151 out of 471 the next afternoon. There may not have been a more genuinely auspicious debut in Australian history, heightened by Clarke's choice of headgear for the milestone: the baggy green cap, which had been presented to him by Warne, looked so fetching.

Clarke's six-hour audition was complemented by Gilchrist's run-a-ball jolly, then the early strikes of McGrath, who bowled Dravid, and Warne, who bowled Laxman. Kasprowicz dismissed Sehwag and Ganguly for good measure, and Australia circumspectly elected not to enforce the follow-on despite a first innings lead of 230. From 2001, the visitors had gleaned that India needed to be taken by stealthy stages; they bowled aggressively to defensive fields; they waited their chances. India chafed their way to a sobering 217-run defeat.

Australia lost their last eight wickets for 46 in the Second Test at Chennai, mainly to Kumble, and conceded 376, mainly to Sehwag, but Shane Warne never bowled better in India, his 6/125 the fruit of a manful forty-over toil. But the keystone to Australia's defensive arch was provided by Damien Martyn, usually the Australian batter easiest on the eye, and Gillespie, probably the hardest. Martyn hit eleven fours and a six in 106, Gillespie survived four hours for 26, and Gilchrist remembered as one of his favourite days of Test cricket a day he did not actually take the field: 'I didn't want to budge. The crowd noise was intense, and it was desperate cricket, pure guts. I'd never been prouder of Marto. He went to another level . . . A group of us sat there, playing music, watching the game, almost pretending that everything was fine. But we were very, very nervous and willing them on.' The nerves were finally soothed by a final day ruining the match but preserving their series lead.

Martyn then proceeded to dominate the Third Test with a bracket of 114 and 97, and by now India had succumbed to former quarrelsome ways. An election at the Board of Control for Cricket in India reinstalling Jagmohan Dalmiya of Kolkata at the expense of powerful Maharashtran politician Sharad Pawar seemed to play out in the preparation of a pitch at Nagpur that would not have been out of place at the Gabba. Kolkata's Ganguly missed the Test; likewise Harbhajan. Dravid substituted, ambivalently, reinforced by Tendulkar, back from injury. Both failed, giving up the Border–Gavaskar Trophy after three years. Recriminations ensued.

The dead Test at Wankhede turned out to be a prelude to Indian pitches in recent vintage, designed for instant turn and rapid deterioration: a 200-over Test ensued in which Clarke, a part-time spinner at best, took 6/9. At Sydney earlier in the year, India's batsmen had piled up 9/916; now they were felt to require the protection of a made-to-measure surface. India prevailed by 13 runs, but the stratagem evidenced how deeply the Australian challenge, and defeat in front of their own crowds, had rattled them. They have taken no chances in the twenty years since, reinforcing their immovability by doubling down on their home ground advantage. Australia, too, have never again proven so irresistible.

Sydney Test 2008
THE BITER BIT (2008)

A week or so ago the cricket world was in a funk about Test cricket, how the inevitable advance of T20 would crush all in its path, how the game desperately needed a five-day game to die for. The Sydney Test was made to measure: five days of high drama and fluctuation with a grandstand finish in which all cricket's skills were on display – except, maybe, umpiring.

Yet somehow the match's only beneficiaries have been India's effigy suppliers, whose stocks of white-coated figures are going up in flames all over the subcontinent – and mainly because one cricketer allegedly called another a 'monkey'. The twist in the tale is that the sledger was an excitable Indian, the sledgee a muscular and aggressive Aussie and his co-accusers more of the same. Otherwise the incident attests to the power of sport to make people lose perspective, proportion and all rationality.

Racism is serious. Racism is about the denial of another person's essential humanity on the basis of their skin and their culture. Racism is about embedded prejudices, institutionalised discrimination, real economic and social deprivation. Racism is South Africa under apartheid – on which, say it soft, Australia was the last cricket country to lower the boom. Racism is Robert Mugabe – against whose country the Australian cricket team would seemingly have been happy to play had it not been for the federal government. To say, then, that one cricketer calling another a monkey on a cricket field is racism is to define the idea frivolously. Was Andrew Symonds belittled? Was he hurt? Was he disadvantaged?

Curiously, when a few score Indians made monkey noises directed at Symonds at Vadodara last October, he went out of his way to state that he had not made any complaint, and affected not to care. 'I'm not the most deadly serious bloke,' he said. 'Life goes on.' Yet somehow Harbhajan's emission is now the gravest of offences and befitting of the severest sanction. Regrettably, the Australian complaint smacks of cricketers who in the process of scaling great heights of excellence have sealed themselves off from reality.

It also smacks of Australian players just a bit peeved about always being seen as the bad guys, who want the world to know that they, poor things, get taunted too. There is a sort of wounded self-righteousness to captain Ricky Ponting's comments in the aftermath of the Sydney Test that recalls those mealy mouthed defences of Australian sledging of the recent past: other teams do it but they don't get criticised because we're more honest and they play the beastly trick of doing it in Hindi and Urdu . . . which, yeah, are their languages . . . but oh, *it's not fair*!

For decades Australian cricketers have been steadfast in maintaining the principle that what happens on the field stays on the field, and regarded as snitches those opponents, such as South Africa's Graeme Smith and Sri Lanka's Arjuna Ranatunga, who abrogated it. Which is fine. Even if you haven't always agreed with it as a philosophy, it has at least been understandable and unambiguous, and in that sense worthy of respect. The common sense of the principle, in fact, is verified by this incident. Because when you abandon it, as Ponting has, you incite others to take grievances beyond the boundary, as the Indians are doing by trumping up their tit-for-tat charge against Brad Hogg.

Perhaps it's worth considering why cricket has a code of conduct, not to mention a preamble in its laws about the game's proper spirit. These exist to deter players from poor sportsmanship. They aren't there to be pushed as far as you can in quest of a short-term competitive advantage. There is a case that both Harbhajan and Symonds should have been punished. There was nothing passionate, committed or red-blooded about their confrontation, nor any of the other boilerplate excuses. It was another unnecessary and completely avoidable face-off between players who are paid pots of money to know better. What was said will be endlessly disputed; what we saw looked bad, boorish, ugly.

There is still a quaint idea that provocateur and respondent in these exchanges are distinguishable. But who knows where the animosity between Harbhajan and the Australians began? And who cares? As for the cartoonish arguments about whether 'monkey' is racist in one culture, or 'bastard' is illegitimacist in another, cricket should be worried first about its own standards – and standing. The Sydney Test should have enriched it; as it is, the game has metaphorically dropped a catch off a hat-trick ball and somehow deflected it for six.

Sydney Test 2008
MONKEY BUSINESS (2008)

A couple of days after the Second Test between Australia and India ended at the Sydney Cricket Ground amid acrimony and indignation, I boarded the tram for an evening's practice at my cricket club with fifteen-year-old Bill. A bright boy, Bill. I knew him to be keen on his cricket and was interested in how his career had progressed since last I'd seen him.

I found that Bill was no longer quite so keen on his cricket. In the nets he was still a tidy player who essayed a pretty cover-drive and lobbed a passable leg-break. But, Bill explained, he wasn't playing so much these days. He'd joined a club where the coaches had impressed on their charges how important it was to be as verbally aggressive as possible – to, as they say, 'sledge'. Why? Well, because everyone does it. And while his club wasn't very good, it had won a few more games than the players' talents justified because they were capable of putting opponents off by being 'in their faces', by appealing for everything that appeared remotely out, by carrying on a bit if they did not get their way. Bill, he thought that was a bit stupid. His parents weren't keen on it either.

121

I'm pretty inured to petulance and cynicism among international cricketers these days, of which Sydney was merely the worst episode since the last episode which was the worst, following the one before that. This conversation with Bill, however – this was dismaying. For it is this aspect of sledging and general malcontentment on the cricket field that has become most pernicious: not that it is ugly or offensive or dehumanising, but the sheer, mindless, rote-learned nature of it. Now and again, there is a flash of exasperation, frustration, anger, even humour. Otherwise, it is a part of the game that has become noisily, and annoyingly, automated.

The skirmish between Harbhajan Singh and Andrew Symonds owed nothing to the spur of the moment or the heat of the contest. Harbhajan knew he had a way of irking Symonds; they had even discussed it off the field. The Australians knew Harbhajan to be a provocateur; the Australians entered willingly into the confrontation, aware of exactly what was acceptable boorishness under Paragraph 3.3 of the ICC Code of Conduct and what was not. Thus did a relatively small objective, a short-term tactical edge on an opponent, masquerade as a very big issue.

The game's ugliest image was provided by neither Harbhajan nor Symonds, but by Australia's captain, Ricky Ponting: finger aloft, bent forward at the waist, daring the umpire to doubt his assertion that a snick to slip had carried, turning even his lip service to good manners – a pre-match agreement with India's Anil Kumble to rely upon the fielders' word where low catches were concerned – into an emblem of Australian aggression. The appeal for a catch at the wicket when Rahul Dravid missed a ball by nine inches, meanwhile, was a miracle of harmony to rival the Beach Boys.

As it usually does, the charge of racism immediately deprived everyone of rational thought, entailing the inevitable

'I said, you said' claim and counterclaim. And if Australia's cricketers are the world's biggest bullies on the field, India's administrators are easily their match off it. At once there were threats that the Indians would take their bat, their ball and, most importantly, their money, and go home. A tit-for-tat charge was laid against Brad Hogg for barking at Kumble and his partner, Mahendra Dhoni: 'I can't wait to go through you bastards.'

And so it became a busy week for the average cricket hack. Peter Roebuck, in *The Age* and *Sydney Morning Herald*, took India's part, not a little impetuously. *The Australian* reopened the culture wars on a new front, passing off hectares of partisan comment in support of star columnist Ponting as news. Kerry O'Keeffe laughed uproariously at his own jokes – so, no change there. I was interviewed by a reporter from a television current-affairs show who, apparently unable to raise Roebuck, solicited my view no fewer than six times on whether Ponting should be sacked. I also participated in a surreal radio debate with a Punjabi editor who insisted that racism in India, presumably like homosexuality in Iran, does not exist.

Between times, just to bring it all back home, I played my weekly club game. While opening the batting I was called a homosexual, a paedophile, a cheat for not walking when I missed a ball by two feet, and a loser merely for existing. While bowling we faced a batsman whose idea of fun was to goad each fielder in turn and who, when a comment was made that this was obviously how they played in Frankston, droned on for several overs about 'racial vilification'. Monkey see, monkey do.

For this is cricket circa 2008, a game still hugely rich and various in its skills yet massively alike in its behaviours, in which you do not merely play to win but to dull your opponents' love of the game, and thus their appetite for the contest. This has become a means, in fact, by which groups define and unite themselves. Brad Hogg wasn't questioning anyone's parentage in Sydney; he was, after more than a decade hankering for Test selection, clamouring for membership of the tough boys' group. And Australian captains have been such noisy apologists for verbal aggression, psychological dominance and 'mental disintegration' over the years that the route to self-exculpation at lower levels of the game is obvious: the role model made me do it!

On reflection, then, part of my conversation with Bill was quite hopeful. People, even fifteen-year-olds, have agency. They can make choices. They can reject recommended and prescribed behaviours. Alas, they might have to leave cricket behind in order to do so. And here the fault is not in our super-stars but in ourselves, in that we have colluded in turning a game with perhaps more scope for individual expression than any other into another means of instilling mass conformity.

Sachin Tendulkar
TWENTY YEARS OF MASTERY (2009)

Many tributes to Sachin Tendulkar this month will begin with a recollection of one of his epic innings. I wish to cite one of the shortest. It was in Melbourne, my home town, on Boxing Day 2003. It was a day rich in entertainment, containing a Virender Sehwag century full of eye-popping strokes. Seldom, however, have I sat in a crowd so obviously awaiting one player, and when Tendulkar appeared they radiated happiness and contentment, bursting into heartfelt applause. Tendulkar at the MCG? Delayed Christmas presents come no better.

Except that it was all wrapping and no gift. Tendulkar feathered his first ball down the leg-side and was caught at the wicket – a miserable way to fall for any batsman, in addition to being a lousy anti-climax. The crowd had hardly ceased cheering than it was compelled to resume, cheering Tendulkar off, and the feeling afterwards was almost devastation. You could hear the sibilance of conversations, as connoisseurs ruminated that cricket sure was a funny game, and fathers tried explaining to sons that even the greats had bad days. About three overs later, three spectators at the end of my row got up and left. It was mid-afternoon, Sehwag was still mid-spectacular, and *they left*. This was not what they had come for, and they would accept no substitute. I had to stay – it was my job – but I could easily have followed them. The hollow feeling persisted all day.

When it comes to communicating Tendulkar's place in cricket history to future generations, I suspect, this is what will be most significant, and also the hardest to convey. In the twenty years of his career, international cricket has changed unrecognisably: elaborate and ceremonial Test cricket has been usurped, economically at least, by the slick, shiny celebrity vehicle of T20. Yet even now, Tendulkar makes time stand still: every time he comes to the wicket, no matter the game, no matter the place, there is a sense of occasion. It needs no pop music, no cheerleaders, no word from his many sponsors. He is announced by his accumulated excellence, the effect somehow magnified by his tininess: little man, big bat, great moment. His entry could not seem more dramatic were he borne to the crease on a bejewelled palanquin by dusky maidens amid a flourish of imperial trumpets.

This, moreover, has been the case almost for longer than one can remember. I first saw Tendulkar bat live in England in 1990. He looked so young, so small, like a novelty item on a key chain. Any sense of frailty, however, was quickly dispelled; instead, there was a sureness of touch not just impressive but altogether ominous. You told yourself to remember him this way; you wanted to be able to say you were there; he was going to be good, so good. By the time he first toured Australia eighteen months later, he simply oozed command. All that held him back, and it would be a theme of his career, especially abroad, was his sorely outclassed team.

Sometimes, this looked almost eerie. Ten years ago in Melbourne, India and Tendulkar played a Test at the MCG. To distinguish between the two was only fair. India were terrible, a shambles. Kumble dropped the simplest catch imaginable from the game's second ball and took 2/150; Dravid batted more than three and a half hours in the match for 23 runs; Laxman and Ganguly failed twice, the latter playing on to Greg Blewett of all people.

Tendulkar batted as if on a different pitch, to different bowlers in a different match. Shane Warne came on with Australia in the ascendant in front of his home crowd. Tendulkar promptly hit him into that crowd beyond mid-off. Brett Lee, in his debut Test, bowled like the wind. Tendulkar treated him as a pleasant, cooling breeze. The follow-on loomed, apparently unavoidable. Tendulkar guided India past it, toying with Steve Waugh's formations, making the fielders look as immobile and ineffectual as croquet hoops.

Had it not been for his ten teammates, Tendulkar could have batted until the crack of doom. As it is, he had to rest content with 116 out of an otherwise bedraggled 238. And this wasn't just an innings; it was, at the time, a synecdoche of Indian cricket. No matter where he went, Tendulkar was the main event, preceded by acute anticipation, followed by grateful wonder, seasoned with sympathy, that such a flyweight figure had to bear such burdens.

There is no discussing Tendulkar, even in cricket terms, as batsman alone. He is also, of course, Indian cricket's original super celebrity; as Pope wrote of Cromwell, 'damn'd to everlasting fame'. In this sense, he has been preternaturally modern, at the forefront of developments in the culture of stardom in his country, with his telephone-number television entanglements and sponsorship deals, and his reclusive private life. Without Tendulkar's prior demonstration of cricket's commercial leverage, Lalit Modi and all his works would have been unthinkable.

What's truly amazing, nonetheless, is that the simulacrum of Tendulkar has never overwhelmed the substance. He has gone on doing what he does best, and has done better than anybody else in his generation, which is bat and bat and bat. Like Warne, albeit for different reasons, cricket grounds have been a haven for him: in the middle, he always knows what to do, and feels confident he can do it. Life is full of complications and ambiguities; cricket by comparison, even shouldering the expectations of a billion people, is sublimely simple.

Tendulkar's fame, then, is of an unusual kind. He is a symbol of change, but also of continuity. What's astonishing about his batting is not how much it has changed but how little. He set himself a standard of excellence, of consistency, of dominance, and challenged the rest of Indian cricket to meet him up there. Gradually, in the twenty-first century, albeit not without set-backs, stumbles, financial excesses and political wranglings, it has. His presence now is an ennobling one. First it was his excellence that rubbed off; now it is his integrity. Cricket today specialises in the manufacture of instant stars, temporary celebrities, glorious nobodies. Tendulkar acts as a kind of fixed price or gold standard. To choose a well-loved and well-worn advertising catchline, he is 'the real thing'.

In his sheer constancy, in fact, Tendulkar unwittingly obscures just how completely cricket has been transformed, to the extent that it is almost impossible to imagine his fame being replicated. Who in future will play international cricket for twenty years, losing neither motivation nor mastery? Who in future will master all three forms of the game, capable of spontaneous spectacle and massive entrenchment alike? Who in future will excite us simply by walking onto the field, just a man and a bat, and disappoint so seldom? Recalling how shocked, even grief stricken, was that crowd in Melbourne six years ago as Tendulkar's back was swallowed by the shadows of the pavilion, I find myself brooding anxiously on the thought of what it will be like when he disappears for the last time.

Sachin Tendulkar v Ricky Ponting

TEST OF TIME (2010)

It's one of those challenges whose resolution will be both satisfying and sad. For nigh on a decade, the statistics of Ricky Ponting and Sachin Tendulkar have stood like pillars, suspending aloft a great arch of batsmanship. When their day is done, one or other will have achieved the monumental proportions of *the* record for Test run-scoring: a record that, given the dwindling incidence of Test matches, may last for all time.

The respective records are already extraordinary. Tendulkar has 13,447 runs at 55.56 from 166 Tests plus 17,598 runs at 45.12 from 442 one-day internationals, including a total of ninety-three hundreds. It's an eloquent attestation of the industrialisation of the global game. Tendulkar has played twenty years, as long as Bradman, and scored four times as many runs, despite several injury-related absences. Could even Bradman have maintained such intensity of productivity? Given the different values of his period, would he even have wanted to?

Ponting, meanwhile, has 11,859 runs at 55.67 from 142 Tests, plus 12,731 runs at 43.30 from 340 one-day internationals, having given Tendulkar a six-year head start, and being eighteen months his junior: Australia's captain turned thirty-five in December, India's champion turns thirty-seven in April. Ponting's 209 against Pakistan at Bellerive in January represented his thirty-ninth three-figure score in Tests, while his 106 against the West Indies at the Gabba a month later was his twenty-ninth three-figure score in limited-overs internationals. It bespeaks an appetite, for runs and for cricket, almost unappeasable.

There is an epic grandeur to the achievements of both men, not least because they have chosen to ennoble the game's oldest international form. In a country that bequeathed pyjama cricket to the world, Ponting has persevered with the cricket equivalent of dressing for dinner. In a country gone crazy for the limerick of T20, Tendulkar has steadily written the *Mahabharata* of batting. In a world of braggarts, both are resolutely humble. In an era when bigger is always assumed better, both are small men punching way above their relative weight and heights. And in a game bent now at every opportunity on selling itself to the highest bidder, both Ponting and Tendulkar have put national responsibilities beyond price. They feel the honour of representing their countries; you, the fan, feel the honour of being represented by them.

Scrutinising their respective records is a little like listening for bum notes in Mozart. Tendulkar's batting may have been slightly inhibited by captaincy: he averaged 51 as leader, 56 otherwise. Ponting averages 55 as leader, having averaged 55 in the ranks.

Tendulkar, on the other hand, averages 55 at home and away. Wherever he is playing somehow becomes Sachinland, a secure principality of batting excellence. The borders of Rickyworld are a little more porous. He averages 60 at home, 50 away, and, strangely, only 44 in England – an oversight that may account for his eagerness to return there for the Ashes of 2013.

Both men have reached that stage where their opponent is time, as much as any particular country or bowler. Whether it's Tendulkar or Ponting who ends with batting's blue riband depends, as did the duel for the wicket-taking record between Shane Warne and Muttiah Muralitharan, on who is the last man standing. Time has taken a toll on the physiques of both, like the elements leaving their mark on a statue. No elbow in history has been as discussed as Tendulkar's; Ponting's back and right wrist are feeling his age.

In recognition of the march of time, both are shunning distractions, as they have sometimes abjured particular strokes. Like silent film stars loath to embrace talkies, they had little impact on the game's newest and most lucrative form. Ponting has quit the IPL and retired from international T20. Tendulkar has been a low-key presence in the Indian Premier League, and played precisely one T20 international, against South Africa in December 2006. Tendulkar approaches Test innings now with such system as to seemingly negate all variables. 'Watching Sachin Tendulkar bat these days is almost like watching a re-run of one's favourite TV show,' wrote *Cricinfo*'s Sriram Veera after studying Tendulkar at work in Chittagong in January, somehow capturing not just Tendulkar's surety of touch, but also the contribution of television to the spread of his legend in this vast, sprawling, populous nation.

Over their futures, the chief influence is probably that of their respective national administrations. Cricket Australia, which has argued at the ICC for a World Test Championship, still takes five-day cricket seriously. The Board of Control for Cricket in India, the largest obstacle to a World Test Championship, eyes five-day fixtures as mistrustfully as a property developer discovering a church occupying a city block: yes, it's pretty and all that, but wouldn't an office building or a car park make more sense? Were the BCCI to acquire the Taj Mahal, it would not be long before a television mast had been thrust through the dome.

CA will ensure that Ponting has a steady supply of Test matches, and thus a solid chance of overhauling whatever benchmark Tendulkar sets. He will finish this year involved in another five-Test series; Tendulkar has played only three such in his entire career, none at home, and his Test engagements are becoming so few that he can hardly afford to fail.

Say it soft, in fact, but Tendulkar the batsman is verging on anachronism. To the most historically and commercially significant game of his era, the final of the World T20 in Johannesburg, which ignited India's passion for the game's newest and richest form, he was an onlooker. For one of the crowning triumphs of his career, his fording of the 12,000 Test-run barrier in Mohali in September 2008, there were virtually no onlookers at all.

So for all the splendour of this batting rivalry, cricket is in the process of debasing it. As observed at the outset, the likelihood is that even if Test cricket survives, nobody will play enough in future to parallel the feats of either man. It is like two mountaineers racing one another to the summit of Everest only to find that there is more kudos in climbing ladders – yet further evidence, if it were needed, of how the fast buck has travestied cricket.

Sachin Tendulkar and Donald Bradman

LONG SHADOWS (2010)

The Little Master: the nickname gives equal weight to both qualities, mastery and littleness. But while the mastery makes sense, the littleness does not so much. Tendulkar stands 165 centimetres tall, the mean height of the Indian male. By rights, then, he should be the Average Master. Or maybe the Average Master Blaster. There is something interesting at work in that abiding Tendulkar alias. What might it be?

Like all really sticky and popular nicknames, its origins and authors are unclear – it seems to have affixed as naturally as 'The Greatest' to Ali or 'The Stilt' to Wilt Chamberlain. The original 'Master' was Sir Jack Hobbs, capable of leaping from the pages of *Wisden* to the denouement of *Slumdog Millionaire*. And the original 'Little Master' was, of course, Sunil Gavaskar – google 'Little Master', in fact, and it is still Gavaskar's smiling features that beam out at you from the right-hand side of the screen. It was Gavaskar who famously handed on his pads to his anointed successor, in the way that WG Grace handed on a bat to Victor Trumper, like a kind of relay baton of cricket, or Olympic torch of excellence; the epithet seems to have been transferred the same way.

The concept has its basis in a famous experiment thirty years ago by two American psychologists, Leslie Martel and Henry Biller, who asked several hundred university students to rate the qualities of men of varying heights, on seventeen different criteria. Knowing nothing else about them, the students ranked the short men, those between 157 centimetres and 165 centi-metres, lowest – they were deemed less mature, secure, positive, confident, capable, successful and even masculine than taller peers. Cross-cultural studies by the anthropologist Thomas Gregor, moreover, have found the attitude pervasive, neither western nor eastern. 'In no case,' he says, 'have I found a prefer-ence for shorter men.'

There is even a Twitter account, Exposing Heightism, which captures and collates evidently heightist tweets – more profuse and vehement than might be imagined. On an average day, it turns up such examples as: 'Why are short guys even a thing?', 'Why does God make short men?', 'Men under 5′7 are females', 'Any man shorter than 5′9 should join the circus!!!!', 'Short men are not men they're children. GROW UP you childish assholes', 'Short men aint useless. They can be used as TV stands or can be useful in the toilet to hold tissues'. No cricket lovers here, evidently.

Because for Tendulkar, 'littleness' has always been a virtue, an addition to his specialness, an enhancement of his exemplary nature. Why? In sport, of course, the little have their day, and the race is not always to the swift or the battle to the strong. While there are games in which standing tall, bulking large or reaching wide are advantageous, just as many exist where such attributes either mean not much or are a mixed blessing: what the tall tennis player may gain in power on serve or net coverage, for example, they might lose in access to low volleys or handling returns at the body. And cricket, of course, prides itself on encompassing perhaps the widest variety of body types, shapes and sizes: it has featured batsmen from Gundappa Viswanath (163 centimetres) to Tony Greig (200 centimetres), fast bowlers from Harold Larwood (170 centimetres) to Mohammad Irfan (216 centimetres), slow bowlers from Rangana Herath (168 centimetres) to Sulieman Benn (201 centimetres).

Plus, there's Bradman. Cricket's most historically exalted figure stood 170 centimetres, and rather relished the cutting of rivals down to size. When he met Babe Ruth in 1932, he is reported to have looked him appreciatively in the eye, and opined in solidarity that 'us little fellows could hit them harder than the big ones'. In his time, others referred to Bradman, in endearment and tribute, as 'the little chap' and 'the little fellow'. In later life, Douglas Jardine is said to have mused that his team's Bodyline victory was far closer than it looked: 'We almost didn't do it, you know. The little fellow was bloody good.' For Tendulkar, then, there have always been big little shoes to fill, as it were.

But this goes a little deeper I think. As observed, Tendulkar's is merely the average male height in India. His 'littleness' was first observed in contrast to the physically larger figures of foreign opponents. The first time I saw the teen Tendulkar, in England in 1990, he did indeed look tiny, relative to the likes of Devon Malcolm and Gus Fraser, hurling themselves down at him from their great heights, not to mention Graham Gooch, whose bat looked wider still and wider than the Empire itself. Into the bargain, Tendulkar appeared impossibly young and fresh-faced, as though in need of a chaperone as much as a batting partner. The impression lasted, of course, for as long as it took for Tendulkar to play a few deliveries, making obvious his precocious certainty. When he batted his team to safety at

Old Trafford, he looked a mature batsman and old soul indeed. But I suspect that Tendulkar came to be 'little' partly because India was seen, and rather saw itself, that way – weak, meek, faintly embattled, vaguely outmatched, generally vulnerable.

And his being 'little' has remained as an artefact of Indian cricket before its great commercial expansion and geopolitical ascendancy – today's 'Indian moment', so to speak, which has all the hallmarks of a long hegemony. 'Little Master' somehow expressed India's culture of victory against the odds, against the grain, against the big boys, and has gone on expressing it long after India became the biggest of all boys itself. With him, then, might go not only among the mightiest of cricketers, but a way of looking at the world – the transition from a time in which India succeeded in spite of to an era in which it succeeds because.

Sachin Tendulkar at fifty
HALF CENTURION (2023)

Sachin Tendulkar fifty? For all that we heard it 264 times in international cricket, his half-century of birthdays arrives today with a jolt.

In our mind's eye, players tend to remain fixed, unchanged and unchanging. Tendulkar, moreover, had an immutable quality, regularity reinforced by his role: 84 per cent of his Test innings began at the fall of the second wicket, at which he emerged as reliably as a cuckoo from a clock announcing the hour.

Not for him the endless prating of more recent cricketers about role ('Everyone knows what their role is'; 'I've discussed my role with the coach/captain/selectors'). Tendulkar grasped his role instantly: his role was to be great.

Still, fifty is fifty. And Tendulkar was so young so long. I first saw him, aged seventeen, in the Lord's Test of 1990 – tiny, cherubic, more closely resembling a jockey than a cricketer. Under that helmet, though, a hard head, as I came to understand at Old Trafford, where his maiden Test century righted a listing team after his elders had failed.

Part of him remained that cool-headed, warm-blooded boy too. To the very end of his career, he retained a youthful passion for the game, blending into every training session as though it was his first. You studied him for signs of boredom, of fatigue, of satiety. Nope, nada, nothing doing. Had it been possible, Tendulkar would have played forever; as it was, it only seemed like he did.

Fifty then – which means that a good many years have passed since the feats that built his stature. The elapse of time has historicised those feats also. Tendulkar was half as old, of course, when he propelled India to victory in the 1998 Coca-Cola Cup with 134 from 131 balls in Sharjah, having helped them qualify for the final with 143 off 131 balls two days earlier. Both at Australia's expense.

He had been eighteen during 1992's Perth Test, when he plucked 114 from India's wrecked first innings; he would be thirty when he dropped anchor in 2004's Sydney Test, famously abjuring the cover-drive for ten hours as he accumulated an unbeaten 241. Tendulkar's 150s in the 2007–08 Border–Gavaskar Trophy came when he was thirty-four, and whole generations had moved on since his debut, but he had not.

Even then the Indian Premier League was appearing on the horizon, over which he pronounced a kind of benediction by playing in the first half dozen seasons, even if the format always seemed a little small for him, like trying to compress *Mughal-E-Azam* into a half hour with advertisements or the *Mahabharata* into a haiku.

Think of what most of us are doing at those ages. Usually we are getting started. At best we are collecting the building blocks of success, which we might then hope to pile. Tendulkar was levelling the site, laying the foundations, erecting the walls, constructing the roof, then doing it again next door, and next door, and next door, until he had laid out a vast, carefully planned city of runs.

Sometimes we talk of the tendency of Test matches in India to suddenly accelerate – to 'go into fast-forward'. Thanks to his early precocity, his rapid maturity, his extended eminence and capacity for reinvention, Tendulkar lived his cricket decades at headlong pace, gathering a momentum that has continued carrying him forward in retirement.

Tendulkar can now be seen, of course, as a foretelling of Indian success, on field and off, by his achieving when it was still uneven, uncertain, unexpected. With a sense of that, he has discerned in the 2011 World Cup a special defining quality, the culmination, as it were, of a two-decade tournament. 'Nothing beats the World Cup final in 2011,' he has said. 'That was the best cricketing day of my life.'

Virat Kohli's tribute after helping to shoulder his elder from the field was so good it sounds apocryphal: 'Tendulkar has carried the burden of the nation for twenty-one years; It was time we carried him. Chak de India.' It is all the more meaningful for being true.

But with the passing of time, Tendulkar has also become something of a hostage of his generation. In youthful India, celebrity is perishable; in modern India, heroes are plentiful. A demographic wave is being inducted in cricket with no independent memory of Tendulkar – the country's median age is twenty-eight. Son Arjun, a twenty-three-year-old left-arm pace bowler last week capped by the Mumbai Indians, is growing up in a very different world.

This generation will be excused wondering how good Tendulkar really could have been, whether fogies like us aren't just getting a little carried away. He'll increasingly be someone for those who saw him to hold on to, to make claims for, to champion. What was true of the Master, Jack Hobbs, in John Arlott's poem, is no less true of the Little Master.

> The Master – records prove the title true,
> Yet fail you for they cannot say
> How many men whose names you never knew
> Are proud to tell their sons they saw you play.

So fifty, which we celebrate, while also sensing it will never be enough. Those who imagined that Bradman would surely live until the age of at least 99.94 will be loath to prophecy. But if ever a cricketer could be backed in the pursuit of a three-figure milestone, by calm, courage and the studious husbandry of energy, it is Sachin Tendulkar.

Sydney Test 2012, Day 3

PONTING STRIKES BACK (2012)

Your best form, says an old cricket dictum, is only ever one innings away. Sometimes, all it takes is a shot – as Ricky Ponting demonstrated at the Sydney Cricket Ground yesterday.

Ponting had moved carefully to 64, about as far as he had come lately in his pursuit of the hundred out of reach for two years. He was facing speedy Ishant Sharma, who had dismissed him seven times in Test cricket previously, and whose success against him four years ago first caused critics to wonder about the encroachments of age on the Australian's technique.

The fourth ball of Sharma's twelfth over was on a good length about middle, of a kind not unlike deliveries that for the last few months have been causing him to topple over to the off side – a tendency of which he has being trying to cure himself with hour upon interminable hour of practice, with bowlers, coaches and machines, lining himself up with mid-on and keeping the face of the bat as open as possible.

In an instant, everything came together. Ponting's body stayed upright, and he kept, as they say these days, his shape:

the ball vanished, not through mid-wicket, where Ponting used to hit naturally, but through mid-on, where the percentages are now more in his favour. Nobody bothered chasing. This was batting in perfect ratio: the minimum of effort, the maximum of return. Well, of course, not quite the maximum, in the sense attached to it in T20, which has made a cargo cult of The Maximum, whether a cow corner mow or a ramp over the keeper. But if you wanted to demonstrate to a lay person what cricket calls 'a stroke', you could hardly have found a better example than this on-drive: a single stride, a pure swing, a fluid movement, like water flooding through a channel.

To a batsman seeking corroboration that his game was in good order, this was the kind of shot to fill him with exultation, flood him with endorphins. Ponting was on his way; so, with its captain Michael Clarke also surging ahead, was Australia. For all the excellence of their country's bowlers this summer, Australians have awaited just such a day as this: one of crushing batting dominance, in which the promises that everyone was working hard, hitting it well in the nets, and feeling a big one around the corner were honoured.

And suddenly, it was on us: a long-awaited reacquaintance with the qualities that make top-notch Test match batting, in a summer in which it has been little seen, with the personal dimensions of Ponting's rehabilitation and Clarke's further habilitation thrown in. There were mighty shots. There was sedulous planning. Ponting and Clarke first scintillated through the pre-lunch session, adding 120 runs: a rate in ancient days we used to call a run-a-minute, before T20 made that seem like undue tardiness. Early on, Ponting swung the first ball of an over from Zaheer Khan for four: another resounding, heartening shot.

At once, with that distinctive hand-puppetry batsmen have popularised, he matter-of-factly signalled for new gloves to come on at the end of the over. During Ponting's hardest times staying in, the gesture would have seemed an affectation. Now it radiated intent: yes, he would be there at the end of the over; yes, he intended to be there quite some time longer; in fact, keep those gloves coming, because there were big runs in the offing.

Clarke was every bit as animated and ambitious. He danced to the spinners; he marched into his drives; he stretched elastically to create half-volleys, including when he punched through extra cover to reach his century. When he played his trademark clip off his legs, he seemed to be running almost before he had connected with the ball.

Yet as attractive as it was, the partnership was also measured. As Australia extended its lead, India's attack, enervated by the heat and taxed by back-to-back Tests, began to look ever-so-slightly medium rare. The fast bowlers' pace fell away; Umesh Yadav bowled a tell-tale half-tracker, smashed for four, bracketed by apologetic wides. But Ravichandran Ashwin, on whom India rely to moderate the workloads of his colleagues, was shrewdly picked off so that Dhoni had to keep throwing them the ball.

Ponting and Clarke were fit. Even after all these years, Ponting shows a colt's enthusiasm in the warm-ups to a day's play; on Clarke's frame hangs not an ounce of spare flesh. They were set on ascertaining exactly how fit were their rivals. As the afternoon unfolded, captains past and present took their toll. Twenty-two relief overs from Kohli and Sehwag were milked in utmost safety. Ishant registered the first Indian century of the series when he gave up his hundredth run, and was emulated by Ashwin and Khan.

Clarke played with immense and indissoluble discipline, passing his double hundred before he played a deliberate stroke in the air, although after a year caulking the Australian middle order he enjoyed an indulgence or two, playing his seldom-seen pull shot with gusto. Beneath his Australian cap and brandishing a cleanskin bat, he looked a sight for nostalgic eyes, his off- and cover-drives off Zaheer Khan after tea sounded as sweetly as the peal of a church bell.

Because of his and Ponting's hard graft earlier, Hussey, so often the redeemer of Australian ruin, then had a rare opportunity to bat under next to no pressure, and permitted himself the frivolity of a couple of straight sixes. The day's headline event, of course, already scarcely needs reliving. Ponting's final supplicating dive to achieve his hundredth run, as if hurling himself on the mercy of the cricket gods, will be limited-edition memorabilia soon enough, probably with genuine SCG dirt mixed in. Have your credit card details ready.

It was a golden moment, to be sure – one of those where technique and training go out the window, and all the cricketer is left with is hope. In point of fact, Ponting almost never dives for the crease: from an old-fashioned bat slider, this was an act of palpable desperation, as revealed by the guilty grin afterwards.

As an image, Ponting's dusty shirt and joyous celebration will inevitably in time stand in for the whole of the innings. This will be poignant, but also a little misleading. Ponting's innings, and Clarke's also, were months in the making – months of dedication and determination to stave off demoralisation and doubt, months of coaching trust and selectorial faith. Some instants in cricket, it is true, *are* accidents. But to play as the Australians did today was not the stuff of chance.

Adelaide Test 2012, Day 4

THE COMING OF KOHLI (2012)

The race is not always to the swift nor battle to the strong, but over four Test matches the odds are in their favour. Yesterday at Adelaide Oval, Peter Siddle and Virat Kohli illustrated the genre's possibilities.

By busting open India's top order like a piñata, Siddle showed why he has become his captain's go-to guy when Australia's going has been, at least momentarily, stopped – ever ready, always eager, full and feisty, capable in his third and fourth spells of hitting velocities still greater than his first.

Kohli showed another dimension of the longer Test series – the opportunity for redemption. After an indifferent start, he has fought his way back into this summer. Even in his comparatively brief first innings in Sydney, he exuded quality; Perth and Adelaide have enabled him to flesh the bones of his case to be a long-term Test cricketer, and his century is the best news for Indian cricket since the World Cup. The trajectory of the series itself was unaltered. But there was some crossfire about the cricket that the verbal interchange on and off the field complemented. That's another aspect of longer series: players play for sufficient time to grow irritated by one another.

During the pre-lunch session, the Australians were as methodical and organised as they have been all season, allowing India just 61 runs in thirty overs. Nine runs accrued in the first half hour before Tendulkar finally worked Siddle wide of mid-on for the day's first boundary, the ball keeping a teasing step ahead of Lyon all the way; the next ball held its line and zoomed just past the outside edge just to keep everyone on tenterhooks.

The bowling nagged like a dripping tap; the field was sealed vacuum tight. A flashing Tendulkar back foot drive looked a certain four until Marsh took advantage of the slight widening of the square boundaries here to arrest it with a sliding save. As he did in Melbourne, Siddle then drew Tendulkar into an overeager push outside the line of his eyes, and the day's Little Mastery was over. Before this series, Siddle had been the only current Australian bowler to have dismissed Tendulkar in a Test; he remains the one who troubles him most.

Siddle's bouncer to unseat Gautam Gambhir in his next over was close on the best ball of the series, steepling off a blameless surface, and startling a well-set batsman with no objective beyond survival. Gambhir is a fastidious, rather intro-verted batsman who fusses about his block like a schoolboy at his geometry homework; Siddle played the part of the annoying classmate jabbing him with a compass.

When Laxman fell tamely soon after, there was a dreadful sameness about it all. Only once in their last eight away Tests have India passed 300. Their collapses have begun blurring into one, as indistinguishable as films starring Jason Statham. Kohli, fortunately, looked anything but daunted. If anything, the position of an ebbing innings and a series already lost licensed him to play with natural freedom.

Before the Test, both captains talked about Adelaide Oval as offering the conditions most akin to those in India; only Kohli has provided empirical evidence to back the assertion, but it was emphatic. His left forearm guided him into drives on the up; his right wrist swivelled like a gimbal as he picked off the pads. When pressed, he manufactured shots, including a leg-stump pick up from Ryan Harris that would have made Royal Challengers Bangalore fans swoon.

The stocks of India's apprentice batsmen – Pujara, Raina, Sharma, Badrinath, Vijay, Mukund – have risen and fallen unpredictably in the years since the retirement of Sourav Ganguly. Kohli himself lost his preferment after an abortive trip to the West Indies, although sitting out the Tests on the subsequent tour of England has ended up doing him little harm and perhaps some good.

Because Kohli also gives Australians the appearance of fancying himself just a little – and after all, anybody who bowled in their sunglasses in club cricket here would be sledged by their own team. Mind you, he has probably been luckier than he knows. Twice he has gone close to incurring the referee's ire for hanging around the crease after dismissal, like a bad tenant insisting on his bond back despite having burned down the house.

Kohli has also, quite visibly, learned a lot, such as the value of strike rotation: with Wriddhiman Saha an alert respondent, he took thirty-two singles. In contradiction of Gambhir's pre-match griping about the summer's pitches, playing on a variety of surfaces has made Kohli look a more complete cricketer.

Only at the last when he found himself nearly deserted by India's detachable tail did Kohli puzzle as to what to do. He scorned to run when he hit to the cover sweeper, then took a single that he was lucky to turn into a second with an overthrow. Having rolled over Ashwin and Zaheer in consecutive deliveries,

Siddle bowled Kohli an inspired over, beating outside and inside edges of his bat. Kohli was then so busy waving his Braveheart broadsword when he passed three figures that he almost forgot to return for a second.

The only real irritant of the day was that the umpires seemed acutely anxious to avoid an international crease incident, perhaps out of respect for the overlapping national holidays. Apologists for video verification are apt to say that it enhances the drama and spectacle of decisions. Going to replays to determine whether front feet have trespassed and requiring batsmen to remain there simply looks ridiculous, and raises questions about the attentiveness of the human officials.

Otherwise, this was a jumbo packed day of Test cricket, rejoiced in by a record crowd. Kohli can jeer all he pleases about them, but at least it was a crowd, in contrast to the thousand people who watched the first day of India's recent Test against the West Indies at Eden Gardens. Had this series ended like so many series these days after two Tests, furthermore, Siddle would have been credited with performances worthy but inconclusive, and Kohli would have returned home with his career in the limbo in which it began the series. This Test may or may not have a winner, but the format yesterday enjoyed a triumph.

Australia v India 2011–12
WALKOVER (2012)

In a series as undeviatingly one-sided as Australia's defeat of India, the question is always: was one team that good, or the other so bad? The answer was, as ever, a little of both. But this both was itself surprising. Australia had lost stunningly to South Africa then New Zealand in its preceding four Tests; India still had the services of its mighty batting quartet – Sachin Tendulkar, Rahul Dravid, Virender Sehwag and VVS Laxman – while Zaheer Khan was also fit at last. What happened was that Australia ascended heights of excellence not seen here for five years, and India plumbed depths not witnessed for nearly a generation.

For Michael Clarke, who as captain appeared a step ahead of each Test throughout in addition to compiling 626 runs at 125.5 and at a helter-skelter strike rate of 70, it was a stunning vindication; the veterans Ricky Ponting (544 runs at 108.8) and Mike Hussey (293 runs at 58.6) found new reserves of resilience too. For MS Dhoni, who was humiliatingly suspended from the Fourth Test because of over-rate transgressions in the Third, it was enough to raise questions about his aptitude as a

Test player let alone as a captain; that the faded four managed just 834 runs at 26 between them reflected poorly on selectors who countenanced just one unforced change in personnel and order all summer.

In hindsight, the hinge point of the series was a spell towards the end of the second day of the First Test, when Peter Siddle first bowled Dravid with a fast no ball then Tendulkar with an even faster fair one. India had been 2/214 chasing 333; they eventually trailed by 51, and were unable to exploit early inroads in the Australian second innings, allowing the home team's tail to add a 100 under next to no pressure. Dhoni's default setting of keeping it tight might have won a World Cup but against a resourceful and flexible Test opponent was revealed as hopelessly inadequate.

India's batsmen certainly arrived confident, on the basis of run-rich tours in 2003–04 and 2007–08, when Australia's fast bowlers operated at lengths that suited their partiality to the ball arriving at waist height. They were caught completely unprepared for the siege that Siddle, Ben Hilfenhaus, Ryan Harris and James Pattinson laid on their front foot techniques, and stuck obdurately to the tried, trusted and failed. Poor Dravid kept having his stumps hit, to the delight of wordsmiths riffing on the theme of 'The Wall', until he had diminished from picket fence through privet hedge to herbaceous border. Tendulkar's wait for his hundredth international hundred became a filibuster; Sehwag repeatedly blew himself up and Laxman was repeatedly blown away.

India's bowlers arguably fared a little better than anticipated, considering that none of them arrived in Australia with much form or fitness to speak of. Zaheer Khan was endlessly crafty; Umesh Yadav and Ishant Sharma showed turns of speed. But they were let down by fielding straight out of Indian cricket's bad old days: it was as though they were disappointed to find that servants hadn't been laid on for them. This was character-istic of an attitude of apathy and arrogance the Indians never shrugged off.

Indian XIs have traditionally been great favourites in Australia. This team won no friends. They dished plenty out on the field then whimpered when this was reciprocated; they kvetched about the pitches, about the crowds, about the media. To press conferences, which by convention involve senior or successful players, they sent individuals who had taken 0/100, who weren't playing, or who spoke little English ... but not once Tendulkar, who declined to speak even when a presenta-tion was made to him in Adelaide in gratitude for his career. They were pampered the length and breadth of the land, to the extent of travelling with their own chef, but not once expressed any pleasure at or enthusiasm for being in Australia. They even groused and grumbled when forced to wait ten minutes to meet Australia's prime minister. Had an Australian team behaved as boorishly in India, there would have been scandal and hand-wringing.

The only Indian to advance was twenty-three-year-old Kohli, who oozes aggression and attitude, if not always good judgement. In the first innings at Adelaide Oval, he surfed a wave of adrenaline; in the second innings, he was dumped, taking an unnecessary run to protect an unnecessary night-watchman and becoming an unnecessary wicket, which somehow summed up the wastefulness of the whole squad. Still, he is going to be some player.

The series' outstanding feats were almost exclusively Australian, although for all the heavy scoring of Clarke, Ponting and Hussey, it was an innings by David Warner that stunned onlookers and stopped traffic. In the nets before the Second Test in Perth, Warner looked like a novice, being knocked over repeatedly and barely hitting a ball off the middle. There might initially have been a 'kill-or-cure' edge to his strokeplay, but it soon turned into a 'kill-or-be-killed' attack. Seldom can a batsman have so outstripped rivals on show: he scored his 180 at a strike rate of 113.12 per hundred balls; other batsmen in the match scavenged their 502 runs at 48.2.

The Australians' top three remained unsettled: Warner failed elsewhere; Ed Cowan debuted promisingly without quite seizing his opportunities; Shaun Marsh had a wretched series coming off injury. Brad Haddin gained a few more detractors with some untidy work. But more than a year seemed to have elapsed since the debacles of last summer, when the same sentiments being applied to India had been applied to Australia.

Rahul Dravid

OVER THE WALL (2012)

R ahul Dravid is a thinking cricketer. But one person
I learned last season that he does not spend a lot of time
thinking about is . . . Rahul Dravid.

It was shortly after the Boxing Day Test, and we were having
dinner with a mutual friend near my home, at a spaghetti joint
in Lygon Street, Carlton. As happens when you're in distinguished sporting company, the subject of conversation turned
to setting down some thoughts about that career when it
ended – as Dravid announced yesterday, it was.

Test cricket's second tallest scorer, and the man who faced
more Test deliveries than any other, would seem to have a tale
to tell. Dravid did not agree. What, after all, had he done? He
had had a comfortable upbringing, a good education, a loving
marriage and . . . well, yes, he'd made more than 24,000 international runs with forty-eight hundreds, but what of it?
Dravid had recently read Andre Agassi's autobiography, *Open*.
Now, *that* was a story. Drugs, girls, money, triumph, disaster.
By comparison, Dravid said seriously, he had hardly lived
at all.

While it seems almost churlish to dispute such a common-sensical self-estimation, on this occasion let's quietly beg to differ. For most of his fifteen years at the top, Dravid was the most immaculate cricketer in the game, a batsman of preter-natural serenity, and a sportsman of model decorum.

That wonderful Indian cricket writer Sujit Mukherjee once said of Dravid's great antecedent Vijay Hazare that his innings had 'no beginning and no end', because 'whether his score was 2 or 20 or 200, he [Hazare] was assessing the bowling with the same exacting concern that characterised his every moment at the crease'.

The same was true of Dravid. He batted as a river runs, at an immemorial pace. You could tune into an innings of his at any time and be unsure whether he had batted six hours or six minutes. He carried himself with the same easy dignity in success or failure, in India or abroad: unlike the other members of his country's prestigious batting elite of Tendulkar, Sehwag, Laxman and Ganguly, he boasted a higher average away than at home.

Dravid's decision to retire will not come as a great surprise to those who watched him struggle through the Australian summer. You arrive at a point in contemplation of any great batsman dealing with poor form where rational explanation no longer suffices. Some little advantage has been lost; some indefinable aura has faded. Bowlers sense it: they attack where they used to be content to keep quiet. Fielders sense it: they crouch in eager expectation of catches, and relax in confidence of accepting them.

Such was the case with Dravid in 2011–12, and he is too per-ceptive not to have sensed it, despite his valiant struggles. He was, as ever, a model guest, his Bradman Oration being quite possibly the season's outstanding Indian performance. It is also characteristic that Dravid waited until the Australian summer was completely done with before making any announcement; it is in line with his view that individuals are at the game's service, not vice versa.

Not every cricketer's cricket faithfully reflects their personality, but Dravid's would seem to. In company, he thinks before speaking, gives his interlocutors undivided attention, is unhurried and unflappable. That evening, dining al fresco, we were perfectly at the mercy of passing rubber-neckers. Every two minutes, it seemed, someone would ask Dravid for an autograph, want him to pose for a photo, or simply stop to gawk. Even the chef came out to shake his hand.

Dravid gave every petitioner perfect partial attention, not once growing flustered, not once losing the thread of a conversation – dealing with them rather like balls wide of off stump, giving them their due but no more. There was, I realised after a while, a well-honed technique to it. Dravid acquiesced to each request politely but straightforwardly, volunteering nothing in addition. People got the message; it was impressive.

Various subjects were discussed that evening, which it seems impolite to divulge, and may even be unenlightening to, because Dravid is so reticent about his career, and so respectful of opponents.

About one opponent, though, he was forthcoming, and that was Ricky Ponting. He recalled being accosted by Ponting, whom he hardly knew and had barely conversed with, during Australia's tour of India in 2010. 'I want to talk to you,' Ponting insisted. Dravid wondered what he had done wrong; on the contrary, Ponting wanted to tell him what he was doing right. Dravid was having a poor series; Ponting urged him to hang in there.

'I know you're not making runs, and I know there's probably a bit of pressure on you at the moment,' Ponting told Dravid. 'But let me tell you: every time you come in, I tell the guys that you look like you're going to get runs today. You've been getting out, but I reckon there are some big scores around the corner for you.'

Dravid was moved by the grace of Ponting's gesture – as indeed were we, his companions that night, to hear of it. He went and proved Ponting right, too, enjoying in 2011 the second-most prolific calendar year of his Test career.

Just over a week after our dinner, Ponting dived headlong for his crease at the SCG, just beating a throw and achieving his first Test century in nearly two years. It was noticeable that while most of the Indian fielders assumed excruciated poses, hands on heads, looking martyred, Dravid moved in from mid-off clapping appreciatively, and perhaps also gratefully.

You would think that having a cricketer play at international level for more than fifteen years might conduce to a little succession planning; this being Indian cricket, you would think wrongly. Nobody stands out in this Indian line-up as an inheritor of his mantle. His retirement will leave the same breach in his team as it would have a decade ago. All the same, there is perhaps no modern cricketer better equipped intellectually and temperamentally to make a contribution to the game's governance and direction. Dravid's greatest impact on cricket might lie ahead of him. And that would be a story worth telling.

Mohali Test 2013

CULTURE VULTURES (2013)

If you're looking for it, it's section 1.5, and it starts on page 20: that is, the 650 words in last season's Argus review, that touchstone of Australian cricket administration, headed 'Improve the Australian Team's culture'.

In a week that culture came under internal and external scrutiny, it's been worth a glance. The report, if you recall, found there to be a 'lack of a strong culture' in the Australian team, and vested great faith in a '360-degree feedback process' and 'adult conversations', with individuals 'agreeing required changes to behaviour as part of an overall development plan'.

Well, that's gone swimmingly, then. How did we get from the methodical, graduated managerialism of Argus to the frantic line-in-the-sandism of Mohali? What has Cricket Australia been doing these last eighteen months?

It's possible that the suspensions of Shane Watson, Mitchell Johnson, James Pattinson and Usman Khawaja will have a salutary effect on attitudes prevalent among elite cricketers. But they are also a tacit admission of management failure, because culture does not form in a vacuum. An honest appraisal of events needs an acknowledgement of the changing macro picture – something that, in hindsight, the Argus review rather neglected.

Much of the most severe commentary this week has come from distinguished ex-players such as Darren Lehmann and Mark Waugh, drawing on their own experiences. But how directly comparable are those experiences now? Lehmann left school aged sixteen to work in a car plant in Elizabeth, and took another twelve years to make his Test debut, by which time he had compiled thirty-three first-class hundreds – a number he had more than doubled by the time his career was over. When picked for his first Test, Waugh had compiled twenty-five first-class hundreds, a number he afterwards more than trebled.

Golden soil, wealth for toil: theirs were classic Australian careers, influenced heavily by elder statesmen in their state teams, David Hookes, Wayne Phillips and Andrew Hilditch in Lehmann's South Australia; Geoff Lawson, Greg Matthews and Mike Whitney in Waugh's New South Wales.

Yet that time-honoured culture has been steadily scaled back, marginalised and even maligned, supplanted by an accent on the hothousing of talent, elite underage cricket, and the dogma of 'professionalism'. This year marks a decade since the commissioning of CA's Centre of Excellence – perversely commencing a period in which quality has been in ever shorter supply.

In some respects, the road to mediocrity has been paved with good intentions, with those responsible oblivious to the possibility that 'pathways' extending privileges on the basis of potential rather than in recognition of achievement might well debauch talent, breed outsized expectations, and stultify self-motivation.

The generation that is becoming the backbone of the Australian team has not, as a rule, lived and breathed cricket, or at least talked it and analysed it up hill and down dale alongside senior players. On the contrary, they have listened to coaches tell them what to do, and played it alongside contemporaries in rigid age bands: under-15, under-17, under-19 etc.

It's no fluke that many seem to lose their way at around twenty, when they suddenly find themselves at the bottom of a pile, merely proficient at the game rather than being truly immersed in it. They're of a generation not particularly confident on their own feet or of their own ideas anyway, with a limited self-awareness, and a rather brittle self-worth.

They certainly do not grieve defeat as did a Ponting, a Katich, or a Clarke. There is, for them, always another game – and in this they are arguably right. After all, their game is run by an administration that half the time seems less involved in cricket than in staging a cricket-themed 'show'.

It's easy to look at the current Australian team and observe merely that it is 'young'. It's certainly that: its ersatz intern, teenager Ashton Agar, could be coach Mickey Arthur's son, and national selector John Inverarity's grandson. But it's more; it's a patchwork of vastly differing maturities. Cricketers no longer grow up at orderly rates, achieving similar milestones, experiencing regular rites of passage.

Thirty-one-year-old Mitchell Johnson, for example, has played the grand total of ninety-one first-class games, fifty of them Test matches. You can criticise Johnson for his delinquency where the much-discussed 'assignment' was concerned. But, frankly, here is a cricketer who at various stages in his career has looked like he wouldn't know what to have for breakfast without consulting Troy Cooley.

Much continues to come to many quite easily, such as those on state rookie contracts while still at home, living the dream of professional sport while staving off the reality. And wealth, of course, can these days accumulate very fast indeed: you're only ever one Indian Premier League auction away from overnight millionaire status.

This brings us to perhaps a less obvious point. The challenge Arthur has set his cricketers is to be 'team players'. But what does 'team' mean anymore? In a cricket world of multiple formats, cricketers are in almost constant circulation, to the point where they must wonder whether they are of a team, in a team, or merely near a team. A month or so ago, there were actually two Australian XIs playing simultaneously: one here, one in India.

Michael Clarke spoke on Tuesday of representing Australia being a 'huge honour'. But has not that sense of common purpose, and that identification between cricketer and country, been rather weakened by the squad mentality, the sense of players being autonomous and interchangeable cricketing units?

Traditionally, Australian cricketers have made linear career progressions shaped by strong allegiances and causes: club, state, country. Shane Watson, by contrast, plays for three quite different Australian teams, and has represented three different states, as well as franchises in the IPL and Big Bash League – and he is far from the most promiscuous of his generation.

In an age so abounding in teams, and so incessant in comings and goings, the bonds between cricketers are growing more superficial and contingent, the objectives of commitment and investment harder for coaches to build.

And for all that this week was about 'sending a message', that message remains subtly mixed: are we *really* looking for more strong leaders in Australian cricket, or simply more disciplined followers to toe all these lines in the sand?

This week, four cricketers were made an example of. They may have had it coming. They may have needed the jolt. But the culture goes well beyond them, and it will not be altered simply by management fiat. We have hardly even started the 'adult conversations' necessary.

Border–Gavaskar Trophy 2013

BROWNWASH (2013)

Three-zip. Three-love. India three, Australia yet to score. The scoreline for the Border–Gavaskar Trophy sounds drastic whichever way it's formulated. And there's another expression of it that in its way is an even greater indictment.

Six-one: that's the ratio of Indian to Australian centuries at Chennai, Hyderabad and Chandigarh. Since Michael Clarke battled his way to three figures on the first day of the series, MS Dhoni, Virat Kohli, Shikhar Dhawan, Cheteshwar Pujara and Murali Vijay have done likewise, the last-named, twice. Nor have they been content with the milestone: the average of their hundreds has been 174. This is despite Australia having had the advantage of batting first in each case, while facing an attack similar to the one that in its previous series late last year conceded six hundreds to England, average 187.

In no other respect, in fact, does Australia's tailing off from its green and golden age show up more clearly than in the inability of batsmen to build big innings. Back in the day, avaricious Australians salted away vast stockpiles of hundreds: Ricky Ponting (41), Matthew Hayden (30), Justin Langer (23),

Steve Waugh (32), Mark Waugh (20), Mike Hussey (19), Mark Taylor (19) and Adam Gilchrist (17). They made them big too. Langer's average century, for example, was 173, and opponents found him harder to remove and nearly as annoying as Jonathan Holmes's smirk.

Today only Clarke (23) retains the three-figure habit, having made eight of the eighteen centuries Australian batsmen have spread over our last twenty Tests. A further six came from the now-retired Ponting and Hussey, leaving David Warner (three) and Matthew Wade (two) as the only other scorers of multiple hundreds in that time.

Drill deeper, and the picture darkens further. Twenty years ago, there were sixty hundreds scored in the Sheffield Shield; this season, there have been thirty-one. Just twenty-three of these have been by specialist batsman, only two of whom, Ponting and the perdurable Chris Rogers, have managed as many as three each.

For that matter, only three other batsmen with a minimum of five games have managed to average 40. Australian representatives Rob Quiney, David Hussey, Adam Voges and Tim Paine have averaged less than 30, Shaun Marsh, George Bailey, Peter Forrest and Michael Klinger less than 20. In other words, our batsmen are not making hundreds *anywhere*; they are bringing with them to international cricket shortcomings instilled at domestic level.

Developing the concentration to bat all day and the skill to accumulate runs at different tempos, which is really what a Test century entails, are not aptitudes that can be nurtured on ProBatter or Merlyn. They are learned by doing; and we neither do them any longer, nor even seem to value them.

India, it would seem, have rediscovered these customs. The mighty partnership between Pujara and Vijay on the second day in Hyderabad, for example, was an exemplary demonstration of cricket in three moods. Before lunch, the Indians garnered 49 runs in twenty-seven overs; from lunch to tea, they collected 106 in thirty-four overs; from tea to stumps, they plundered 151 from thirty overs. Australia has players capable of batting in each of these three moods, but only Clarke has demonstrated an aptitude for all of them.

Pujara and Vijay recalled that charming French expression *reculer pour mieux sauter*, meaning to run back in order to jump further forwards, or to give way a little in order to take up a stronger position. By contrast, Australian batting this series has been a mixture of carte blanche and cul-de-sacs, leading to regular and profound senses of déjà vu.

But then, what precisely did anyone expect? Surrender cricket to the priorities of mass marketing and television scheduling, transform your first-class season into the hurried prelude and subdued postlude of a puffed-up T20 tournament, create a cricket system that accords greater prestige to making 20 from ten balls than 100 from 250 . . . well then, frankly, you'll get what you deserve. And if we're to recover some capacity to bat for the durations necessary to make big Test scores, then the first priority must be to restore some sense of proportion, coherence and continuity to our summers, rather than treating our batsmen like professional automata, somehow infinitely flexible.

Time was, if you recall, when summer was carefully scheduled in blocks on grounds that batting in five-day and one-day formats were essentially different crafts. For evidence that times have changed, consider the 2012–13 of Tasmania's George Bailey.

It runs like this: from 25 August to 3 September, four one-day internationals; from 5 September to 5 October, nine T20 internationals; from 14 October to 1 December, four Sheffield Shield four-dayers interspersed with five Ryobi Cup one-dayers; from

9 December to 5 January, seven Big Bash League T20s; from 11 January to 23 January, five ODIs; from 26 to 28 January, two T20Is; from 1 to 6 February, three ODIs; 13 February, a T20I; 19 February, a Ryobi Cup one-dayer; 21 February to today, four Sheffield Shield matches.

Fans who carp about the season's many guises should try imagining it from the perspective of Bailey, compelled to endure no fewer than eighteen separate changes of format. This has been mainly at the expense of his long-form cricket: in a summer Bailey should have been challenging for an Ashes berth, he has managed a single first-class half-century. What a waste of a smart, resourceful cricketer.

For batsmen to have the opportunity to bat long, team innings also need to last. Under present circumstances, the tough love for batsmen that curators have been extending is a better idea in theory than in practice. In only a fifth of Sheffield Shield matches this season have both first innings exceeded 300; twenty-six first innings have folded up for less than 250. Pitches that psych out batsmen, flatter modest seamers and lead to games that don't last long enough to afford opportunities for spinners assist precisely nobody.

Here, then, is the line in the sand we should be drawing. To be sure, Chennai, Hyderabad and Chandigarh have been shambolic failures. But it's arguable that the games were lost even before Australia arrived.

THE LONGEST DECADE

In the last decade, Australia and India have played five series. Australia won only the first, at home, playing on the adrenaline released by the shocking death of Phillip Hughes. This series also heralded the combative captaincy of Virat Kohli, making good the loss of Sachin Tendulkar and MS Dhoni put together. Funnily enough, however, India's skipper when they regained the Border–Gavaskar Trophy in March 2017 in Dharamsala and when they retained it in Brisbane in January 2021 was the under-sung Ajinkya Rahane. And last year Kohli's successor Rohit Sharma led India to defeat in the finals of the World Test Championship and the World Cup. The Border–Gavaskar Trophy begins at Perth Stadium on 22 November. Let the games begin.

First Test, Adelaide 2014, Day 1
HELL FOR LEATHER (2014)

Periodically at Adelaide Oval yesterday, the big screen was emblazoned with the new slogan of Cricket Australia's all-action website: 'Where play never stops'.

Yet cricket is stopping all the time: no game has such an action-to-waiting quotient, is so full of pauses and longueurs. And lately, of course, it has been in actual shock rather than simple repose, suspended for a fortnight in the light of the death of Philip Hughes, frozen in time. Even David Warner stops, every so often, or at least decelerates and consolidates, and in doing so on this first day he gave Australia's delayed Test summer an emphatic, stirring beginning.

All the same, the day's most pregnant pause involved Australia's captain, and it trailed off in a series of dots. These might echo through the summer. Michael Clarke had earlier seized his day's first opportunity. The statue of Colonel Light at the top of Montefiore Hill overlooking Adelaide Oval holds a map in his left hand and points with his right. He would project similarly positivity were he miming a front foot defensive shot to the dressing room having won the toss and elected to bat: both are invitations to get building.

Warner, as is his wont, burst from the gate, with circles of the arms and a gaze at the heavens, partner Chris Rogers following mutedly in his wake. For the first half hour he directed his nervous energy into a fusillade of off-side shots, seven boundaries in fifteen deliveries, all rousing, none genuinely risky, as India's bowlers searched in vain for satisfactory ranges.

Then, with the game apparently at his mercy, but his adrenaline overdrawn, Warner took stock. He accorded the bowlers and the occasion some deference, went in to what for him passes for a shell. Curiously, the defensive shots were perhaps more ominous for his opponents, in Warner's balance and composure, in his pointed holding of his pose after each one. For even when not pummelling boundaries, Warner suggests energy at the crease – in limboing to stretch his quads, in telescoping his arms to keep them loose, in his sprinter's explosion as he sets off for a single, in his tumble turns as he takes a second or third.

The authority returned after drinks, when Warner surged to his first 50 and started on his second with two pull shots and a lofted drive, whereupon Aaron asked for the ball to be looked at. Understandably so: much more such pummelling and the Kookaburra would be refashioned as a cube.

The pause that mattered – everyone was awaiting it – came when Warner lapped for two to reach 63, where death left Hughes's score suspended two weeks ago, and sank knowingly to his haunches. It was, he said later, 'the hardest point of the day' – and the whole day was hard. He drew to one side; the whole ground drew breath.

The moment passed, and Warner and the game pushed on, as though refreshed: it was a milestone but, after all, also just a score. Warner made a hundred here two years ago by laying about everything in reach; here he contented himself with what was within his grasp. The emotional effort of the nineties had him panting, puffing and communing with himself; the technique, now so tight and trustworthy, saw him through.

Not once did he play and miss, and it was possible to remember only a few mistimings, including a failure to slot away Karn Sharma's first ball in Test cricket, a tentative full toss. Warner's first moment of indiscretion was his last, a pardonably light-headed waft to the tenanted cow corner. He departed with a final tiny pause, to take in a panorama of the field.

The aforementioned halt in the forty-fourth over caused immediate alarm. Concerned players. Medical staff. Distress and confusion. It was all just a little too reminiscent of recent, horrifying events. Alarming at first was the apparent insignificance of the cause, Clarke aggravating his chronically bad back with the merest twist of the hips, no more apparently incapacitating than a sneeze. Then there was the flustered clustering around Clarke's prone form. When Clarke goes down on his front to bend his back, usually, he demonstrates an enviable, and hard-won, suppleness; now, for almost ten minutes, he resembled a tottering pensioner trying to recompose themselves after a fall. If not a surrender, his departure from the field was in the nature of a retreat.

Not even Cricket Australia's spokesperson bothered obfuscating, using the technical term for Clarke's condition of 'considerable pain', a description that may also apply to the sensations experienced by Australia's selectors. For two hours, he had batted in reasonable control. The effect may have been nullified if Australia has to go on with ten. It's arguable that Clarke's problems now extend beyond the physical – that they are aggravated by his tendency to see them as a function of 'toughness', or his 'record', or otherwise. His desire to play every match is manful. It is simply looking ever less realistic – a hardly necessary rod for his already-aching back. Australia's captain may now be facing an enforced pause for reflection.

In India's efforts there were a few too many pauses: their over rate, despite thirty-four overs of spin, was lethargic, and forced them into a rather mechanical hurry after tea. But when they pitched the second new ball up as they had not the first, they belatedly drew the day back into something approaching balance. Wriddhiman Saha kept alertly and Shikhar Dhawan accepted two sharp chances. They will have worse days on this tour.

The pitch, however, is already hinting of fissures, which will widen in the predicted heat, and Steve O'Keefe took a cheap bag of five here a few weeks ago, foretelling a role for spin. The occasional nick failed to carry, too, perhaps presaging some unevenness in bounce. Even when events seem stalled, the time in a Test match is marching on.

First Test, Adelaide 2014, Day 2
CLARKE FIGHTS ON (2014)

'Johnson' said the world's loveliest scoreboard yesterday morning in the corner that tracks the running total and the current batsmen, with a pardonable desire to keep patrons informed ahead of the game. It was perfectly plausible, a wicket having fallen from the last ball of the previous day, and Mitchell Johnson being the next batsman in the nominal order.

Michael Clarke? Well, he had not so much 'retired hurt' the previous day as withdrawn into seclusion, visibly distraught, barely able to put one foot in front of the other. What price his return, for the day, the game, the series, the summer? And then, with one bound, ten minutes of throwdowns, and an all-but-sleepless night of treatment, Australia's captain was free. Well, perhaps not free – more properly the opposite, actually, having himself lashed to his fate, as naval captains would have themselves lashed to their helms during storms, entwining their fates with those of their ships.

Was that Clarke coming to bat? It was Clarke. Compared to publicly and privately farewelling your dearest friend in cricket, perhaps resuming this innings was a cinch. It wasn't,

171

of course: it was the pursuit of a Test century with a peculiar sort of valiance, physical and mental. During his death-before-dishonour 161 in Cape Town earlier this year, Clarke visibly earned his fractured shoulder and other contusions, and came to wear them as medals of valour. Here the enemy was within, from an injury incurred in the course of a tiny sideways jink, and part of an innings always on the brink of a repeat mishap.

As the bowler approached, Clarke stood tall and still at the crease, the tap-tap that keeps the beat of his batting now a thready pulse. His torso was thickened by some supporting garment, his feet confined to a tiny square of activity, leaving his arms and hands to do almost all the work; you saw him wince every so often, and found yourself doing the same; you heard his occasional groan through the stump mic, and wondered how long he might last.

The former England captain Tony Lewis tells a story about Majid Khan when he played at Glamorgan in the early 1970s, who settled a debate about the insignificance of footwork in batsmanship by undertaking a half hour net in which he did not shift from a standing position, and nonetheless met every ball in the middle of the bat. For the limitations to be involuntary . . . well, that is something else. We are used to the idea of bowlers being injured by their explosive exertions; batsmen, still as pillars, are what teams are built on.

Clarke here reminded us of the physical vagaries of batting's movements, its swivels, pivots and levers, its calls on agility, endurance, ability to generate power and capacity to weather blows, because they were all in his case restricted. When he directed Mohammed Shami over the slip cordon and shovelled Karn Sharma through mid-wicket yesterday from a standing position, they were epics of minimalism. When he jogged between wickets and gingerly dabbed his bat into the crease, they were testaments of frailty.

It was, of course, a personal sense of mission that drove Clarke on, the physical pain of success paling before the mental pain of failure. Clarke lost some of his future with the death of Phillip Hughes: it was possible to envision him going on to be a mentor to the younger man of whom he prophesied so much, a hundred Tests and more. One day, in all probability, Clarke will be a father, and know paternal pride; in his relationship with Hughes, I suspect, he experienced a sporting equivalent. Runs will not have remotely made good the loss, but they are a currency in which Hughes jubilantly transacted, and thus part of their bond. A hundred was all Clarke could do, just as he had said all the words that could be said.

It was grim all the same. Clarke began his Test career with among the sunniest smiles in cricket; he is approaching that career's conclusion with teeth often gritted, lips pursed and bitten. On reaching his hundred, and upon dismissal, his responses were, in the context of recent effusions, almost austere – calm of mind, all passion spent.

It is hard to be overshadowed while passing 150 for the first time, but that was almost Steve Smith's fate, even if this was partly an outcome of expectations of his batting he himself has raised. His bearing was once as fresh and spry as that of a PMG boy bearing telegrams; he now appears as reliably as the postman with the daily delivery. His back and across step is slightly more pronounced than last season, and his bat sponsor new. Otherwise he continues on the smoothest of ascents, having averaged 62 in his last dozen Tests.

Smith solemnised his century with a steady and deliberate step towards the '408' embossed on the outfield, then celebrated it with strokes that composed their own sort of tribute, clearing his front leg and smashing overhanded down the ground. Radar timed the deliveries from Varun Aaron at in excess of 140 km/h; it was a shame there was no reverse radar to measure their speed coming back. Flailing cuts and reverse sweeps ensued, with hints of a declaration.

All the Australians have batted in this match with Hughes on their mind; these were the shots perhaps closest to the Hughes spirit, full of generous abandon, including the chance Smith offered to slip from Karn Sharma from a metre wide of leg stump. The beginning was the end, the scoreboard finally having to drag the nameboard for Johnson out at 5.51 p.m., just ahead of the gloom's descent. With two days elapsed and more than 500 runs hoarded, it's probably time to see his name on the other side of the scoreboard. But that's up to the captain – a man very sure of his own mind.

First Test, Adelaide 2014, Day 3
I GET KNOCKED DOWN . . . (2014)

It was perfect – in the absence of consequences, it is allowable to say so. Mitchell Johnson's first ball to Virat Kohli at Adelaide Oval yesterday was the kind of short delivery every pace bowler would wish to reproduce to a fresh batsman: fast, straight, rearing, deceptive.

Kohli played it badly too – that, thankfully, it is also possible to report. India's captain pressed forward, went up on his toes too early, ducked too late, took his eyes off the ball when he was squared up, and absorbed the impact flush on the crest of his helmet, the symbol of the Board of Control for Cricket in India.

I can digress from here to tell you that the aforementioned crest is derived from the Most Exalted Order of the Star of India, a chivalric order founded in 1861, dormant for the last five years. Interesting, huh? I have the licence to do so because, as the technology of the helmet means it to be, nothing happened – the way nothing, or at least nothing much, has been happening for a good many years, at least until the tragedy whose ghostly imprint registers on the outfield here, and commemorated in the very black band round Johnson's bowling arm.

Nothing happened in a vaguely chilling fashion, of course. Johnson himself was visibly anxious, approaching reticently, and being consoled by his captain Michael Clarke as he withdrew. The umpires converged. Fielders came in solicitous relays.

Four years ago, Kohli was a burr beneath Australia's saddle, chock full of chat, the kind of opponent you would hardly have minded seeing roughed up a little. But it's only eight days since he attended Phillip Hughes's funeral. There was relief, therefore, as Kohli removed his helmet with all the nonchalance of a shopper scanning a piece of fruit for bruising, then donned it again with apparent satisfaction. And so the game moved on – a little step closer to normality, if not without a jitter.

This was always going to happen, and probably sooner than later. People wondered how the first bouncer would feel after the tragedy of Hughes; head blows have grown so normalised in recent times that an actual impact was never destined to be far behind. The real test was the next ball, and the participants passed it well. Johnson again bowled short and fast; Kohli tucked in defensively behind it. They were, at least momentarily, protagonists rather than antagonists, taking cricket forward together, out of its dark weeks and despondent thoughts.

Since Hughes's death, Johnson has pronounced himself 'ready to go', and Kohli described the bouncer as 'part of cricket' and 'every bowler's right'. Their deeds here spoke still louder. Two deliveries later, Kohli eased forward then punched confidently down the ground.

In the main, it was a day of mild cricket in mild weather before a mild crowd. Bowling was made challenging by blustery conditions, brisk enough to blow off bails. There was hard work for fielders without competitive cricket in their legs. The convalescent Clarke avoided slip, spending much of the day at mid-on, a position Sir Robert Menzies once described as 'the last refuge of mankind', turning to chase only as long as it took him to detect a younger and more mobile fielder in the vicinity.

The benignity of the pitch was encapsulated in two early cuts by Pujara off Harris, the first square as the ball sat up, the second fine as the ball came back slightly – adjustment made easy. Suitably reassured, Indian batsmen exorcised some of the demons by which they were possessed in the northern summer. Pujara, troubled in England by the ball that came back as he tried to cover deliveries going away, faced no risk of such whip-sawing by seam here. Kohli, for whom a fourth stump line in England might nearly have been surrounded by crime scene tape, looked ever more secure and authoritative.

A determination to assert himself was most obvious in Ajinkya Rahane, who tried to sweep from outside off, pull from above head height, slash square, hit over the top and drive on the up all in his first twenty-five balls, before settling down. The short ball, nonetheless, remained a useful threat. After tea, Siddle bowled a waspish and accurate spell, encouraging the pull shot, menacing the helmeted heads, and Rahane's top edge landed in space between equidistant fielders. In his day's con-cluding sally, Johnson then slipped himself, and looked again like the bowler who a year ago made it almost look necessary to wear two helmets. Kohli, who in reaching a hundred kissed his badge as if to atone for its earlier rough treatment, was suddenly defending it again, and fell to a cramped pull shot. With a leg gully and short leg in close attendance, Wriddhiman Saha had eleven deliveries to negotiate from the world's fastest bowler, and handled them well, remaining inside the line, keeping his eye on the ball, timing his sway, on guard for the fuller variation – hostility handled with skill. The Australians bristled, the crowd crowed, and everyone, perhaps, felt a little better afterwards.

Brisbane Test 2014
JOHNSON STRIKES AGAIN (2014)

Having made an inconspicuous start to the series, Mitchell Johnson intervened twice to devastating effect at the venue of his Test comeback a year earlier. Australia was drifting at 6/247 on the third morning in pursuit of India's 404 when he surged to 88 from ninety-three balls, leading a rally that yielded a 101-run lead. The next morning, he splintered India's top order like matchwood with a spell of 3/10 in eleven balls; Johnson was then at the crease when the winning runs were scored late in the afternoon, extending Australia's undefeated streak at the Gabba to twenty-six Tests, composed of nineteen wins and seven draws.

Man of the match, nonetheless, was Steve Smith, who in his first Test as captain lost the toss on a day of enervating heat, and watched India pile up 4/311 by stumps, Murali Vijay compiling a polished 144 (213 balls, twenty-two fours), adding 124 in 165 deliveries with Ajinkya Rahane. Bowlers sagged, Mitchell Marsh tweaking a hamstring that kept him from bowling for a month; catches went down, Shaun Marsh spilling Vijay at gully and short cover; officials and medical staff in the dressing room had to maintain a constant cycle of instant treatments and sub-stitute fieldsmen; over rates slumped. It was a harsh initiation in the office Smith had temporarily inherited from the injured Michael Clarke, ahead of the official vice-captain Brad Haddin.

Yet Smith's composure never left him; nor did his form. After Josh Hazlewood, making his Test debut, forced his way through India's lower order on the second morning, Smith took breezy command of Australia's innings, scoring the first first-innings hundred by a new Australian captain in thirty-nine years, and his sixth in thirteen matches since his maiden in August 2013. MS Dhoni, who resumed India's captaincy after recovering from his long-term hand injury, seemed to have no plan for him: it was almost as though India had budgeted for a hundred, and were intent merely on keeping him quiet, which they signally failed to do.

Smith's 133 (191 balls, thirteen fours, two sixes) wanted only for support, which Johnson finally provided. Their riotous partnership, 148 in twenty-six overs, fed off some feckless short-pitched bowling and some reckless on-field banter, Rohit Sharma apparently reminding Johnson when he came in of his previously indifferent bowling. Far from taking umbrage, Johnson played like a man unburdened, while Smith for a period was very nearly forgotten. Australia's last four eventually added 258 in just 48.3 overs.

With India 1/71 coming into the fourth morning and still in touching distance, there were confused and confusing advices from their dressing room. In warming up, Shikhar Dhawan was struck on a wrist and decided he could not resume; Virat Kohli walked out at 10 a.m. with Cheteshwar Pujara and was shortly walked back, having dragged Johnson on. Rahane was bounced out, Rohit nicked off, and when Dhoni lurched forward to Hazlewood and was hit lethally on the pads, India was 4/111. Dhawan at last recommenced at the fall of the wicket of Ashwin, unluckily deemed caught behind when a ball brushed his thigh, and mysteriously showed no ill effects – indeed, after Pujara fell to an unplayable lifter from Hazlewood, he batted breezily, putting on 60 in eighty-seven balls with Umesh Yadav. It was a mysterious interlude and a muted one: the Indian camp made a complaint about the quality of the practice pitches, but only an 'unofficial' one; they denied rumours of a dressing-room contretemps between Dhawan and Kohli; they left Dhoni to summarise after the match in inimitable fashion: 'That kind of scenario can create a bit of unrest – not like a typhoon coming sort of unrest, but the calmness of the dressing room goes for a toss.'

Australia were left 128 to chase, and were grateful to Chris Rogers, who batted with unaccustomed fluency to reach a second half-century in the match: 55 in fifty-seven deliveries with ten boundaries. The satisfaction of seeing Australia to victory eluded Smith only when he had to detour round bowler Varun Aaron returning for a second and was found short of his ground by a pinpoint throw from Umesh Yadav, who bounced Haddin out at the same score. The accuracy and purpose were too late; Haddin had also the satisfaction that his nine catches were the second most for an Australian in a Test.

The overall run rate of 4.12 was the highest in Australian history and the ninth highest of all time. The over rate, unfortunately, was consistently poor, the number of visits by groups of supernumeraries bearing gloves, drinks and even bananas increasingly exasperating: Smith was fined 60 per cent of his match fee, his teammates 30 per cent of theirs. Ishant Sharma dropped 15 per cent of his match fee into the ICC swearbox for a send-off to Smith.

Melbourne Test 2014, Day 3

RAHANE'S ROMP (2014)

India's young top six batsmen must dodge some long shadows. Comparisons to the previous gilded generation come readily – in part they are invited.

Virat Kohli arrived at number four like a boy emperor, preceded by a one-man dynasty, that of Sachin Tendulkar. Cheteshwar Pujara has been saddled from the first with the mantle of Rahul Dravid; Shikhar Dhawan's brio and insouciance follows in the tradition of Virender Sehwag. Rohit Sharma? He may be there as a cautionary tale, of India's capacity to waste talent in the era since it divided between the haves and the have yachts.

The one on whom it is hardest to get a fix is twenty-six-year-old Ajinkya Rahane, neither left-handed like Sourav Ganguly nor rubber-wristed like VVS Laxman, neither as cavalier as Navjot Sidhu nor as roundhead as Sanjay Manjrekar. At 168 centimetres and 61 kilograms, he is the shortest and the slightest of his present group – round-shouldered, undemonstrative, unassuming. Apparently he does not use a credit card and has eschewed the endorsements which descend on young Indian cricketers like so much gold dust.

181

That lovely prose stylist Rajan Bala once described cricket as sparing Indians 'the anonymity of clerical serfdom', and that is how you kind of imagine Rahane in a world without cricket – as a methodical, scrupulous and uncomplaining clerk, keeping a ledger in a nice, round hand. Right now, however, cricket is making Rahane welcome indeed. He has streaked ahead on this tour, much as his partner in yesterday's huge stand, Kohli, did in Australia four years ago.

Rahane arrived here with a reputation for solid technique, sound temperament and a steady Test strike rate of 52 (not to mention a nondescript domestic T20 strike rate of 115). In five innings so far, he has breezed along at 77 per hundred balls, outpacing every other specialist batsman in this series – Kohli, Dhawan, David Warner, Steve Smith and all. Three good deliveries, one poor decision and one slight misjudgement have been necessary to remove him.

You can feel the urgency when he pushes the ball a little in front of himself and takes a few dancing steps down the pitch, inviting his partner to take him up, daring the field to take him on. He backs up a long way, calls decisively, dashes between wickets, and looks ready at all events. That readiness is no accident. Like the team itself, many an Indian batsman has been a lion at home and a lamb korma abroad: Pujara, who averages 75 in India and 29 everywhere else looks more and more an example of the genus.

Rahane, who has played but a single Test, his first, in India, has set himself single-mindedly to batting overseas, to coping with seam movement in England and New Zealand, speed in South Africa, bounce in Australia. His coach, Pravin Amre, himself a disciple of Tendulkar's guru Ramakant Achrekar, has run a cricket academy in Mumbai for the last three years and in that time made over the techniques of Robin Uthappa, Suresh Raina and Naman Ojha, among others.

Rahane is now undoubtedly Amre's star pupil and best advertisement: seldom has a young Indian batsman in Australia pulled and cut with such alacrity. It very nearly cost him his wicket early at the Gabba. He stayed the cross-bat course. When the space beckoned yesterday, Rahane hit in the air; when the man went back, he hit down. He pulled in front of square and behind, full-bloodedly then cool-headedly. He went deep in the crease to crash Johnson through mid-wicket after tea with a flourish, then leaned alertly into the ensuing half-volley.

To surge through the 80s, he flailed Harris through point then glanced him with a gossamer touch for four. To proceed from there to three figures, he explored the airspace over slip. Nathan Lyon alone gave him pause, inducing an unpunished nick, then dropping a return catch that he would have been embarrassed to miss had it been lobbed back by the wicket-keeper. Otherwise there was not a semblance of doubt let alone risk.

Preceding Rahane by an hour and outstaying him by another hour, Kohli played with the same application he showed in the first innings at Adelaide, mixed with some of the panache he displayed in the second. It was an innings made to measure, and not just for his girlfriend Anushka Sharma, keeping glamorous vigil and causing Twitter to swerve in the Great Southern Stand.

Kohli set simply to survive the relentlessly probing Harris – just eleven scoring strokes in fifty-two deliveries. But from Johnson, India's nemesis in Brisbane, he looted 68 from seventy-three balls with eleven boundaries, including three disdainful pull shots in an over after tea. The rivals tangled again before the umpires again ensured that the flickering needle on their patented ICC banter-o-meter did not trespass on the red zone. Johnson seethed and perhaps regretted not hitting the batsman's badge harder in Adelaide. Kohli pouted and blew a kiss, missing Anushka by 180 degrees.

Cricket's caprices had the second last word: a relatively straightforward chance having gone down earlier, a far harder one was taken from the day's final delivery. Kohli, who still seems more mischievous sprite than public nuisance, added a few dot points in the post-play media conference.

At the press conference twenty-four hours earlier, Ravi Ashwin had fantasised of India amassing 650. His muted duck at the top of the last hour yesterday militated against it, even if the pitch continues to play irreproachably, and might in the end prove too good to provide a conclusion. Certain conclusions, however, it will be possible to draw, like those about the emerging qualities of Ajinkya Rahane.

Under the Southern Cross: in the unofficial Australians on their pioneering 1935–36 tour of India (*above*), impresario Frank Tarrant is flanked by Charlie Macartney and Jack Ryder. In the Australian XI for whom he scored his hundredth first-class hundred in 1947–48 (*below*), Donald Bradman is unmistakable.

Captains Courageous: Bob Simpson (*above left*) and Bill Lawry (*above right*) formed a great Australian opening partnership and were consecutive captains against India. The Nawab of Pataudi Jnr (*below*) was their valiant and admired rival.

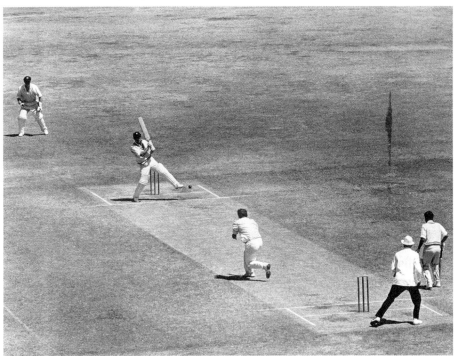

Scoreboard Pressure: the second of Bhagwat Chandrasekhar's 6/52s looks down from the scoreboard after India's triumph in 1977's Melbourne Test (*above*). 5/28 from Kapil Dev (*below left*) won a Test in Melbourne too, and 10/194 from Bishan Bedi (*below right*) almost won a Test in Perth.

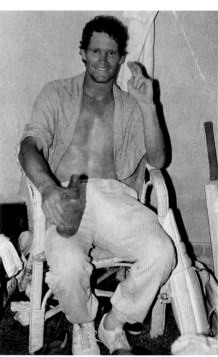

Trophy Cabinet: the feats of Allan Border (*above left*) and Sunil Gavaskar (*below*) are honoured in the trophy for which Australia and India have competed since 1996. The courage of Dean Jones (*above right*) during his death-defying 210 at Chepauk in 1986 may be the benchmark by which batting in the trophy is judged.

The Little Master: for twenty years Indians were transfixed by the batting of Sachin Tendulkar. Almost to the same degree, so were Australians.

The Wall, The Pall: Rahul Dravid (*above*) never tired of batting, exhausting bowlers with his immaculate defence. Harbhajan Singh (*below left*) and Andrew Symonds (*below right*) brought more combustible temperaments to the Border-Gavaskar Trophy in a dispute that threatened Indian–Australian relations.

One In, One Out: Virat Kohli launches his tally of Test hundreds in Adelaide in 2012 (*above*); Michael Clarke wearily grinds out his last in Adelaide in 2014 (*right*).

Congratulations All Round: the visiting Indians savour their triumph in the Brisbane Test of 2021, retaining the hard-won Border-Gavaskar Trophy (*above*); Jasprit Bumrah congratulates Travis Head on his decisive innings in Ahmedabad which secured the 2023 ODI World Cup for Australia (*below*).

Melbourne Test 2014, Day 5

DHONI DEPARTS, KOHLI ARRIVES (2014)

Mahendra Singh Dhoni has retired from Test cricket. A cynic would say it might be hard to tell the difference. That would be unfair, but he has assuredly been like the Grand Old Duke of York, marching India to the top of the hill and marching them down again. Five years ago, under Dhoni's captaincy, they became the world's number one Test team; by the end of this series, they will be seventh, ranking behind New Zealand.

Dhoni has been the only international captain to hoist all of cricket's most gilded trophies: the ICC Test Championship, the Champions Trophy, the Champions League, the Indian Premier League and, of course, the World Cup, which he'll shortly defend. But he has in that time finished second an awful lot, and an enduring image will be his sitting at a losing captain's press conference transacting in a mixture of obscure ironies and management speak. Had Dhoni been a captain at the White Star Line, he would have pronounced the *Titanic*'s maiden voyage a success in all non-iceberg processes. In his favour can be said that he retained

185

his dignity always; more sardonically, that so he should, having had so much practice.

Still, we're missing the point of Dhoni if we're to labour this. For a great many Indians, Dhoni's quitting Test matches will be no biggie. They did not follow them anyway. And Dhoni is not in any case a purely cricket story. He has not so much changed the game as incarnated a change in it.

Wisden is the first volume you would consult for the measure of most great cricketers. For an assessment of Dhoni, the first periodical to consult would be the business magazine *Forbes*: he is perhaps the game's first eminent practitioner to be known chiefly by his wealth. *Forbes*'s latest list, published in June, placed Dhoni fifth among the world's most valuable athletes, having accumulated more than $US20 million in the preceding year, ahead of the likes of Ronaldo, Messi, Rafa Nadal, Usain Bolt and Kobe Bryant. Using the bat with which he blocked out the final overs of the Melbourne Test earned him $US4 million alone.

In India, Dhoni's cricket vies for attention with his mammoth home in Ranchi and his vast collection of motor-cycles and cars. Walk a mile in Chennai, whose IPL franchise he leads, and you will encounter his face fifty times, gazing beatifically down from Pepsi signs above streetside refreshment bars, almost like a religious icon. He is a symbol not just of sport but of aspiration itself.

Indians, with their latter-day experience of global economic heft and gaudy mass media, are zealous apostles of the cult of brand value. One of the most thorough instant assessments of Dhoni's retirement was published yesterday in the *Economic Times*, a business paper, which polled pundits on the impact on 'Brand Dhoni'. You'll be pleased to know, I'm sure, that it's all going to be okay: 'Retirement not to affect popularity, Brand Mahendra Singh Dhoni is not over, say experts'. Phew.

This, mind you, arguably had it the wrong way round. Dhoni was not important because he was a Test cricketer; Test cricket remained significant by his playing it. And now he does not. With the departures of Dhoni, and Sachin Tendulkar a year ago, in fact, the Indian team has lost its last connection to the world in which international cricket was the be-all and end-all. The XI that the mercurial Virat Kohli will lead at the SCG next week has grown up since the advent of IPL and Champions League lent Indian cricket the assurance of being the centre of the financial universe. That contains some interesting implications. We may already be detecting them.

When Virat Kohli and Mitchell Johnson exchanged unpleasantries in Melbourne, the punchiest phrase was not the standard all-purpose Australianism, unfit in any case for a family newspaper: it was that migratory Americanism, 'spoiled brat'.

Australians in the past have often objected to arch competitors and provocateurs – with more than a whiff of hypocrisy, invoking 'the line' as though they own it. But with Kohli, I suspect, there's a slightly different kind of irritation, the sort engendered by a petulant son of privilege – too much money, not enough runs.

For his part, Kohli in Melbourne made extensive use of the R-word. Australia weren't showing him 'respect' so he wasn't going to 'respect' them back, not that he needed their 'respect' given their absence of 'respect'. A similar postcolonial abrasion was on show in the Jadeja–Anderson affair during the Pataudi Trophy, and you detect it more generally in modern estimations of who in world cricket owes what to whom.

For all that, there's much to welcome about Kohli's new ascendancy in Indian cricket. Dhoni's last few years as a Test cricketer were honest and dutiful but sort of solemn and world weary, like someone growingly perplexed by all the format's manifold possibilities – and the bounded realities and unambiguous tasks of one-day internationals always seemed to suit him better.

Kohli is ambitious, driven, volatile on the field yet surprisingly poised off it – he cut an impressive figure, for example, at the funeral of Phillip Hughes. His game is in tip-top shape – albeit it was in terrible shape as little as six months ago, and the inevitable checks on his batting progress will challenge him. His body will not be worn down as Dhoni's by the wear and tear of wicketkeeping. His pride will make for intriguing relations with administrators.

The Indian captain begins to divide his public the minute he steps on the field – actually he hardly even needs to do that. So let's be sympathetic and also frank: brand Kohli is a good one for Test cricket to have on its side. In all likelihood, it will be a rocky ride, at least in the foreseeable future. But retiring is not a word you will ever associate with it.

Pune Test 2017, Day 1

NO WAITING (2017)

The injunction to control the controllables in sport comes with the implication that the uncontrollables are best ignored. Sometimes they cannot be; sometimes there is no avoiding them.

For almost two hours before lunch yesterday at MCA Pune International Cricket Stadium, Matt Renshaw looked like he had digested only the most wholesome influences of his touring experiences. He had left judiciously, defended decisively, with a long forward press. He had coped coolly with Ravi Ashwin, profitably employed the lofted on-drive as his release shot against Ravi Jadeja. As lean and angular as Bill Lawry, he revealed a head prefect's boyish features when he shed his helmet.

India, however, throws up unique challenges. It is, after all, a land with more mobile phones than toilets. And when Renshaw had sudden need of the scarcer of these, he started back-pedalling faster than a conservative panjandrum from Milo Yiannopolous. This did not endear him to the bleed-green-and-gold brigade, maybe even to his captain, drawn into the tripartite negotiations with the umpires. But it was also a lesson of sorts. This is the tour of lurking, unforeseeable danger. Batsmen will look settled in, until they aren't. Four hundred will appear like a good total, until it isn't. Sessions will drift by as if in a dream, then overs unfold like gory hallucinations. That's India.

It happened that just before Renshaw's unscheduled pit stop, Australia had met with its first crash, Umesh Yadav coaxing David Warner into playing down a fifth stump line with an ambivalent bat. As Renshaw scampered up the steps, Australia abruptly had two scoreless batsmen at the crease, and for the next fifteen minutes what had been a picturesque landscape of batsmanship grew more like a washed-out still life. Steve Smith and Shaun Marsh scratched about under the attention of a newly excited crowd and a seemingly more hostile sun.

Australia had made the best of the day's first uncontrollable at least. Smith was so ecstatic on winning the toss that when asked for his 'combination' by Ravi Shastri could offer no more than, well, two fast bowlers, some batters ... errrr ... a few other guys ... eleven basically ... but, y'know, phew.

Virat Kohli appeared sanguine, as though India would be happy to take their turn at the crease in the dark and under-water. But after a wicketless ninety minutes, India's captain was assuming a stance that is his equivalent of Allan Border's old 'teapot' of annoyance; in Kohli's case, his eyes narrow, his arms fold tightly across his chest and he tilts slightly backwards at the waist. Kohli had cause to tilt tightly, for Jayant Yadav, included ahead of Bhuvneshwar Kumar here, had managed to bowl Warner round his legs with a no ball – and a Jayant one at that. The SG ball, fast shedding its lacquer, was doing little untoward, while the openers were showing an impressive pre-paredness to concede inches in order to gain feet – stretching wide of off stump with bat ahead of pad to the left-armers to stave off lbw; playing down the line of off stump to the off-spinners, countenancing defeat of the outside edge in order to protect the inside.

Of the two teams, India were at this stage arguably the less patient, expending both reviews by 12.30 p.m. With five left-handers to pick over, Ashwin and Jadeja looked determined to live up to their billing as numbers one and two on the ICC Test rankings, and to offer Pune something by which to remember its inaugural Test. Australia made them wait. In the afternoon, however, momentum took another of those Newton's cradle shifts, when Smith and Peter Handscomb went from calmly established to dejectedly dismissed within five deliveries. Smith departed with a helmet slap – cricket's equivalent of the facepalm.

Renshaw reappeared, a little wiser and perhaps a little lighter. Australian fans were experiencing sensations akin to his in the morning. The 30 runs Renshaw added were Australia's most fluent of the day. He reached the boundaries of backward square leg, mid-wicket, and mid-on with strokes of youthful conviction. He was unhurried, found gaps, worked singles, protected his off stump, but pushed no wider. He was obliged to play the Ashwin delivery that dismissed him; he can take some comfort from being worked over by a master.

Australia was blessed thereafter that Mitchell Starc had one of those days where his 360-degree batting arcs make solid connection. Under the circumstances, the temptation of the mid-wicket boundary was worth giving in to. Having scored at 2.5 an over from the first new ball, Australia took 4.5 an over from the second. The assurance with which he did rather belied Australia's dark glances at the pitch over the days preceding the Test. It is as dry as the state of Maharashtra during its recent election; succeeding days will reveal how hard it is beneath.

Having gone nineteen Tests without tasting defeat, Kohli will be confident. But there is no doubt that batting last here will be worthy of his mettle, and uncontrollables impact on even such as him.

Pune Test 2017, Day 2

EARLY WARNEING SIGNS (2017)

The night before this first Test, Shane Warne was holding
court amid an Indian audience in a Pune hotel when he
was asked about Virat Kohli. Warne smiled, made a gesture
of assent, and spoke admiringly of Kohli for a full minute:
the best in the business, the star of the show.

Mind you, Warne added, Kohli was inclined to go a bit hard
at deliveries pushed wide, wasn't he? If Warne was out there
now – and part of him has never quite left the middle – then
he would challenge Kohli on a fifth or even sixth stump line,
where India's captain was inclined to chase the ball with an
angled and open blade.

Cue 10.45 a.m. local time on the Test's second day. Kohli
descends the white-washed staircase from the home dressing
room amid universal acclaim, almost as though he is not about
to bat but to host the Oscars. Stepping onto the playing surface,
Kohli does not stride or strut. Rather does he saunter, reminiscent of RC Robertson-Glasgow's description of the English
amateur Cyril Walters approaching the crease 'like a free man,
one going out to a hard but agreeable task'.

No wonder, really. For thirty months he has been lousy with runs – he has almost had more than he has known what to do with, and could conceivably have donated a surplus to charity. More beckon. There is little ceremony or ostentation about Kohli taking guard: as usual, he can hardly wait to get started. He holds his bat from harm as the first ball from Mitchell Starc zooms along a fourth stump line.

Starc's left-armer's angle will always tend to tempt a batsman wider, but the second ball floats wider still, deviating about a foot from its basic flight path in the last half of its journey. Kohli is unconcerned by this movement, impatient to make contact, to go about his business of being best. With the benefit of a little time to acclimatise, Kohli's second ball might next have been seen bouncing back halfway from the boundary boards at deep backward point. Instead, Pete Handscomb has just time for the half-formed thought that he must hold onto this heaven-sent offering: bending his knees, he watches it all the way into his midriff, as does Kohli, eyewitness to his self-destruction.

Maharashtra Cricket Association International Cricket Stadium is a ground as atmospheric as its name, but what little Kohli's arrival has introduced now escapes until the ground feels depressurised. Except perhaps the Australian huddle, towards which Starc runs as though into the arms of a long-lost family.

Of Warne the pundit, the rest of the day is a little less flattering. Steve O'Keefe's low-slung round-arms and minimalist variations do not appeal to him; in that same hotel gathering, Warne had scattered stardust over the junior leggie Mitchell Swepson. But it is O'Keefe who, having opened the bowling with Starc, commences after lunch to widen the breach in India's batting until it gapes.

Twenty-four deliveries can go by in these parts without time seeming to pass at all. Now they encompass six wickets for O'Keefe, and the home dressing room might as well have a revolving door: India, having looked a tad impatient on the first day, are as panicky and adrift in the conditions as some touring teams have been over the years.

Smith is moving fields as if drawing on divine inspiration. Nathan Lyon is bowling his best spell in Asia since Delhi in 2013, at speeds comparable to Ravi Ashwin, at the expense of his drift but with an enhancement of his threat to the stumps. It is not a raging turner of the kind folkloric in the subcontinent. If anything it is the ball travelling straight on and tunnelling through that is causing gravest consternation. Nothing goes along the ground or menaces the clavicle. Batting should be possible, yet the batters are almost aphasic.

The gregarious O'Keefe grows ever more nonchalant about his wickets. As he has Umesh Yadav caught to secure Australia a 145-run lead, he hitches his trousers, exchanges a few high fives, and saunters off almost as casually as Kohli had arrived before lunch. In hindsight, the day can be said to have turned on that Kohli walk and that Kohli wicket. It is as if the hosts have simply never factored in the possibility of his failure, or taken at face value all the tributes they have paid themselves about home ground advantage, improved athleticism and bench strength. They are, today, all duck and no dinner.

Out the back of the media area, Warne can be seen smiling with Michael Clarke. Like their radio colleague Simon Katich, Australian coach Darren Lehmann and visiting Cricket Australia director Michael Kasprowicz, they were playing when Australia last won a Test in India twelve and a half years ago; they have been in all likelihood watching the next win, on a day to reward and defy everyone's best guesses.

Pune Test 2017, Day 3

MISSION POSSIBLE (2017)

To the third ball of the third day of this First Test, Steve Smith played forward and guided it behind point for an easy single. At first glance anyway. Before one knew it, he had turned and begun pelting back. Jayant Yadav did his best to trap and release swiftly, and a direct hit would have been opportune. But Australia's captain was quicker still, and his dive perfectly executed – so perfectly that he almost picked himself in the same motion, wearing a bit of Pune dust as do-it-yourself desert camouflage.

The clock had barely nudged 9.30 a.m., his team was comfortably positioned, and a day stretched out ahead. Yet Smith had started the allocated overs as he meant to finish them, by winning every trick, however trifling. There was no risk of Australia being the dog that caught the car and didn't know what to do with it. The quarry was to be shaken till its teeth rattled.

So it went. Less than five and a half hours later, stump in one hand, other arm round David Warner, Smith was leading his team off MCA Stadium in what used to be called Indian file, but so thoroughly have his team assimilated local conditions might almost be deemed an Australian walk.

His first break here was luck: winning the toss. All the rest have been pluck, preparation, perseverance and finely honed skill. At the tail of the line, as if to make the moment last, trailed unlikely man-of-the-match Steve O'Keefe: not young, not flash, absent discernible X-factor, finding a home away. His was not a bold charge or frontal assault; it was more like a denial-of-service attack, launched from all angles.

For those with long memories, O'Keefe's mirror six-fors paralleled Bhagwat Chandrasekhar's in Melbourne forty years ago. Australia and India have shared a rich cricket history, and O'Keefe makes a wonderfully improbable addition to its lists. '4502 days': the length of time since Australia's last Test win here tripped from Smith's tongue as he and O'Keefe took their media turns soon after. The adaptability Australia has shown here suggests that the next will not take so long.

Credit was spread throughout this Australian side, but each individual owed something to Smith, and his 109 was an expression of cumulative purpose as much as an individual feat. Third-innings hundreds can be casual canters: this was a monument of self-control. Even Smith's wriggly mannerisms, which used to make him look like someone who'd had ice dropped down the back of his shirt, now conform to a sort-of check list: helmet, gloves, pad flaps, box pat, bat tap, knee bend, bring it. When he leans on his bat, legs crossed, at the non-striker's end, he might almost be any other player.

Except that he's not. The next highest score in this match was 68, made on the first day. As he passed that minor milestone yesterday, Australia's captain came down the pitch at Jadeja and slapped a delivery nine inches outside off stump in the air between mid-on and mid-wicket. There is not even a name for this shot. It should be a Smith. He had been dismissed playing a version of this strike on the first day; once bitten, never shy.

Some have quibbled that Smith's century cannot be judged as among the best, or even his best, on the grounds that he enjoyed several lives. But a dropped catch isn't so much a flaw as an event; it mars only a surface purity rather than substance. It's arguable, too, that a few of the chances went begging because of the sheer gold-platedness of Smith's wicket. The Englishman Joe Hardstaff once said that every time he thought of Bradman his feet felt tired; mention of Smith must cause at least a little anticipatory tenderness among players in these parts too. Against this opposition, he has scored hundreds in five consecutive Tests and averages nearly 90.

At Galle and Colombo last year, having himself referred to the heinousness of the offence, Smith was twice bowled by Rangana Herath as the ball passed by his inside edge. Here, until he played across Jadeja, it was hard to recall a similar instance. And although deliveries often caressed his outside edge, if anything they deepened his defiance, and a play-and-miss is no use to a bowling side if it sows no doubt.

As for Smith, so for his team. The analysts totted up no fewer than fifty outside edges beaten during Australia's second innings. Yet one seldom felt the imminence of a wicket. Beat me all you like, each Australian seemed to say: I'm still standing.

India did not present such a united front. Before their second innings had been in progress twenty-five minutes, they had lost both openers and squandered both reviews: a BCCI campaign for the repeal of the DRS, perhaps, starts here. Smith's counterpart Virat Kohli then provided a symbol of India's veering expectations. On the first day he had waved his bat like a cutlass; now, committing too early to a leave, he kept it sheathed. As the Australians celebrated the loss of Kohli's off stump, he paused in apparent supplication. His teammates proceeded to lose seven for 30 to go with their seven for 11 the day before, and 'soft' hardly begins to describe some of the dismissals: they were soft like a Pillsbury Doughboy full of Cool Whip.

Towards the end, the Australian effort was infinitesimally marred by an overthrow. Smith looked ever so slightly peeved. He wants to win it, win it all.

Pune Test 2017
COUP D'ÉTAT (2017)

In years to come, my recollections of the Pune Test will be in terms of a toilet. Although not in a Matt Renshaw way. Bear with me on this.

In the malodorous gents on the northern side of MCA Stadium, beneath the media area, there were three cubicles. Of the last of these, the installers had made a bit of a hash, screwing the lock with its 'vacant/occupied' dial to the inside of the door with the result that the user could not close it. As is standard in these parts, a solution had been improvised: a bolt on the front of the door. This meant that it could be closed only from outside – the purpose of privacy was thereby lost. I won't elaborate on the interior of the gents more generally as you may be reading this at breakfast.

Anyway, as information steadily emerged about the eleventh hour intervention of the Board of Control for Cricket in India in the preparation of the Pune pitch, this lavatory cubicle developed an ever stronger resemblance to the home side's predicament. Aiming to shut the visitors out, they actually left the door ajar; and while the Indians were busy within, Australia swiftly locked the door behind them.

In their comments during and after the game, captain Virat Kohli, coach Anil Kumble and opener Murali Vijay conspicuously played the pitch down. 'I don't think it was any different from the turners that we played in the past,' said Kohli. 'We just didn't play good cricket.'

Superficially, this was a manful refusal to blame conditions for his team's deficiencies; at a deeper level, it smacked of deflection. Whatever the case, it has turned into an omni-shambles. Various local newspapers, notably the *Indian Express*, have blamed 'team management', abetted by BCCI officials, for the decision to shave the pitch and withhold water for the three days before the game. The International Cricket Council's match referee, Chris Broad, has subsequently graded the pitch 'poor' under a new four-point criteria penalising surfaces for 'excessive' seam movement, turn and uneven bounce.

The irony is that the popular conspiracy theory before the match was that the pitches for the series would be quicker and bouncier than usual, manifesting tensions between the new administration at the BCCI and its disinherited predecessors: Pune is the stronghold of former secretary Ajay Shirke, Ranchi the seat of former secretary Amitabh Chaudhary, Dharamsala the fiefdom of erstwhile president Anurag Thakur.

India has form in this respect. Thirteen years ago, the Nagpur Test was played on, of all things, a green seamer, chalked up to tensions between the BCCI's poohbah Jagmohan Dalmiya and restless rivals led by Sharad Pawar. Pawar's allies at the time included Nagpur's Shashank Manohar, since gone on to chair the ICC.

No wonder Shirke is now demanding the interim committee placed in charge of the BCCI by the Lodha Commission of India's Supreme Court refer the matter to the Central Bureau of Investigation: 'Since the spot-fixing [in IPL 2013] came to light, the whole board has been thrown out. Now let us see what steps the court-appointed administrators take to get to the root of pitch-fixing.' Chaudhary, meanwhile, is shortly to be heard in the Supreme Court on the plea that the interim committee is overstepping its remit of overseeing governance transition by 'passing directions which give an impression that they are to administer the BCCI'. Damned if you don't, damned if you do . . .

The team of Kohli and Kumble has done a remarkable job this summer of holding aloof from upheaval in Indian administrative circles. They may inadvertently have made themselves into an exhibit in the case against their new overseers. Certainly, the BCCI badly needs the story to go away, preferably under cover of a Kohli-led comeback by the Indians from this afternoon in Bengaluru; trouble is, under new measures agreed by the ICC chief executives' committee last month, it will, down the line, almost certainly result in an embarrassing fine, compounding the original ignominy of getting stuck in their own toilet.

Personally, I held no hardline objection to the pitch in Pune. Steve Smith made a fine hundred; nine wickets fell to pace; nobody was injured; the cricket was absorbing; the better team won. Where pitches are concerned, we can be too much like Goldilocks, anxious that everything be 'just right'.

Australians would do well not to be too pious in such matters too. It's not because Brisbane is pleasant at the time of year that Australia has traditionally commenced Test summers at the Gabba: it happens to be a stronghold at which the hosts have not lost since 1988. We have also rolled out our share of bad pitches. Comfortably the worst in Australia these past couple of years was the WACA's Nullarbor-flat surface fifteen months ago, preluding a bore draw with New Zealand. Mitchell Johnson liked it so little that he retired. The most positive aspect of the CEC's new criteria for assessing pitches is that it also penalises those that display 'little or no seam movement or turn at any stage in the match together with no significant bounce or carry, thereby depriving the bowlers of a fair contest between bat and ball'. Hopefully Australian curators take note.

What pitches friendly to bowlers reveal, meanwhile, is the flipside of modern batting: batters have hardly been more explosive, innovative, virile; with that has come a disconcerting negativity and impotence faced with even minimal deviations, and almost neurotic frailty under pressure. By *Cricinfo*'s count, there were twenty-nine batting collapses in forty-seven Tests in 2016, generally in perfectly fair conditions and under only standard pressure. Three-innings defeats were incurred by teams that had accumulated more than 400 in their first innings – a fate that had befallen only four teams in the preceding fourteen decades of Test cricket.

So while India's fate in Pune of losing 7 for 11 in the first innings and 7 for 30 in the second reads grimly, it could hardly be deemed an outlier. Administrators care little: the propensity has brought closer the four-day Test matches that many of them quietly favour. They might want to be careful what they wish for. Another feature of that toilet in Pune was noticeable: I never observed anyone trying to use it.

Bangalore Test 2017
THE GHOST IN THE MACHINE (2017)

The only way to deal with an open can of worms is, proverbially, to obtain a much larger can. Thus this week's agreement between the Board of Control for Cricket in India and Cricket Australia, after they had issued violently clashing statements in support of their captains after the Second Test at Bangalore.

There had already been a conspicuous clatter as the International Cricket Council tucked its code of conduct can opener away in the disciplinary drawer, enjoining the antagonists to 'focus their energies on the Third Test'. And people did just need to cool it, for as long as necessary for perspective to dawn.

Steve Smith was wrong; Peter Handscomb, while inexperienced and well-meaning, was wronger still. Indeed it beggars belief that modern cricketers could be so obtuse about the conduct of the game as to start studying player viewing areas for escape clauses. Under the circumstances, Kohli's suspicion was perfectly pardonable.

Yet this is also a grey area in the Playing Conditions. Consultation about a review, it is true, can only be on-field; but

Bangalore was the first occasion anyone could recall umpires needing to define that line. Some aspects of DRS protocols, moreover, remain ambiguous. In the Chappell-Hadlee Trophy thirteen months ago at Seddon Park, umpires referred a caught and bowled after a big screen replay revealed that Mitchell Marsh had hit the ball into his boot and Brendon McCullum on seeing it reiterated his appeal. Smith opted not to make an issue of this, but made a useful point: 'He was out, there was no doubt about that. But if I get hit on the pad next time and it's missing leg, do I stand there and wait until it's going to show that on the big screen?'

In a general sense, too, cricket's playing area is scarcely sealed. The modern field hosts a seemingly unregulated parade of reserves and helpmates, with drinks, gloves, tablets etc., and also, as we know, from time to time, messages. And messages can come in all forms. Cricket frowned on Hansie Cronje's earpiece; but boundaries have grown, if anything, more porous. Under the circumstances, the umpires did very well, acting promptly, decisively and firmly. Virat Kohli did not need to say anything at all, during the incident or after the match. Regrettably he could not contain himself. Private suspicion is one thing; noisy public allegation of a pattern of behaviour, on the basis of assertion rather than evidence, is a leaf from Donald Trump's playbook. To let a journalist then interpolate the word 'cheat' was then just too cute. Had Smith acquiesced in a similar description of Kohli, one suspects that this might already have been ruled off as a two-Test series.

The only subsequent informal emanation from the Indian camp was disquiet about the response on the Australian balcony to Mitchell Marsh's first innings lbw. Yet this was almost certainly related to its occurrence on the last ball of the eightieth over, shortly before the recharge of reviews. And, of course, it availed Marsh precisely nought.

Kohli is such a glorious cricketer and vivid personality that one is inclined to excuse his occasional verbal incontinence. But this was a lapse of taste and intelligence. The BCCI may have felt no choice but to back him – in the search for a minuscule patch of high moral ground after being caught in the act of cooking the Pune pitch – but succeeded in doubling down the crassness.

At the same time, there is a point or two to be made in India's favour. Such smug vindication has surrounded India's final assimilation of the DRS it has been overlooked that many of its initial criticisms were valid. When the BCCI made its objections known nine years ago, the technology was inadequate, the protocols unclear, the adoption decidedly casual. It's thanks to the need to win Indian support that we have as effective a system as we do.

There have also remained solid grounds for objection, not least the mission creep of what started as a television gimmick being allowed to mutate into cricket's ultimate appeals court, and what was originally a means of redress for 'howlers' making welcome gamblers and chancers. The technology is still inconsistently applied and subsidised by broadcasters rather than the ICC. On the field, DRS has become cricket's ghost in the machine, subtly distorting surrounding behaviour, essentially providing a legal channel for dissent, on which the game has traditionally frowned. Availability is unevenly distributed – the later you bat and bowl, the less likely reviews will be on offer. Benefit of the doubt is no longer extended to the batter – it accrues instead to the umpire.

These aren't necessarily arguments for its repeal. The best case for DRS is watching a game without it, like India's last Test defeat in Australia, when Cheteshwar Pujara was caught behind off his helmet and Ravi Ashwin off his thigh; or India's last win against England, when Joe Root was lbw despite virtually leaving a splinter in the ball. But crude as he was, Kohli showed that the DRS is a conversation cricket has rather failed to have. And if there is sufficient of an incentive, every system will interest its users in gaming it.

While denying his own team so indulged, Australian assistant coach David Saker conceded on Thursday that malpractice was perfectly conceivable: 'Because there is a lot of time, that could actually happen if you wanted to do it.' The incident at Bangalore recalled a fleeting interlude in England's first innings in 2013's Old Trafford Test, when Australia hesitated to refer an lbw appeal against Kevin Pietersen – the confidence of bowler Shane Watson was insufficient for captain Michael Clarke and vice-captain Brad Haddin to seek a review.

At the time, Darren Lehmann was enjoying somewhat of a burlesque relationship with Sky, based on his ever-present earpiece: a reaction shot of the hearty Australian coach to commentary banter and on-field events had become almost a meme. This reaction shot was different: on the player balcony, Lehmann was revealed signalling lugubriously with his right index finger. Clarke recalled the moment in his tour diary. 'It was out,' Haddin said. 'Who said that?' Clarke replied. The keeper gestured to the dressing room. Look in that direction today and you'd best have a big empty can handy . . .

Adelaide Test 2018, Day 5

INDIA OUTPACES AUSTRALIA (2018)

Under the entry 'snakes', the fabled Irish encyclopedia was said to read: 'There are no snakes in Ireland.' Time was when the encyclopedia of Indian cricket contained a similar entry for 'fast bowling'. The climate was too hot, the pitches too dry, even the national diet too deficient in protein.

That time, to be fair, was long ago – India has brought fine pace bowlers to Australia, such as Kapil Dev, Javagal Srinath and Zaheer Khan. But it has never verifiably outpaced Australia in its own conditions, until this first victory here in almost eleven years.

Ishant Sharma survives from that victory; Mohammed Shami was here four years ago; Jasprit Bumrah is new, fresh, and will take some getting used to, with his rasping pace, oblique angles and low but strong front arm, his saunter and surge style like a meandering sentence concluding in an exclamation mark.

It was not merely the wickets the trio divided here that so impressed, but their consistent hostility and hostile consistency, challenging the stumps and the Australian defensive techniques, but also clanging headgear, banging gloves, menacing splices and clavicles.

India have, moreover, something in reserve. Umesh Yadav, probably the quickest among them, and Bhuvneshwar Kumar, perhaps the swingingest, have been drinks wallahs here, but will almost certainly get their turn this summer. Virat Kohli is still feeling his way in managing such equipment, but he is learning. This was the tenth Test match out of a dozen this year in which India have taken twenty wickets. They have not won as many as they should have with such a record, but if they prolong it will finish more often first than second.

With as many as ninety-eight overs possible yesterday, the gold dollars dropped into their donation buckets in the morning like coins into a wishing well. Each run, however sketchy, drew a ripple of applause; each passed edge and half shout drew a little intake of collective breath. An enclave of flag-waving Indians swooned every time Kohli handled the ball.

When India's captain won the toss and batted on Thursday, he'd probably have envisioned a rather different-looking fifth-day pitch – darker, dustier, more deeply eroded. But the mission of pressing for victory in a fourth innings, always akin to drawing teeth from an unwilling mouth, was on this drop-in surface even harder yakka than usual, especially for a four-man attack with overs on the clock already, who eventually enjoyed but one break during the day.

Kohli clapped till his hands must have been sore; Rishabh Pant bore three helmets back and forth like an overburdened waiter; Ravi Ashwin wasted a review, as if in a hurry for a kettle to boil. It was not Ashwin who particularly harried the Australians, though he kept it tight and taut, bustling through his overs. Rather did Ishant set India on its road with a bouncer that, from round the wicket, would have done more than muss

209

Travis Head's hair had his gloves not got in the way; he later hit Mitchell Starc's helmet for good measure.

Shaun Marsh looked the part as always, in the leanness of his physique, the geometry of his stance, the daintiness of his defence. He turned the strike over effectively, middled a pull, played the shot of the day off his pads. A corollary of Marsh's being a poor starter is that he has been an effective goer on – he is some duck and some dinner. Before this game, one in six of his Test innings had ended at 0, one in ten with a hundred; between 70 and a century, he had fallen only thrice. If he could just get there . . . but at 60 he was nicked off by Bumrah, who also bounced out Tim Paine.

Shami had by then nearly had the greatest impact of all, with a seething lifter jamming Paine's finger against his bat handle – with his awful surgical misfortunes, Australia's captain must feel queasy every time he hears a door slam. In the event, blessedly, he was cleared of injury.

If Australia's pacemen were outbowled, they arguably held their own with the bat. Starc showcased his 360-degree swing; Pat Cummins displayed a scholar's diligence in defence; Josh Hazlewood applied himself bravely. Above all there was Nathan Lyon, who met some scepticism on Sunday night when he stated that 'the wicket's good enough for us to really knuckle down tomorrow and have the belief we can score these runs' but looked intent on doing the job himself. He had a superb match.

For all their pluck, however, Australia have lost five of their last six Tests, and will not change that trend if they can scratch together only two half-centuries and a best partnership of 50 across two innings. Man of the match Cheteshwar Pujara provided an object lesson in batting discipline, so abstemious against Starc, Hazlewood and Cummins, so nimble against Lyon, so trusting in his defence that he could afford to hasten slowly.

Individuals have problems to solve, but there is a confidence lacking that can only be stimulated by achievement and example. Aaron Finch's permeable defence is one thing; his strange reticence about reviewing his second innings decision offers a suitable case for treatment. Had Australia gone into tea on Sunday without losing a wicket, there's no telling how yesterday's chase would have turned out. An imaginary encyclopedia of Australia would confirm that there are still batsmen. But they need to believe it themselves.

Perth Test 2018, Day 2
GOOD TO BE KING (2018)

Yesterday a newspaper pronounced Virat Kohli 'super duper' and an 'uber-success story', and a commentator praised the positivity of his body language as he walked to the crease. For India's captain, it was all in a day's hyperbole. What a challenge – unique in world cricket. He must be Virat Kohli without succumbing to the unavoidable distractions of being *Virat Kohli*.

With India 2/8, Kohli perhaps felt the tug each way. It was a situation in need of his powers and his presence. The flag-waving Indian claque welcomed him with lusty salaams, the Australian pace attack with probing lengths. Kohli had gone eight innings without a half-century in the Border–Gavaskar Trophy, but soon made this seem less like a matter of form than a piece of trivia: 109 deliveries set it to rights. It was a holding operation – India still trail, on the scoreboard and in the match scenario. But while Kohli batted the match imperceptibly stabilised. It was not quite 'Kohli v Australia', but you'd have been forgiven for thinking it so; on 'Kohli v the second new ball' this morning could this match hinge.

Milder temperatures than the first day eased the bowlers' burden yesterday, while perhaps also slowing the pitch's deterioration, with help from a morning's rolling. For the first hour, in fact, India's bowlers appeared grooved at a classic 'pretty length', grunting as bouncers flew, sighing as edges were beaten, overlooking the accruing runs, which swelled Australia's first innings past 300 for the first time in seven Test matches – for the first time since Australia last won a Test, in Durban in March. Only a handful of deliveries would have hit the stumps; finally a couple did.

The Australian bowlers had batted attentively. As pundits searched for positive readings on their body-language-o-meters, Starc insinuated an inswinger between Murali Vijay's bat and pad, and Hazlewood torpedoed KL Rahul with the batsman shaping towards mid-on – sharp bowling, muddled batting, and astute analysis.

Kohli got going with a crisp drive down the ground, repeated in Hazlewood's next over, bracketed by boundaries through mid-wicket: positive batting, nine inches out of his ground, meeting ambitious bowling, probing away at the stumps, molesting the pads.

With India 2/38 from ten overs, Australia's bowlers imposed an austerity policy. Between 1.35 p.m. and 2.20 p.m., Cummins and Lyon yielded only 12 runs in twelve overs. The batsmen did not so much grow passive as assume a posture of armed neutrality. To adapt the vernacular, Pujara padded away with intent while Kohli left in good areas, if one delivery from Nathan Lyon, turning back sharply, sniffed around off bail.

At one point the off-spinner's figures were a pristine 7-3-5-0 – more like the combination on a briefcase than a bowling analysis. At length, Kohli broke the spell with a cover-drive so scintillating that it almost threw off sparkles.

For a figure who personifies action and vitality, Kohli also has a gift for non-motion, so still as the bowler approaches that a butterfly could alight on the peak of his helmet, so sculpted in defence that he inclines to holding the pose half a beat for personal appraisal. He has a purist's preferences, taking as much pleasure in a decisive leave as a virile stroke.

This was Test match special Kohli, humble in the face of the bowling's demands and the match's stage, sometimes becalmed although seldom long. The only delivery that caused him regular trouble was on a fifth stump line, his hands sometimes stretching outside his eyeline as his bat searched busily for contact. Beaten, he would give a wry smile, adjust the wristbands on his gloves, and penitently re-mark his guard. Passed by Cummins, he gave an appreciative nod. Recuperating from a painful blow on his bottom hand by Hazlewood, he check drove immaculately to the long-on boundary.

The impasse ended when Pujara feathered Starc down the leg side, although that brought Ajinkya Rahane, whose back foot power suited the pitch's bounce, and contributed nearly two-thirds of their unbroken 91-run partnership. Kohli passed 50 by carving Cummins over slip, then eked out only singles for the next half hour. A few overs from stumps, he drilled to mid-on, gestured in the fielder's direction, then rehearsed a kind of T20 onside flick over the top, which would have brought the house down at Chinnaswamy Stadium on a hot night in the Indian Premier League. It was the nearest he came to indulging himself all day, enhancing his legend all the same. As he walked off unbeaten, his being Virat Kohli had contributed just a little more to his being *Virat Kohli*.

Perth Test 2018, Day 4

FACE OFF (2018)

Perth Stadium boasts a playing surface area of more than 21,000 square metres, yet before lunch yesterday Virat Kohli and Tim Paine found themselves competing for more or less the same spot.

The former was approaching the stumps as the latter completed a run. Belly-to-belly while studiously looking different ways, the captains resembled two people trying to squeeze past one another in a narrow hallway.

No sandpaper was seen. No soft signal needed to be given. The snickometer was not used to determine whether actual friction occurred. But it was one of those moments on which the camera cannot but dwell: cricket, of course, has been a contact sport in Perth before. The stump microphones, which this week have been the hardest working listening devices in sport, overheard umpire Chris Gaffaney calling the captains into line.

The Australians have had an abundance of advice about how to handle the volatile Kohli this summer. 'A few words' and 'hostile body language', Ricky Ponting urged.

'Make him your best mate,' Dean Jones advised. Looks like Ponting's counsel is carrying the day; it may not be his only weakness.

Kohli has annoyed the Australians in Perth, and not merely by his masterful hundred. His celebrations, his gesticulations, his standing his ground when caught, his enjoining Indian fans to make themselves heard: he has carried the reddest rag since Steve Waugh's. The Australians should now have the last laugh on the scoreboard in this match. They kept their cool yesterday. They understood their limits. But Kohli is also in their heads as few visiting captains have been.

There is an undertone to Australian complaints about Kohli: that he is a provocateur; that he 'gets away' with stuff that they do not; that he is the beneficiary of 'double standards'. And sure, there is a hint of hypocrisy about a cricketer who affects to let his bat do the talking, then in the next breath has his talk do the baiting. But the cry of 'double standards' is a feeble one. The world contains multiple different standards, not only because people and cultures and heritages differ, but also because minds and attitudes change.

The Australians have, of course, lately been recalibrating their standards, dogged by the reputation for abrasiveness they used to relish – indeed, it is precisely this on which India's skipper has been playing, working away in their corridor of behavioural uncertainty. By grumbling about Kohli, the Australians are in danger of reintroducing the jaded concept of 'the line' in another guise, and essentially insisting on their right to draw it. The public, rightly, sickened of that. Paine's men looked better off yesterday enjoying what Kohli brings to the contest: not just a standard of excellence, against which it is exciting to be measured, but also a kind of unifying enemy, of whom it is exhilarating to get the better, as when Nathan Lyon found his outside edge after tea.

In Kohli's approach there also lies risk to himself and others. His tour is becoming like that fabulous French documentary a decade or so ago about Zinedine Zidane, where the camera followed the great footballer for a whole game, capturing the stages he was off the ball as well as on – the exhortations, the feints, the lunges of anticipation, the periods of repose.

An equivalent movie of Kohli would reveal precious few of the last. He is more often still at the crease than he is in the field, prowling mid-off, pervading second slip. He beckons and despatches, claps and chivvies, even polishes the ball with a manic energy. As the field changed over at one stage yesterday, he leaned forward and caught a ball behind his back. He looks, in short, like a man in his element, of contagious mood. He lights his team up; he could also, potentially, cast it in shadow.

In India last year, the Australians lost the series but had the better of Kohli. He appeared in a state of constant distraction. The extremes of his moods were summed up by his batting at Pune, where he threw his hands at a wide delivery in the first innings, let a ball hit his off stump in the second. His relationship with his coach Anil Kumble deteriorated so markedly that it was over within months.

Who now could tell Kohli that he had gone too far? Who are his confidants? Who moderates and balances him? He personifies an extraordinary world. After play concludes at Perth Stadium today, world cricket's attention will turn to an annual rite: the auction, now in Jaipur, of 350 of the world's best cricketers, for tens of millions of dollars, to the corporate owners of Indian Premier League franchises. In such a system coils enormous potential chaos. Kohli's personality is what binds it; it could just as easily split it. Going toe-to-toe with Kohli is one way of challenging him. But the space Kohli has to himself is, for India, just as much of an issue.

Melbourne Test 2018, Day 3
HAZARD LIGHTS (2018)

It's proverbially a recession when your neighbour loses their job, a depression when you lose yours. The Boxing Day Test may have marked a similar transition in Australian batsmanship.

It is eighty days since an Australian Test batsman passed 72; yesterday, nobody passed 22. There was no blaming the pitch, the overhead conditions, the DRS, the stump mics, the Illuminati, or any other miscellaneous uncontrollables. This was routine, humdrum, common or garden mediocrity.

It's arguable that the presence of two outstanding batsmen, Steve Smith and David Warner, has for some time masked the depths of batting recession in this country; without them, at any rate, depression seems to have well and truly set in.

The Test year began in Sydney with the Marsh brothers seeming to come of age with fraternal hundreds; yesterday, with no Smith and Warner to beat the path for them, Shaun and Mitchell eked out 28 between them in nearly a hundred balls. They toiled willingly at least. But work is not the issue, any more than the batsmen's 2 kilometre time trials and skin folds.

It is a lacklustre system that underlies batting so confused and directionless.

Nobody but nobody seemed capable of coming to terms with the pursuit of more than 400. There was a guileless virility about the clutching at aggressive options, using horizontal bats, playing against the spin, taking on fielders – Aaron Finch, Marcus Harris and Travis Head were dismissed playing Russian roulette with intent.

And while in Adelaide and Perth the batting was shored up by captain Tim Paine and the tail, here the second half of the innings fell open like a trap door. When last an Australian batting unit failed so abjectly, in the corresponding Test here eight years ago, the line-up still contained Ponting, Hussey, Clarke; Justin Langer has no such resources to draw on.

There was, to be fair, some fine Indian bowling into the bargain. Ishant Sharma and Mohammed Shami were an established, effective formula coming into this series. Jasprit Bumrah has brought the combination to a kind of critical mass.

Bumrah clops in like a man riding a pretend horse. It is mainly cosmetic; his action is all in its final surge. He would be very nearly as fast and as awkward from a step or two, thanks to his powerful shoulders and the oblique angle of his arm, veering his stock delivery in, with a natural bias that straightens the ball as it ages.

The Indians apparently call him 'Crofty', for Colin Croft, who bowled malevolent sidewinders from the edge of the crease for the West Indies in the 1980s. His inclination of attack bears a likeness to that of Ben Stokes too. But Bumrah will probably prove better than either. Unlike most fast bowlers, he threatens the inside rather than the outside edge, seeks the stumps rather than the slips – a method as challenging to prepare for as to play, which also leaves him less dependent on India's fallible catching cordon.

His variations, meanwhile, are subtle, adept and abrupt. His slower ball to Shaun Marsh yesterday on the stroke of lunch, following on five deliveries of uniform speed, was the cricket equivalent of Donald Trump's stealth fighter – to Marsh at least, literally invisible.

There is no need to describe Ravi Jadeja's run-up as it does not exist. He is either bowling or walking back to bowl, as looped as a duck in a shooting gallery. His Rajasthan Royals captain Shane Warne dubbed him 'Rockstar' for his confident airs, although his minimalism is more of the twelve-bar-blues variety.

Here he was vital. His dismissal of Usman Khawaja removed Australia's best player; his accuracy enabled Virat Kohli to keep his precious pace bowlers fresh; his rapidity was a boon for India's over rate, which threatened to coagulate in Perth, but here circulated healthily.

As ever, Australia's bowlers were left to make good the failings of their batting colleagues. And just when it appeared nothing awaited the home team but further downtrend, there was an uptick – maybe a technical correction, but one cannot afford to be fussy. Pat Cummins has bowled with pace, patience and a poor ration of luck in his last five innings. An over in which Pujara and Kohli fended identically to leg gully amounted to karmic payback. Rahane's leg-side strangulation was on the batsman's part almost a random act of kindness.

In truth, India's batsmen were as neglectful as Australia's had been, if from nonchalance rather than naivety – with a lead swollen to more than 300, you can get a bit casual. It completed a turnabout in the skill ascendancies: from 7/451 on days one and two to 15/197 on day three. But who will provide Australia with the stimulus it needs to alleviate this depression?

Sydney Test 2019, Day 1

CHE-MANIA (2019)

There were traces of Sachin Tendulkar at the Sydney Cricket Ground yesterday in the armbands worn by the Indians in memory of Ramakant Achrekar, the Shivaji Park coach who had the Little Master as a littler pupil. And there was Cheteshwar Pujara.

India is a cricket nation with an almost religious devotion to huge scores. Fifteen years ago here, with a Border–Gavaskar Trophy on the line, Tendulkar made a legendary double-century by completely abjuring the cover-drive, an epic of passive resistance. The following year, as if to present his own credentials, Pujara made a double hundred on his under-19 Test debut.

He has been a stalwart servant: more than 5000 Test runs at an average, as of yesterday, better than 50. But this summer has been his career's meridian. While King Kohli has been cynosure of all eyes, his sole century came in a losing cause in Perth. It is plebeian Pujara who presaged victory at Adelaide and Melbourne with his long methodical entrenchments, and might have threepeated the effort here.

Yesterday Pujara took his batting in the series into its twenty-ninth hour, during which the Indians have added 1059 runs. He has faced more than 1138 deliveries, before each of which he has readied with a preparatory glance at his splice, like an act of communion with his bat. In doing so, Pujara has become a kind of Medium Height Master, similar to Tendulkar in his dedication and piety.

What Achrekar was to Tendulkar, Pujara's father Arvind has been to him. A Ranji Trophy player for Saurashtra, Arvind began coaching his son in Rajkot aged three, every day, before and after school, and every weekend and festival, eventually persuading the railways for whom he worked to lay a cement pitch for his 'academy'. To this day, father and son train together, their tie so tight that when Arvind talks of his son's batting he uses the word 'we'.

Pujara builds an innings with an according orderliness, approaching it like a capable camper approaches erecting a tent – patiently, systematically, in a sequence tidily logical. He clears the area; he lays the ground sheet; he knows the ropes – also the pegs, the nets, the flaps.

In a decade of Test cricket, it's hard to remember Pujara ever, as they say, 'getting away to a flier' – opening his innings with a cluster of early boundaries. You imagine he might not like it, think it a little frantic, ostentatious. For while some batsmen pursue big scores with avidity, a Narevian greed, Pujara's innings are an endless process of settling in, in full cognisance of the bowling, the conditions, the scenario. The runs accumulate as though via sedimentation. Left too long he almost merges into the pitch. Which is why yesterday when Pujara was 12, Paine sent a rejected caught behind appeal from the bowling of Cummins for DRS analysis.

It was a speculation. The bowler had stifled his appeal; umpire Richard Kettleborough does not get much wrong; but if Pujara was to be had, it must be soon. So Australia forfeited a review – an advantage for India that eludes calculation, but that was wrung for them by their number three's reputation.

There were no further alarms, not a chance, no memorable miscues, not the merest concession. Even when clocked in the back of his helmet by Hazlewood just before lunch, Pujara submitted to only a routine panel beating from the physiotherapist.

There were a few extremes in Pujara's batting last year. He took fifty-three balls to get off the mark in a Test at Wanderers, ran himself out hopelessly at Lord's, top-edged a hook to fine leg on the stroke of lunch at Trent Bridge. At one stage he even lost his place. But from the instant he came to the wicket in the second over of this series, he has given Australia no help, in addition to looking more versatile than the batsman of four years ago. After eking a single out of twenty-three balls yesterday afternoon, for example, he poached 21 from twelve in the last three overs before tea. Marnus Labuschagne will bowl poorer overs, but not many to a better batsman.

As Lyon wearied after tea, Pujara twice came down the wicket and worked him past short leg and between a straight mid-wicket and a wide mid-on – a stroke every bit as much his signature as Tendulkar's cover-drive. When Starc returned for a final listless spell, he cut incisively and flicked commandingly twice, the last boundary raising his eighteenth Test century. Pujara marked this with a fist pump – restrained and decorous, but unmistakably a fist pump. Here, perhaps, the comparison with Tendulkar broke down. Indeed, it was rather like watching Jascha Heifetz indulge in a spot of air guitar.

But as the Australian bowlers felt the efforts of their Melbourne exertions and the pitch mellowed in the last hour, Pujara resumed his natural manner, towards a glimmering objective of something even Tendulkar never accomplished: a decisive role in victory in a series in Australia.

Sydney Test 2019, Day 2
SMITHEREENS (2019)

Cricket grounds have a shape-shifting character. At times when you're batting, they can seem as claustrophobic as a cupboard; at times when you're bowling, they can feel vast, open, undefendable, your nine fielders like a Boy Scout troop trying to hold Thermopylae.

A fielding captain in the situation of Tim Paine after tea at the SCG yesterday feels his powerlessness acutely. On the first morning here, his pace bowlers were ferocious, intimidating, and might have had India four down at lunch had they not defaulted to lengths too short.

A day and a bit on and they were paying the price, assigned a third new ball against a runaway partnership with a lickety-split outfield – not an attack, not even a defence, but a full-blown retreat. You understood the appeal to House Republicans of a wall. Paine could not afford his either. Even patrolled by as many as five fielders, the SCG's circumference has seldom looked so vulnerable.

Rishabh Pant and Ravi Jadeja put on 204 in 224 deliveries, a seventh-wicket record for India against Australia, although 'put on' hardly does it justice. They looted it, ran their fingers through it with maniacal laughter, then carried it away in a swag, playing shots with a Sehwagian insouciance. Marnus Labuschagne bowled, Travis Head, even Usman Khawaja – at a pace so slow that he could have run after the ball and caught it up had he felt so moved.

In contrast to Cheteshwar Pujara, the earnest Test specialist who dominated the first day, Pant and Jadeja are cricketers carried forward on India's T20 wave, chased at auction, exalted to stardom. They are young, bold, cheeky, have two and a half million Twitter followers; Pant, of course, has 'gone viral' in the last week, while Jadeja has the tribute of a parody account.

Yet their career foundations are strikingly solid. Twenty-one-year-old Pant averages 50 in first-class cricket, has made six hundreds including a triple-century. And while pitches might be flat in India they are still 22 yards in length, and the air through which Pant likes hitting provides similar wind resistance.

So far in his brief international career, Pant has been in search of a comfortable tempo. His first Test scoring shot was a six at Trent Bridge; he pottered forty-seven balls over a duck at Southampton; he made a run-a-ball hundred at The Oval. He scored 92 in consecutive home Tests against the West Indies, in an allegro eighty-four balls and an andantino 134. In Australia, Pant has been compromised by the weakness of the Indian tail. At Perth in particular, where he was essentially left to corral four number elevens, he seemed unsure whether to stick or twist.

Jadeja's busy acquisitiveness and lickety-split running was here an ideal complement. Pant went to his century with his forty-eighth single, unflustered by conservative fields and defensive lines, with only a few flecks of flamboyance like a peachy reverse sweep from Lyon.

After tea, all came alike. In consecutive overs from Labuschagne and Lyon, Pant nailed conventional sweeps just as hard, as if to demonstrate there was no safe place to bowl to him. A pull shot from Hazlewood brought cheers for his 150; a switch hit from Head was as celebratory as New Year's fireworks.

Jadeja, as trivia buffs know, has the bizarre distinction of three first-class triple-centuries; also, recently, a Test hundred. He must have glimpsed another as he put even Pat Cummins to the sword, clearing his front leg to launch into the Bradman Stand, drawing back to scythe over point. The four boundaries Jadeja poached when Cummins took the third new ball with four men on the perimeter somehow summed up Australia's helplessness. Deep square leg and fine leg were close enough to be communicating with two soup cans connected by a piece of string, but neither moved as hook shots bisected them twice. When Cummins pitched in the batsman's half, he was wellied down the ground to the unprotected straight boundary. When Cummins dropped wearily short again, he was pulled contemptuously in front of square.

Australia's only solace is that the pitch is without blemish even for two days' play, and that a leg-weary Pant shelled Khawaja in the third over of their brief reply – a reminder that but for Wriddhiman Saha's stubborn shoulder injury, his stump mic repartee would not have obtained him such a cult following this summer. Australia must hope he has a lot more talking to do.

Earlier, Pujara had prolonged his batting time in the series to nigh on thirty-three hours, a full day and a night of concentration and stamina, leaving a midden of discarded gloves at the boundary's edge, and a trail of civilly detained bowlers in his wake. Again, he batted as if in his own Test match, aslant to cricket generally, a cricketer rather than an athlete, with his round shoulders and broad haunches – run-bearing hips, you might call them.

Pujara is cricket's 'Desiderata'. You could watch him all day as a form of therapy, like listening to whale sounds or wind chimes. He threw his head back when he fell seven runs short of a double-century, trying to make a little too much of a straight ball from Lyon: he will be nearly thirty-five by the time India tours again, and may not make it back. The Australians breathed a collective sigh of relief, unaware that the field was about to change shape around them.

Virat Kohli

HISTORY MAKER (2019)

On the afternoon of 4 December 2018, the day before India began its defence of the Border–Gavaskar Trophy, Virat Kohli went to the nets behind the Western Stand at Adelaide Oval for a final workout. He held his bat side-on to check leg stump, marked his guard with four brisk scratches, and batted twenty minutes against first his pace bowlers then his spinners. Behind him crouched a cameraman from the website of Cricket Australia, lens tilted slightly up so that 175-centimetre Kohli filled the frame, catching every detail for a minute-long edited package that went live a few hours later, and proceeded to take on a life of its own. In the next twenty-four, it was watched more than three million times.

Of the thirty-one strokes, twenty-eight are aggressive. Kohli pirouettes into pull shots, launches into long drives, runs to third man with an urgent reflex call: 'Yes one!' At a solitary miscue, the microphone also picks up a self-admonition: 'Ah no.' Otherwise the soundtrack is a succession of improbably deep detonations from Kohli's bat, echoing off the stand's bricks like a skeet-shooting rifle. Twitter echoed the echo.

228

'Wow!!!!' exclaimed an awestruck Adam Gilchrist. 'Don't think it used to sound like that off my bat …' murmured a droll Paul Collingwood. Hashtags were hung: #intensity, #freak, #Supercharged and the inevitable #KingKohli. In a column for *The Times*, Mike Atherton called the footage 'a paean to modern batsmanship', deciding finally: 'I'm not sure I've ever seen a better batsman'.

There has assuredly never been a batsman watched more closely and more widely. Last year in Adelaide was hardly the first time he has been studied in the nets – YouTube offers a thriving sub-genre of Kohli in training, with scores of videos bearing titles such as 'Virat Kohli Smashing Bowlers in Nets' and 'Virat Kohli Batting with Pure Technique!!' The day may come time when these interludes are policed, when the sound of Kohli's bat is monetised as part of his intellectual property like the Harley-Davidson growl. But not, thankfully, yet: it remains a public event every time Kohli picks up a bat, because it is an event when he does most anything.

In the last two decades, India has grown into substantially the world's largest cricket country, culture and market. Its captain is both cause and effect. 'Kohli embodies a new and self-confident nationalism in India,' says James Crabtree, author of the new study of Indian wealth, *The Billionaire's Raj*. 'One which is somehow entitled, which grew up thinking India was rightly top dog.' At thirty, Kohli is the outstanding batsman of his generation in all three formats, and leads the world's best team in Test and one-day cricket; but the world bows down as much before his concentrated star power, his estimated $US60 million net worth, $US180 million brand value, and thirty million-plus Twitter and Instagram followers.

Kohli did not invent the business of sport, marketing and media in the subcontinent. Its heritage is long: when Denis

Compton was taming his locks with Brylcreem in England, Vinoo Mankad was doing the same in India; when Fred Trueman and Trevor Bailey were synonymous with 'BBC Test Match Special', 'Cricket with Vijay Merchant' had a far vaster audience on All-India Radio. In India, cricket has also had the glamorous shadow partner of movies, first aligned fifty years ago when the Nawab of Pataudi Jnr married the Bollywood beauty Sharmila Tagore. You can distinguish members of the lineage of great pan-Indian batsmen by reference to their screen lives. Sunil Gavaskar appeared as himself, somewhat awkwardly, in 1980s movies like *The Kabhi Ajnabi* and *Maalamaal*; Sachin Tendulkar inspired a deferential and earnest documentary, *Sachin: A Billion Dreams* (2017); MS Dhoni was the subject of a florid three-hour biopic, *Dhoni: The Untold Story* (2016). Kohli? Last September, Kohli starred in a knowing one-minute superhero spoof, *Trailer: The Movie*, rolling it out in a droll Tweet: 'Check it out while I prepare my Oscar acceptance speech.' It is no less funny for being an undisguised brand-building exercise for the apparel range, Wrogn, that Kohli owns with Anjana Reddy's Universal Sportsbiz. 'Watch while one man rises above the rest,' says a stentorian voice-over as Kohli dodges about between aliens, zombies and dinosaurs, 'by standing . . . on a really . . . tall . . . building'. So far, for Kohli, fame has been only a one-edged sword, something with which to shave his perfectly kempt facial hair.

This shrewd containment of his own image makes him, in a way, unknowable. Kohli is seldom interviewed. It is hardly worth his trouble. In May 2016, he agreed to sit down with *India Today*'s Boria Majumdar where he was staying, in Kolkata's ITC Hotel. When Majumdar advised him where the cameras were located, Kohli replied: 'I will be there by 6 p.m. as discussed. I just need to arrange for security to get to the part of the hotel where you have set up.' Tendulkar famously found it almost impossible to move around in public; Kohli cannot even cross a hotel lobby. When he married his own Bollywood belle nine months later, the ceremony had for convenience's sake to be held in Tuscany and the honeymooners to adjourn to Finland. Still, rather than seek total seclusion, Kohli and his bride Anushka Sharma shared scenes on social media, embracing their lives' inhibitions and artificialities and making them part of the fun.

Those seeking an essence of Kohli often do so ethnically and geographically, that he is a Punjabi from Delhi. 'The saying about people from Delhi is that if they can be heard in a whisper they still want to shout,' says the cricket veteran columnist Ajaz Memon. 'There's something of that in Virat.' Cricketers from Delhi are defined by their dash and volatility: Lala Amarnath, said a teammate, was 'quick to fight and quick to love'; Bishan Bedi, said his biographer, 'refused to come down from the heights of attacking'; Raman Lamba was so mettlesome he got himself chased by a bowler wielding a stump in a Duleep Trophy final. Kohli, what's more, hales from the 1980s apartment blocks of the city's west: Virender Sehwag, Ishant Sharma, Shikhar Dhawan and Ashish Nehra are other products of their noisy, crammed and competitive confines.

Kohli's family were perhaps slightly better off. Father Prem was a lawyer; Virat and brother Vikas were polished by a convent school. But by his own admission, Virat was a 'cricket brat' from the age of nine when Prem enrolled him in the West Delhi Cricket Academy in Paschim Vihar – one of a host of such sporting colleges, always thronged with hopefuls. Coach Rajkumar Sharma, who had played a handful of games for Delhi as an off-spinner, charged the princely monthly tuition fee of 200 rupees.

Rajkumar intuited the boy's talent at once. Kohli threw and hit with precocious power. He was noisy, energetic, hated only not being involved, would sit brooding in his pads after a dismissal, fret if there were too few runs to chase and there was a chance he might not bat. He was undaunted by competing against older boys, undismayed when local selectors looked the other way. Delhi cricket is ill-famed for its nepotism – the Delhi and District Cricket Association is colloquially known as the 'Delhi Daddies Cricket Academy' – and Kohli notoriously found his path temporarily blocked at under-14 level. His determination doubled.

Still, nothing was foreordained when he reached senior level. Test opener Aakash Chopra was impressed when the teenage Kohli joined Delhi's Ranji Trophy squad but unconvinced. 'He came across as a very confident lad, but not so out of the ordinary,' Chopra recalls. 'Yes talented, yes passionate, yes aggressive. But you also know that when you play in Delhi you see a lot of kids like that, and he had some technical difficulties.'

The most famous incident of Kohli's cricket youth is his fourth game for Delhi, where he went into the second evening against Karnataka on 40 not out, then learned overnight that his father Prem had suffered a mortal stroke. After consulting Rajkumar, he elected to continue his innings, falling just before lunch for a five-hour 90. When Rajkumar checked back, his prodigy was annoyed: 'Sir, I was given out wrongly when I was just ten short of a century . . .'

It is a great story. It evokes doggedness, destiny, filial piety, preternatural focus. But there were no headlines at the time. India has more than thirty first-class teams, numberless unacknowledged daily tales of misfortune defied. Kohli's advance owed more to changes underway in Indian cricket, which was finally achieving a wealth to match its abiding scale and ardour. However hard the scrabble of his boyhood, Kohli's youth was fortunate. In the twenty-first century, Indian cricket has not just been finding talent but looking. India's win in the 2000 under-19 World Cup, with its starring roles for Yuvraj Singh and Mohammad Kaif, pointed the way. When Kohli led India to repeating that success in Malaysia in February 2008, he was guaranteed even swifter recognition, thanks to the looming Indian Premier League – cricket amplified, accelerated and monetised as T20.

Scooped up for a nominal fee by the Royal Challengers Bangalore, Kohli played in the IPL's inaugural game. He made 1. He averaged 15 in thirteen matches, of which RCB won only four. But this was a new cricket economy, more forgiving than of yore. Opportunities were more numerous; fruit hung lower. Kohli obtained a bat contract with BDM, was gifted a job as 'manager' by Oil & Gas Corporation, was included in elite youth teams. And during the second IPL, held in South Africa, Kohli was wooed by an aspiring sports agent, thirty-year-old Bunty Sajdeh.

It was not Kohli's run-making that appealed to Sajdeh so much as his relatable qualities: youth, vitality, the flair of his designer wardrobe, the flash of his eye-catching ink, the face of a mischievous cherub. Under Dhoni, India was remaking its fifty-over team after the disaster of the 2007 World Cup, building towards hosting the next. Yet this was also the phase of Tendulkar's long fade, when his every innings was a game within the game, when results appeared at times secondary to the laborious pursuit of his hundredth international hundred. A country three-quarters of whose population is younger than thirty-five, Sajdeh reasoned, would soon be searching for younger heroes.

Sajdeh's may be one of the savviest management calls of all time. Capped for India in one-day international cricket after just eleven Ranji Trophy matches with a single hundred, Kohli found it a snug fit. In his first forty ODIs, he averaged nearly 50; he achieved a similarly healthy strike rate for endorsements, mainly of youth-accented fashion accessories. When the 2011 World Cup came round, Kohli opened the tournament with an unbeaten hundred against Bangladesh, concluding it with a composed 35 in the final; he was also one of a handful of younger co-stars in Dhoni's campaign for Pepsi. As Dhoni accepted the Cup, Kohli loyally helped chair Tendulkar from the field, and led a dressing room chorus of a song from the movie *Rab Ne Bana Di Jodi*: 'What to do, my friend, in you we see God himself!' The movie, a 2008 romantic comedy, starred Kohli's future wife.

India's Test team proved harder for Kohli to infiltrate: he did not find a regular slot until its experienced batting unit began to fray and fissure in Australia in 2011–12. But smart money was on him. Chopra remembers a conversation with Rahul Dravid around this time, in which India's venerable number three compared Mumbai's Rohit Sharma with Kohli as next generation players. Rohit, Dravid felt, was the more naturally gifted. But Kohli had a rarer aptitude, for improvement. He had already set to remedying an early fault against the short ball, showcasing a powerful pull shot in his maiden Test hundred at Adelaide Oval. He looked the kind of batsman who would be better a year hence, then again a year after that. The prophecy was as far-sighted as Sajdeh's.

Kohli's relationship with Anushka has now drawn him to a luxury apartment in Mumbai's plush Worli, and it is a Mumbai expression that best summarises his cricket. *Khadoos* is a traditional exhortation to the batsmen that have made the city famous – Gavaskar, Tendulkar, Vengsarkar, Merchant, Manjrekar. Its nearest translation is something like 'relentless' or 'inflexible'. Remember, *khadoos*! Kohli's era might be more lucrative, more comfortable; somehow he has risen above all the potentially negative entailments of such a world. With each passing year, he seems harder, leaner and keener, if not meaner. Like every great batsman, Kohli has his signature faculties – a conquering stride, a supersonic bat speed, gimballing wrists that access the leg side to a degree's precision, a strong bottom hand that imparts top spin to his cover-drive, a purist's regard for hitting the ball along the ground unless absolutely necessary. But what chiefly marks Kohli out is his untiring pursuit of broad-based excellence – from the battening of his defence against the moving ball to the expansion of his T20 attacking options. He is batting's supreme evolutionary specimen. Gavaskar was the great master of Test cricket; Tendulkar excelled in Tests and ODIs; only AB de Villiers rivals Kohli in his mastery of cricket in all durations, and the South African lost the taste for the five-day format that in the Indian remains as sharp as ever. De Villiers' recent autobiography ends with a piquant story of the pair, teammates at RCB, having breakfast one morning.

> 'So I was wondering,' I said, out of the blue, 'how long do you think you're going to keep playing cricket?'
> Virat's face broke into a beaming smile, his eyes alight.
> 'I'm going to play forever,' he replied.
> 'If only that were possible,' I smiled, 'if only that were possible.'

The reality of cricket immortality not being possible does not prevent Kohli approaching cricket as though it is. It took television host Rajdeep Sardesai six months to organise an interview with Kohli in June 2016, but it was worth it. Rajdeep is the son of another great Mumbai batsman, Dilip; by Kohli, who emerged from his private gym, replenished himself with a protein shake, and expounded on cricket and life from three hours, he was enthralled. 'He was brilliant,' says Sardesai. 'I was impressed by his knowledge and passion. He is completely in love with the sport. He has an intense understanding of his own game and of contemporary cricket, and a very sharp grasp of what it will take for him to continue this level of sporting excellence, form, fitness, diet.'

Kohli's *khadoos* is perhaps most pronounced in his athleticism. Since shedding a youthful chubbiness, Kohli has made a cult of his lean muscle mass that is almost Djokovician, but which clearly has tripartite cricket ends in mind – endurance for Test cricket, explosive energy for one-day cricket, explosive power for T20. India has had fit cricketers before: Dhoni is built like the mountains he hails from. But fitness for Dhoni was personal; for Kohli it is philosophical. He has likened himself to 'a monk in civil society'. His left arm bears tattoos symbolising contemplation and asceticism – Lord Shiva meditating on Mount Kailash, alongside a monastery. And in a country where adequate *quantity* of food has more often been the issue, Kohli's obsession with the *quality* of his wheat-free, gluten-free diet, the quotient of protein and the choice of vitamins, is revelatory. That India's cricket team has never been fitter can be ascribed directly to his *idée fixe*.

Captaincy came to Kohli steadily then suddenly, on a tour of Australia in 2014–15. It was the trip where everything about Kohli's batting seemed to click and whirr. He peeled off four hundreds in four matches. He stared down Mitchell Johnson in a Boxing Day Test. Then, at the end of that game, thirty-three-year-old Dhoni matter-of-factly gave Test cricket away.

By his own account, Kohli returned to his hotel room and broke down. For all his modernity, Kohli has a distinctly Indian sentimentality about his mentors. On 5 September 2014, Teachers' Day in India, his brother Vikas had turned up at Rajkumar Sharma's doorstep and on Virat's behalf presented his former guru with a Skoda. At the altar of Dhoni, Kohli still downright genuflects; he will not hear of the thirty-seven-year-old giving up one-day and T20 cricket. 'Kohli is fiercely loyal to Dhoni, which is interesting because they are so different,' observes the columnist Memon. 'Dhoni is reclusive, unavailable, never gives a press conference, and has made his cricket personality around an enigma. Virat is in your face, frequently on Twitter, interacting with fans. But Virat leans on Dhoni a lot, and the team is loyal to Dhoni too.'

All the same, Kohli has felt no need to emulate Dhoni's impassive, low-temperature personality. He has recast captaincy in his own death-before-dishonour image, leading an unapologetically confident team. Since January 2016, India have been the number one ranked Test nation for all but eight months. On his heaped-up burdens, Kohli has stood ever taller. No sooner had Kohli succeeded Dhoni as one-day and T20 captain than he churned out double-centuries in four consecutive Test series, including an epic 235 against England in Mumbai in eight and a half hours. It was the first Test at Wankhede since Tendulkar's last, but even the mighty Sachin already felt like prehistory. The love of Kohli admits no nostalgia. He constitutes a one-man golden age.

In accord, Kohli has begun sounding less the 'cricket brat', more the sporting statesman, a custodian, even a traditionalist ('I feel somewhere the commercial aspect is taking over the real quality of cricket and that hurts me'). Where insouciant Dhoni always looked like he could take or leave Test cricket, Kohli is the 142-year-old form's foremost ambassador ('I think if Indian cricket respects Test cricket . . . then Test cricket will stay at the top because of the fan base that we have all over the world').

Where insular Tendulkar could appear completely sunk in his own performance, Kohli accents collective achievement ('We strive to play well as a team. Single innings and single spells don't win games of Test cricket. We play to make the team win'). Where Dhoni and Tendulkar led India's obstinate distrust of cricket's video-assisted DRS, Kohli has been an unreconstructed technophile ('There are significant decisions that the DRS has been able to overrule and . . . it's something I think all cricketers should be happy with'). At the same time, he has exhibited grace in defeat ('There's no good reason why we should win every game, and I've naturally started feeling happy for the other team if they outplay us, because they are playing the same sport') and generosity to rivals – including the humbled Australians Steve Smith and David Warner, whose public humiliations he deplored ('I've known David and I know Steve as well . . . the things that happened after should never have happened').

Through his off-field duties, Kohli moves with similar confidence. England's former captain Mike Brearley tells a story of observing Kohli at a reception for his team at Lord's last year organised by India's High Commission. As can happen at such gatherings, the noise rose to uncomfortable levels that failed to abate when it came time for speeches. Commandeering the microphone, Kohli firmly shushed the audience. 'I would never have had the nerve to do it myself,' says Brearley. 'Perhaps I would have insinuated something when my turn came to speak, to persuade people to listen . . . But it was so crisp, impressive, unfussy, and, I thought, so correct.' It's central to his conception of Kohli. 'The impressive thing about Kohli is that he doesn't become bland,' argues Brearley. 'He keeps his energy, his articulacy, his sharpness.' Not merely a captain, then, but a leader.

*

But what *is* a leader in contemporary India? Another aspect of Kohli's personality to emerge through his captaincy over the last four years is its unilateralism. India is playing extraordinary volumes of cricket, but Kohli exhibits little desire to defray his workload or dilute his authority. A management diagram of India's cricket team, perhaps even of Indian cricket, would reveal a bunch of straight lines back to him. This is a mode of operation that reminds some of Narendra Modi, which Sardesai calls 'the cult of the supremo'.

'This is an age where people are looking to the strongman, the muscular individualist,' Sardesai says. 'Mr Modi is like that. He runs his government less through the cabinet system than by sheer force of personality – a very top-down governance style. Most of our political parties and movements are one-man or one-family shows with very little internal democracy too. And our cricket is moving in the same direction, with less scope for discussion and dissent. Kohli approaches cricket as a team sport. He's completely invested in the team. In a T20 match, Kohli will run from long-off to long-on as captain, leave Dhoni to manage the inner circle. But at the end of the day, all the decisions vest in him. It works at times, but it can be vexing for those whose personalities are not like that.'

One of these was Anil Kumble, Test cricket's third-highest wicket-taker, a figure revered for his skill, courage and integrity. The Board of Control for Cricket in India appointed Kumble as India's coach in June 2016. During his year working with Kohli, India won twelve Test matches and lost one. Yet for reasons neither has deigned to divulge, Kumble departed. Kumble's tweeted resignation remains his only statement on the matter: 'I was informed for the first time yesterday by the BCCI that the Captain had reservations with my "style" and about my continuing as the Head Coach. I was surprised since I have always respected the role boundaries between Captain and Coach.

239

Though the BCCI attempted to resolve the misunderstandings between the Captain and me, it was apparent that the partnership was untenable, and I therefore believe it is best for me to move on.'

Kohli has not said that much, leading to the perception of the interlude as a new variation on an old theme. 'In India, we have always glorified the individual more than the team,' says Sardesai. 'As long as Tendulkar was making runs, we never really cared about winning and losing. Under Kohli, that's changed for the better. But there are aspects of him that remind me of the India of the past where the individual becomes the focus, and the clash with Anil was emblematic of that.'

Kohli's accumulation of power has also coincided with power's diffusion within the BCCI following 2013 allegations of corruption in the Indian Premier League. India's Supreme Court first appointed a judicial commission to overhaul the board's governance, then a bureaucratic committee to enforce that commission's recommendations. The result has been a mix of administrative timidity and caprice at the top of Indian cricket, even as Kohli has enhanced his own stature.

Briefly a member of the committee until he quit in disgust at Kumble's axing, historian Ramachandra Guha describes the atmosphere round Kohli as craven and appeasing, like that of a Manchu court with the courtiers speaking of 'Virat' to advertise their closeness to him. 'There was an incident when I was on the committee when the Future Tours Programme came up, and games were discussed with Zimbabwe and Bangladesh,' says Guha. 'This board official says: "Oh, why should we waste Virat's time playing against these lesser-ranked nations?" Forgetting that for quite a lot of our cricket history, India was a lesser-ranked nation.'

Perhaps that's just a recognition that the worship of a figure comes more readily than investment in an institution. Social media here both reflects and leads. Consider that @BCCI, the Twitter handle for Indian cricket, has eight million followers, while @ImKohli has thirty million – a ratio not dissimilar, incidentally, to @BJP4India's ten million followers versus @narendramodi's forty-six million. Social media's amplifications, moreover, are set to grow: in a few years India is expected to have more Facebook users than the US has citizens. 'Most Indians are in stultifyingly boring jobs they are looking for any escape from,' says Keshava Guha, a novelist and writer for *Scroll*. 'Many of them have limited social life because work has taken them away from their families, or if they are working where they come from they want to get out. Social media brings the world to them.' Only a select few will ever be able to rise above its hubbub, intensified by India's ethnic, religious and linguistic differences. Kohli, then, suits these times also: a kind of everywhere figure, raised in Delhi, based in Mumbai, representing Bangalore, materialistic some days, spiritual others, brash occasionally, suave often, exciting always.

How to handle such eminence? Kohli has applied himself to the question with the same earnestness as he does cricket. For the last six years, for example, he has funded an eponymous charitable foundation whose causes have ranged from under-privileged children to underprivileged sport – that is, basically any sport in India bar cricket. For a time, Anushka herself was a cause. When she was first publicly acknowledged as his girl-friend, Kohli pushed back strongly against the idea, popular on social media, that she was Indian cricket's Yoko Ono, distracting and divisive.

Anushka herself is an unapologetic career woman, socially conscious, publicly aware, favouring positive roles as smart, strong, talkative young women – she played a cricketer's feisty girlfriend in *Patiala House* (2011). Her net worth has been put

241

at $US35 million. She has veered into movie producing, owns her own clothing line, supports charities advocating female empowerment and gender equality, even providing a voice-over to India's first openly transgender musical group, the 6-Pack Band. Some also detect Anushka's influence on Kohli's sudden interest in animal welfare – an army officer's daughter, she is renowned for her love of dogs.

Certainly, having moved on from his days as a simple clothes horse, Kohli evinces increasing fastidiousness about his stable of endorsements. In September 2017, for example, he cut ties with Pepsi, which by sports sponsorship standards was almost an abdication. Pepsi, India's cola market leader, had been enmeshed in cricket since the 1996 World Cup, when it launched a famous ambush marketing campaign featuring Tendulkar, his boyhood pal Vinod Kambli and their captain Mohammad Azharuddin. The endorsement had been passed down to Kohli via Dhoni like an ancestral heirloom. A sugary drink, however, was now at odds with Kohli's commitments to good nutrition and hard work; in similar spirit, Kohli also abjures sponsorships from makers of junk food and fairness creams, the skin tone cosmetics that still sell widely to India's self-conscious. He hews to products he can use, such as Chisel, a gymnasium chain, Puma, for whom he has designed a sneaker (the Basket Classic one8), and MRF, in the advertisement for which he props a tattooed bicep on a tyre (the Wanderer).

Among values expected of public figures in modern India, however, views on cola rank well behind views on country – Modi, of course, exhibits a canny sense of what the anthropologist Arjun Appadurai has called 'the erotics of nationhood'. For the captain of the national cricket team, the outcomes have been less predictable. Responding on video to fan questions when he launched an 'official app' on his thirtieth birthday last year, he appeared to bridle at a correspondent who described him as 'overrated', and expressed a preference for watching English and Australian batsman over 'these Indians'. 'Why are you living in our country and loving other countries?' Kohli retorted. 'I don't mind you not liking me, but I don't think you should live in our country and like other things.' The tone was perhaps half-facetious, the content strangely intemperate. There ensued a Twitter backlash, the actor Siddharth Suryanarayan chastising Kohli for his 'idiotic set of words', and a frontlash, fans leaping to Kohli's defence with such hashtags as #pride and #ISupportKohli. Even Kohli seemed faintly disconcerted. 'I guess trolling isn't for me guys, I'll stick to getting trolled!' he tweeted assuagingly. 'I spoke about how "these Indians" was mentioned in the comment and that's all. I'm all for freedom of choice. Keep it light guys and enjoy the festive season. Love and peace to all.'

Well, not quite all. In February, a suicide bomber from the Islamist cell Jaish-e-Mohammed attacked an armoured convoy in the Pulwama district of Jammu and Kashmir, killing forty military personnel. India blamed Pakistan for suc-couring the perpetrators. Tit-for-tat airstrikes were launched around the line of control that separates the irascible neigh-bours, while social media seethed with patriotic effusions and memes – Kohli was even criticised for not posting his 'heartfelt condolences to the martyred soldiers' fast enough, and hurriedly cancelled a fundraiser for his foundation. Then Dhoni, an honorary lieutenant-colonel in the Territorial Army, organised for the Indian team to wear military-style camouflage caps into a one-day international against Australia in Ranchi. Kohli announced that players would donate their match fees to the National Defence Fund, a state-run military welfare charity, also urging countrymen to give generously.

Some were disconcerted by the explicit identification of cricketers with a warrior culture. 'Dhoni I understand,' says

243

Ram Guha. 'He is from the hill country where people have traditionally gone into the army – three of India's five Victoria
Crosses hailed from his area. Kohli, however, is from a business
community that has resolutely stayed out of the armed forces.
Yet here he was addressing the nation like Winston Churchill.
That's what living in a bubble can do to you.' But when the
bubble is so influential, who dares gainsay its occupants?

Here, though, is something of a paradox to Kohli – that for
all his personification of India, his country has never fielded
a more international cricketer. His tastes are cosmopolitan,
his English fluent and expressive. He makes runs everywhere,
thrives on mastering different conditions, is compelled by
the desire to win away from home, which even Dhoni and
Tendulkar seemed to think a nice thing to do if possible but not
to be too fussed over. Not only is he linked with global brands
such as Tissot, Colgate, Mattel and Audi but he is one himself,
in the league of sportsmen he admires like Roger Federer and
Real Madrid, a cricket counterpart to corporate exports like
Infosys and ArcelorMittal; for her part, Anushka's next projects
are for Netflix and Amazon Video. It's a decade since Harvard's
Nirmalya Kumar profiled *India's Global Powerhouses*, in which
he argued that Indian companies had gone 'from passive
resistors to active promotors of globalization'. The same could
apply to the Kohli household.

To watch him in Australia last summer was a fascinating
study. Aussies do not surrender readily to awe, not even of their
own. Skipper Tim Paine tried to take Kohli down a peg, to little
avail. Crowds brooded on the Indian captain's every gesture in
the field, sat up straight when he came into bat. Sizeable con-
tingents of Indian Australians attended every Test and one-day
international – migrants from India now constitute Australia's
largest source of permanent migration. The media, notoriously

hostile to visiting captains, was transfixed, almost meek. As noteworthy as that much-watched video of him batting in the nets is that it was created at all, so admiring, so deferential. During the last Ashes, Ricky Ponting, these days in Australia the game's most resonant voice, derided England's captain Joe Root as 'soft' and 'a little boy'; during the Border–Gavaskar Trophy, Ponting chided a tiny handful of Australian contrarians with the temerity to boo Kohli in one Test: 'I don't like seeing it at all'. In a recent interview with *CricBuzz*, Ponting echoed Atherton's view of Kohli's place in cricket's firmament: 'His numbers show that he is the best. How old is he? Maybe 30, and he is going to play another 200 games. I don't think there will be many people who are going to argue against him being the best.'

In the same interview, Ponting based a brisk case for Indian's status as World Cup favourites on Kohli's presence: 'If Virat has a good World Cup, India will win.' It cannot be so simple, can it? After all, no batsman takes more than a single ball to dismiss. But it's a capacity of the truly great that they encourage crisp judgements, straightforward conclusions. Kohli will lead India into its first World Cup fixture, against South Africa at Southampton's Rose Bowl, on 5 June. He will be expected, six weeks later, to lead them into the final at Lord's; he will expect it of himself. The world will be watching. It always is.

Virat Kohli
VIRUSHKA (2020)

There's been Bennifer. There's been Brangelina. But no portmanteau super couple in the world enjoys such a following as Virushka: the amalgam of Virat Kohli and his Anushka Sharma, fusing cricket, Bollywood and elite lifestyle for 1.3 billion Indians.

In Australian cricket's book of days, 27 August is known for being the anniversary of the birth of Sir Donald Bradman. In the realm of Indian celebrity, it was dominated this year by the announcement, inevitably on social media, that the couple would be blessed by the arrival of their first child.

'It is an incredible feeling,' India's captain was quoted as saying. 'It puts things into perspective for you. It is a beautiful feeling. It is difficult to describe how you feel, but when we found it, we were over the moon.'

India rejoiced that, moon-wise, Kohli was over it. At Cricket Australia, the sense was of imminent lunar eclipse. Because there was never any serious doubt that this most visibly uxorious of cricketers would put parenthood before participation in a cricket series, however important. Airy talk

246

of Anushka coming to Australia for the nativity was never a prospect.

What's noteworthy about Kohli's attitude in this respect is not simply that he wishes to be present for the birth, but that he wants clear air around it. He wishes to be an attentive husband as well as an attendant father, to be with Anushka in the final stage of the pregnancy and in the first bloom of motherhood.

There may be something else at work, too, to do with Kohli's own supremely exacting professional standards. Kohli gives himself to sport with the totality of a Novak Djokovic. He aims for peak physicality and mental proficiency in everything he does. When he films himself in the gym performing one of his fitness routines, you feel sorry for the weights and treadmills – they don't stand a chance.

Part of Kohli may have feared he could not, under the circumstances, achieve in Australia the degree of clarity and total immersion to which he is accustomed. It will certainly be interesting to see, in years ahead, how Kohli is shaped by parenthood. Cricket and marriage have coexisted peacefully in his life; cricket and children will be harder to reconcile.

It did not seem coincidental that Kohli chose last week to make some pertinent remarks about the pressures of a cricket life spent hopping from one biosecure lily pad to another: 'These things will have to be considered. Like what length of the tournament or series one is going to play and what impact it will have on players mentally to stay in a similar environment for 80 days and not do anything different. Or have space to just go and see family or small things like that.' It was spoken like a man with family very much on his mind.

Times have clearly changed. It was regarded as extraordinarily enlightened that Shane Warne was permitted to fly home from the 1997 Ashes tour when he became a father.

The actual birth of Warne's daughter Brooke, in fact, occurred during Australia's tour match against Oxford University, and Warne had to take 6/48 in the Manchester Test before his brief furlough.

Being busy in a World Cup two years later, Warne was not inclined to a similar step for the birth of his son Jackson. 'I was fine about it,' he wrote in his autobiography. 'I had a great vibe about Jacko. I think it was a boy thing.'

Expectant cricketers either delaying tour arrivals or flying home for births have since become a relative commonplace, but they've still tended to be low-key base-touchings. Kohli, as in his cricket, is taking things to a new level. Why? Because he can. He is Kohli. And good for him.

Not so good, alas, for India. It's not that there's no show without Punch so much as that touring teams here need every advantage. India is a superior ensemble to England in 2017–18, who went from Buckley's chance with Ben Stokes to none without him. But Kohli, by his constant challenging and chivvying in all three formats, provides India's cricket with a continuity of tone and tempo that will now be missing.

Ajinkya Rahane appears the likeliest locum, although Rohit Sharma and KL Rahul will have advocates, and an Indian set-up without a strong overseer can be a restless place. Rohit's omission from the initial squad due to a 'hamstring tear' was a classic BCCI selection riddle wrapped in a mystery inside an enigma, coming as it did, we now know, on the day Kohli apparently advised the selectors of his intentions.

Rohit's re-inclusion now, the day before the IPL final in which he will apparently play despite already having been ruled out of India's short-form games in Australia to rest said hamstring, is still more opaque. Has Rohit, some wondered, been signifying displeasure by dropping 'Indian cricket' from his various social media handles? When you have 16.4 million

Instagram and 17.7 million Twitter followers, it's hard to do anything without inviting interpretation.

Kohli's absence will assuredly peel some of the gilt from this Border–Gavaskar Trophy. The Australian team itself will miss him. His captaincy rivalry with Tim Paine and batting rivalry with Steve Smith are the sort of stimuli that draws from cricketers their best. And there's no getting round it: the Australian media will miss Kohli. He reminds me of that story Ian Chappell tells of going to his first Test as a boy, and his father repeating: 'Watch Miller. Watch Miller. Watch Miller.' You could watch Kohli all day and not get bored. About Virushka, with the best will in the world, it is hard to feel the same.

Adelaide Test 2020, Day 3

THIRTY-SIX AND ALL THAT (2020)

Thirty-six. Or, if you prefer, 36. If you're Virat Kohli, you'd prefer neither. If you're the eye of cricket history, you would have to blink.

Australia was once bowled out for 36, but that was on a wet wicket in 1902. Modern cricket teams, pampered, primped and prepared at enormous expense, have no business being dismissed for what a club cricket team would be ashamed to rack up. But there you have it: never before has a Test team been dismissed with neither batsmen nor extras using only a second column in the scorecard.

So the world's foremost cricket personality will depart Australia next week a loser – a gracious loser, but a heavy one. And he will leave his team trailing 0–1 in the series for the Border–Gavaskar Trophy after a match dominated by the bowlers and shaped by the pitch. From the point Kohli fell, in fact, the result was more or less foreordained.

As Kohli faced Patrick Cummins this afternoon, India was 72 ahead, cornered but still competing. Kohli's first innings had been the match's most distinguished; again he looked earnest and unflustered; he had guided a soothing boundary to third man; hope still sprang eternal.

But Australia have long fancied Kohli on a sixth stump line, jabbing square. And again such a delivery drew India's captain in, Cameron Green taking a fumbling catch from a flying edge at gully, Cummins clocking up a 150th Test wicket.

Kohli loitered while the replay was checked, as if reluctant to take his leave; he turned when it was confirmed, taking his team's chance with him. Within seven overs, India had been bundled out for their lowest total in Test cricket; twenty-one overs later, Australia had concluded an eight-wicket victory. Kohli said afterwards he was 'struggling for words' to describe the experience; those whose job it was find them felt somewhat similarly.

This was the slowest scoring Test in Australia this millennium, batsmen eking out barely 2.5 runs an over, but also among the fastest moving, ending in barely half the allotted time. The bowling was fast though not furious; on the contrary, it today attained a precision that could only be called clinical. A television graphic of where the ball passed through the batting crease during India's second innings revealed a tight crescent, like the bullet holes a firing squad might leave.

These days in Test cricket everything is measured, producing columns of figures, clouds of data. It could be condensed here to 0.68 degrees, the average seam deviation in India's second innings. It does not sound much, representing about a quarter of a bat's width, but at the sort of speeds Pat Cummins and Josh Hazlewood achieve it is enough to shoot rays through a batting line-up.

It rather vindicated Tim Paine's intuition of granting Cummins the new pink ball in the second innings, seam rather than swing having menaced the batsmen's edges and stumps throughout the match. It brought Prithvi Shaw's wicket in the dark on Friday night; but we hadn't seen anything yet.

In theory, day 3 should offer the best batting conditions of a Test, the pitch's early life having drained away, deterioration yet to have set in. It usually features bowlers applying themselves, patiently and frugally, to prising their opponents out.

Adelaide, moreover, has a reputation for sun-soaked, run-soaked Test matches. When these countries met here in 2003, Ricky Ponting and Rahul Dravid traded double hundreds and thirty-six wickets fell for 1506 runs; in 2014, there were six individual centuries amid thirty-two wickets for 1566 runs.

From the outset, however, this Adelaide Oval pitch has belied all our understanding of drop-in pitches, offering encouragement sideways and upwards, to which batsmen out of practice against red balls let alone pink were unequal. What unfolded was a demolition, although less like the action of a wrecking ball on a building than the implosion of a smokestack – sudden, total, self-feeding, pace-gathering.

Cummins knocked out the keystone in the day's fifth over, angling a delivery that Cheteshwar Pujara was good enough to nick as it nipped away. India's hard-won first-innings advantage no longer looked quite so commanding.

Hazlewood from the River End then hit a line that demanded a stroke and a length that made this perilous, nicking off Mayank Agarwal and Ajinkya Rahane in a double wicket maiden. The big screen's tracing of it had an onomatopoeic character: WOOOWO.

India's tail again sold itself cheaply, Ashwin providing Hazlewood with his 200th Test wicket, Hanuma Vihari providing his eighth five-for. The thwack of the ball into Paine's gloves was audible, the collective wince when Cummins struck Mohammad Shami's arm palpable. The last did not take the field when India came out to defend 90, of which Australia made short work.

Joe Burns, last man picked for this Test after a ruinous run of outs, took fifteen balls and twenty-seven minutes to edge a boundary to third man; Umesh Yadav and Jasprit Bumrah then offered generous long hops, each pulled eagerly for four.

Later, like a captive slipping his bonds, he used his feet to drive Ashwin in the V along the ground and in the air. As if in celebration, he finished the match with a top-edged hook that bounced out of long leg's hands for six, bringing up his first Test half-century in more than a year. For him a new beginning, for India's captain an uncomfortable pause. With fond memories of Test feats there, Brian Lara called his first-born child Sydney; whatever can be predicted of the imminent Kohli offspring, it will not be named Adelaide.

Melbourne Test 2020, Day 2

RAHANE TAKES CHARGE (2020)

On the eve of the Second Test, Ajinkya Rahane was asked, inevitably, for impressions of the First. He replied succinctly. India, he explained, had played well for two days, badly on the third. Yes, he consented, very badly. But only, mark him, for a day.

Well, onlookers nodded cautiously, that was one way of putting it, although it was also a kind of comment on the modern game. It might sound to us like a version of the clash of civilisations when 'Australia' crush 'India'. But to the participants, it's ultimately one cricket match among many, and available to be rationalised away. Tomorrow is another day, even if that day might be Boxing Day.

Rahane is also, by nature, an unobtrusive, matter-of-fact cricketer. At the fall of the second wicket yesterday, necks craned to establish who was coming in next. It had been unclear in advance whether Rahane would remain in his usual number five, or take on Virat Kohli's batting responsibilities in addition to the leadership.

It took a few steps before confirmation that the figure beneath the helmet was not Hanuma Vihari. Indian batsmen are rather more recognisable than the days when a WACA Ground announcer heralded the arrival of 'Sir Neil Gavaskar'. Still, India's locum captain hardly possesses the star power of its permanent captain.

Where Kohli projects potency and athleticism, Ajinkya Rahane is round-shouldered, slightly stooped, with the air of a middling bureaucrat, not out of place in a railway ticket box or stamping passports. He looks much the same as when he first came to Australia nine years ago without forcing himself into the Test XI: unassuming, self-contained, quietly determined.

Rahane made a dashing hundred at the MCG in the Boxing Day Test of 2014, full of hawk-eyed hooks and pulls. That pitch was flatter than the Deccan Plateau, but he looked set to conquer the world. He has not, quite. The reasons are elusive. Rahane is an unusual Indian batsman for playing pace better than spin, scoring better away than at home and, these days, happier in Tests than shorter formats; he has not played a one-day international since February 2018; he had a lousy time in the recent Indian Premier League. He is also a slightly sketchy starter, who likes bat on ball, and the confidence boost of early boundaries.

If confidence is an issue, the captaincy may have come as a fillip. On the previous occasion on which Rahane deputised against Australia, at Dharamsala three and a half years ago, Kohli prowled the dressing room, attended the press conferences and generally continued to personify the team. Rahane's new commission is unqualified. He led the team out; he led the team in; he fielded sharply in the gully; he generalled his fielders from beneath a faded cap subtly marking his seniority.

Yesterday Rahane batted with calm and skill, as befits a sixty-six-Test veteran. In the first 50, off 111 balls, there were some choice boundaries: a delectable late cut from Lyon, a fearless pull from Hazlewood with two men back, an exquisitely fine glance off Starc to reach his half-century. But there was also a lot of leaving, after fencing away from the body cost him his wicket in the tour matches, and a few not-how-but-how-many shots, glides to third man without pretence to style. When Paine pushed his solitary slip wider, sod's law dictated that Rahane's nick would find that gap too.

In Rahane's second 50, off eighty-four balls, the class showed through, including off-drives from Lyon and Cummins that veritably hummed off the bat, and a square cut from the latter to reach his century that recalled Gundappa Viswanath here forty years ago – and there is no higher praise than that. The crowd of 23,841 did a passable impression of many more, a score of tricolours fluttering. Tim Paine led chagrined but genuine applause on the field.

Rahane's rival captain had earlier provided probably the day's most brilliant moment, a perfectly timed full-length dive to ensnare a dying edge from Pujara. Pat Cummins bowled a leonine spell for an hour and a quarter from the Southern Stand End, maintaining his velocities, wobbling the seam, with 8-4-12-2 barely doing it justice.

When Cummins resumed after lunch, however, Rishabh Pant took 12 from his first over, recalling his bonny strokes here in India's victory two years ago. Though Pant perished to a flat-footed cut and Shubman Gill to a careless drive, their intent prevented the innings growing becalmed. Vihari showed commendable stickability, Ravi Jadeja consummate spunk.

The second new ball might have done the trick for Australia, but Steve Smith, perhaps a yard close, could only parry a fast-flying edge from Rahane (73) in Starc's first over. Thereafter, Rahane and Jadeja took advantage of the harder ball and attacking fields, adding 41 in nine rather ragged overs.

Rahane raised the pair's hundred partnership, by powering Hazlewood through mid-off and not troubling to run. The 200th delivery he faced, from Starc, then clonked him on the glove and helmet, but the looping edge was jolted from the grasp of a diving Travis Head. With rain swirling, he left the field holding his headgear like one of those Elizabethan ghosts that haunt palaces with heads beneath their arms.

It was a suitably reverberating conclusion to a fantastic day's cricket, and pause in a fantastic innings. Just a reminder: 128 balls was all it took to sweep all India away in Adelaide. But that was eight whole days ago.

Melbourne Test 2020, Day 3

BOXING DAY MASSACRE (2020)

History does not repeat, but does rhyme. Forty years ago in Melbourne, an Indian team that looked utterly outmatched and demoralised surged to win a Test and tie up a series. It's on the brink of happening again.

In that earlier Test, India was led by Sunil Gavaskar, so disgruntled by Australian umpiring that he famously almost forfeited the match. India's current captain is no longer even here, Virat Kohli having heard the call of family. It has been his proxy, the self-effacing Ajinkya Rahane, making the case for the leadership of character rather than charisma.

Australia, meanwhile, have had their worst Boxing Day Test for ten years, recapitulating the 2010 Ashes match with a costly decision to bat first, a stumbling first innings, a listless bowling and fielding effort, and a gradual fade from there. Hubris? If so, say hello to nemesis.

Two years ago, for the parallels keep coming, Australia subsided to India, in a defeat that could be explained in some degree by the absence through suspension of David Warner and Steve Smith. Thanks to injury, Warner is now missing again. Something else is missing from Smith.

It remains possible to argue that, as they say, 'a big one is round the corner' for Australia's most prolific modern batsman – he has made too many runs, too many centuries for it to be otherwise. Still, we are coming to terms with it being a long block. Three years have now elapsed since his last Test hundred in Australia; his four innings in this Border–Gavaskar Trophy have produced 10 uneasy runs. A corollary of Smith's unique methods of success, moreover, is that he has always been capable of finding idiosyncratic ways to fail. Yesterday's was a case in point. Ask not for whom the bail falls; it falls for thee.

At 2/71 on the eve of tea, Smith faced Ravi Ashwin, who has confounded him with drift. Smith reverted to a former method, dancing a few steps; he had recourse to a new method, essaying a rare sweep; he revisited the first innings, softer hands this time causing the deflection to fall a foot short of Pujara at leg slip.

Then, just after tea, Smith shaped to glance Jasprit Bumrah. About five years ago, Smith was bowled behind his legs twice in a World Cup, but quickly adjusted his guard; this delivery was subtler, like a barely audible twig snap in a horror movie as it passed the leg stump.

Smith set off and Bumrah winced as the deflected ball eluded Rishabh Pant's grasp. Then, pointing fingers, excited cries. The larkish Australian opener Sid Barnes liked it as a trivia question: 'What does a bail weigh?' It's a trick: Law 8 (3) (b) specifies no weight. A heavier leg bail might have remained in place; this one, almost retrospectively, dropped.

The knell had already tolled on Joe Burns. He faced ten deliveries in each innings of the match. Nearly half of these might conceivably have dismissed him. He was beaten thrice before nicking off in the first innings; in the second he was nearly run out getting off the mark then exonerated from lbw by an umpire's call before being given out caught at the wicket.

Even then, Burns sought a video Hail Mary – anything to prolong his career, it seemed, if only by a few seconds. Matthew Wade acquiesced – it would have been a hard heart that did otherwise. When the hanging chad went against him, Burns moved off until swallowed in the shadows of the race, fate no longer his own, although curiously entwined now with his coach.

This is a bigger problem than it should be. By identifying so closely with Burns's second innings success at Adelaide, coach Justin Langer has entwined himself in the opener's fate. In appreciation of their bond, the batsman described his unbeaten 51 as 'our innings'; does the Melbourne Test now become 'our 0 and 4'?

Wade, at least, has fulfilled his brief as ersatz opener. He hit a fine straight drive to the fence, ran a hard-working four to fine leg, showed sound judgement around off stump and absorbed a blow to the helmet like he was catching a bullet between the teeth. But with a good delivery to Marnus Labuschagne and a wretched shot by Travis Head, Australia sagged further. They live to fight a fourth day, and, after Adelaide, nothing can be ruled out. But the simply sensible way Cameron Green and Pat Cummins approached batting in the last hour rather mocked the efforts of their nominal betters.

What has happened in this Test so far that the polarities of Adelaide should have reversed themselves so utterly? It will be a rich subject for conjecture. But the match has recalled a story that Graeme Swann related about the Headingley Test of 2009, where England were stuffed out of sight in barely three days. It was a game where if it could go wrong it did, and of that, after the match, the players persuaded each other: their performance had been so feeble that the events could be dismissed as an outlier. They won the next match, and the Ashes, convincingly.

Thirty-six all out is nothing if not an outlier. Neither India nor Australia have ever made fewer. The visitors have tackled this Melbourne Test as though Adelaide was an anomaly, Australia as though it was a trend. For the latter, it has not gone well.

Sydney Test 2021, Day 3

THE SIRAJ INCIDENT (2021)

There are many pleasing and vivid images in *India's 71-Year Test*, a pictorial history of India's cricket tours of Australia launched during the Sydney Test. None is quite so happy as those capturing Indian cricketers on the touring parts of their tours, being welcomed, heralded and embraced.

Images of Indian supporters down under, perhaps surprisingly, go back to the 1960s. But the enthusiasm takes off in this most recent generation: we see disembodied hands stretching to touch Cheteshwar Pujara, fans posing for selfies with a beaming Virat Kohli, and Sachin Tendulkar on his famous pilgrimage to the home of Sir Donald Bradman.

If the book is ever updated, sad to say, there will be few such images of the summer of 2020–21. Is it possible to tour a country without actually visiting it? For that has been the fate of this admirable Indian team, pinned down and penned up since their first fortnight's quarantine, far from home, cut off from their families, and a plaything of overmighty bureaucrats, absurdly execrated for a minuscule quarantine breach in a country that has long since lost any sense of proportion in dealing with COVID-19.

In the foreword to *India's 71-Year Test*, India's coach Ravi Shastri, a visitor to these shores for thirty-five years, calls Australia his favourite touring destination: 'The patronage of the crowds and the big grounds contributed to the ambience. The women are wonderful, the men are sporting and the beer is great.' One wonders whether he'll now be able to convince Mohammed Siraj of this wholehearted endorsement.

It was Siraj who brought yesterday's Test match to a standstill at 2.55 p.m., coming in from fine leg and with a wave of his arms signifying his weariness of the hometown heckling from the Brewongle Stand. Was this heckling racist? Prepare for it to be minimised as 'friendly banter', and for jokes about lip-reading through masks. For a certain proportion of cricket's followers will defend to the death their right to abuse players from other countries in whatever terms they wish.

Bear in mind, however, that yesterday's events came on top of crowd behaviours of which the Indian team complained after play on Saturday, whose reported content sounds more serious. In any event, what we should be prepared to say is that it's at least ungrateful, certainly distasteful and arguably disgusting to jeer or harangue any visitor to this country put through the ordeal this Indian team has experienced in the summer of 2020–21 so that we comparatively fortunate Australians might have something to watch.

Siraj is on his first tour. He is the son of an auto-rickshaw driver from Hyderabad. His father died six weeks ago; he remained on the tour rather than return for the funeral. As India's national anthem played before play on Thursday, a single tear was observed descending from his eye.

Otherwise, of course, we hardly know him; we cannot get close enough to do so, nor he to us. What we have seen, though, speaks well of him: he has toiled manfully on flat wickets in Melbourne and Sydney; he dropped his bat and hastened to the aid of Cameron Green when the young all-rounder suffered his concussion in the tour match at Drummoyne Oval. Siraj is also a Muslim, an increasingly problematic identity in his own nation, where chauvinism and sectarianism has a tightening grip. The scope for misunderstanding is huge.

The Indian team, we are told, are fed up. They glimpse life going round them that looks close to normal – huge crowds in shopping plazas, on beaches, in pubs and restaurants, even as they're confined to hotel rooms, whose walls must by now be closing in. They're confused. Hell, I'm confused and I live here. Restrictions change every day, as governments make it up as they go along, playing politics with public safety, treating their own people as pawns, and our cricket visitors barely as draughts.

Tensions in this series were 'starting to boil', Tim Paine admitted on the eve of the Test. Not even he, the home captain enjoying nothing but support, has been immune – witness his uncharacteristic remonstration with Blocker Wilson on Saturday. And nobody's calling him anything but 'Skipper'.

In Adelaide and Melbourne, there were pockets of exuberant Indian support in the crowd. Here, probably thanks to the hot spot status of Sydney's west, those voices have been fewer. Australian fans have had the ground largely to themselves, and perhaps have mistaken this for licence.

There has been nothing to leaven the visitors' sense of isolation either, although Paine, to his credit, kept the Indian team company during their representations to the on-field officials, and while security was consulted.

The shame was that the incident overshadowed another spirited and well-contested day of Test cricket, Cameron Green growing in stature with each passing over – not bad for a figure already 200 centimetres.

For one so tall, Green keeps solid contact with terra firma, taking a long stride and getting his nose over the ball, punching strongly in the V but quick to reprove error of length with a full-blooded pull. He deferred only to Bumrah, who somehow went wicketless despite repeatedly beating the outside edge, and somehow also kept smiling throughout.

But against everyone else, he stayed busy and even bold. He used his feet to bomb Ashwin over wide mid-on, and with a 360-degree swing thrice deposited Siraj beyond the long-on boundary. I dare say that this also contributed to Siraj's disenchantment; the irony was that the ten-minute break in proceedings probably thwarted Green's ambitions for a century.

As time ran short with the declaration imminent, Green v Bumrah climaxed: a straight drive to the rope, a pump-action pull onto the terraces, and a nick to the keeper. The crowd united in appreciation – all save those already ejected.

Sydney Test 2021, Day 5

THE NEW WALL (2021)

Astrological determinism? Yesterday was Rahul Dravid's birthday. India faced a task at the Sydney Cricket Ground that called forth all the gifts of the batsman they called 'The Wall'. Between them they formed just such an obstacle: call them 'The Barricade', evoking their alert, improvised collective defiance.

India trailed in this Third Test from the moment Tim Paine won the toss on a flat pitch with a quick outfield then encountered a resurgent Steve Smith. They were missing their charismatic captain; they were absent key fast bowlers; they copped injuries, irritations, and, unhappily, abuse. Around them raged a debate about the venue of the next Test. It wasn't only the home team they were keeping out, but the sense of gathering misfortune. This draw was a feat to rank with their victory in Melbourne.

They did it, paradoxically, by first pressing for an improbable win, chasing more than 400. In their first innings, India had been hemmed in by Australian accuracy and persistence, Cheteshwar Pujara eking out his half-century from

176 deliveries, and others falling rather in step. Here they had the brainstorm of swapping Rishabh Pant for Hanuma Vihari, breaking up the succession of right-handers and injecting a note of youthful brio.

Teams are strangely averse to this: Australia made an ersatz opener of Matthew Wade in Adelaide and Melbourne rather than have Marnus Labuschagne and Steve Smith move up a slot. But perhaps the Indians were persuaded by the extremity of their plight, chasing 400 to win with one batsman *hors de combat*. To achieve a different outcome required a different approach.

Pant, of course, had last been seen looking a dejected figure with his arm in a sling after sustaining the painful blow on the elbow from Mitchell Starc that had kept him off the field in Australia's second innings – a little like a fallen cherub. He had already had a poor first day with the gloves; he would have completed a sorry match yesterday had Tim Paine held him at the wicket on 3, but the edge was just too thick, the deviation too sharp.

From this moment, however, Pant made himself right at home. He hit Lyon out of the attack at the Randwick End, then at the Paddington End, then at the Randwick End again. He hit with the spin and against the spin; he hit with the field up and the field back. He cut and drove the pace bowlers too.

He is a fun cricketer, breezy and nonchalant; when you watch him, worldly cares slip away, save perhaps if you're batting next, or the opposition captain. Third slip would have caught him on 32, but Paine had by then elected to save runs. Pant also seemed to ginger Pujara, who was able to go about his quiet, methodical business without worrying too much about tempo, which in turn improved his own.

The pitch, meanwhile, continued in its enigmatic character, less reminiscent of last year, when Lyon took the wickets, than twenty years ago, when Stuart MacGill took seven wickets in the first innings and went wicketless in the second. Not even Starc's heavy footfall made much of an impression on it.

There were flickers of reverse swing, dramas with the DRS. But after the roller's effects wore off, uneven bounce posed the greatest threat to the batsmen, particularly when the ball was short; in the game's last 320 overs only four wickets fell to slow bowlers.

Five minutes before lunch, Pujara raised the century partnership with a deft flick through mid-wicket; having not made a Test half-century for two years, Pant carried on breezily towards an improbable Test century, until a wild shot on 97 spiralled to point with the second new ball just four deliveries away. Nothing so good has ended so badly since *Huckleberry Finn*.

A fine delivery from Josh Hazlewood accounted for Pujara, an untimely hamstring almost invalided Hanuma Vihari, and a fierce first over after tea from Pat Cummins nearly removed Ravi Ashwin. But by now, India had pivoted. It was an old wisdom of Richie Benaud's: commit totally to what you do. If you're pressing for victory, go all out; if you want to draw, do not muck around with attacking gestures.

So Ashwin and Vihari tried nothing. Ashwin donned a chest guard like a knight's cuirass; Vihari limped occasionally between wickets like a gouty laird. Otherwise they set to defend over by over, ball by ball, minute by minute.

Ashwin, in delivering his media titbits the night before from his little quarantine cubicle, had responded to the question of the team's unity with a firm: 'Absolutely.' The team, he insisted, had 'come together', and this last day was 'an opportunity to show what sort of mettle we are made of'. The Australians tested that mettle, even by some sly psy ops, Paine needling Ashwin about his Indian Premier League career and his relations with the rest of his team. Ashwin kept his own counsel, even when

Paine dropped Vihari with 9.1 overs remaining: Australia's captain did not have one of his better days.

Two years ago here, Australia escaped defeat thanks to rain; India relied on their own resources and determination. It was cricket not only in Dravid's technical vein, but in his spirit. 'I have failed at times,' said the great man, 'but never stopped trying.'

Sydney Test 2021
TO SIRAJ WITH LOVE (2021)

O ut of the unprecedented actions of Mohammed Siraj in objecting to the behaviour of a group at the Sydney Test has emerged a discussion worth having about the rights and responsibilities of the modern live fan. Yet it is also almost impossible to generalise about them. Crowds are diverse; they are fickle; they are volatile. They do not merely observe the play; they observe one another, and unite or differ. They like to be noticed; they can also object to it.

There is also in Australia an ancient tradition of raucous demotic demonstration, even in cricket, and especially at the Sydney Cricket Ground. It was the scene of our first riot, in 1879. It was the scene, fifty years ago, of the first abandonment of a Test field due to a physical altercation with a player, England's John Snow.

A hundred years ago, meanwhile, there was another incident in an Ashes Test which has long fascinated me – and which affords some parallels with *l'affaire Siraj*. An English amateur vice-captain, Rockley Wilson, wrote an article for London's *Daily Express* deploring the behaviour of a Sydney crowd towards his teammate Jack Hobbs, whom they had heckled for his slow movement in the field when he was publicly known to be suffering a leg strain. There might then have been no internet, but there was a lively trade in cables to Australia of sections of the Fleet Street press, and Wilson's comments were quickly played back to their subject. An account in Melbourne's *Herald* gives the flavour of the response when Wilson came out to bat.

> Everywhere else round the ground thoughts were forcibly expressed. 'Liar! Liar! Liar!' roared the spectators. The roar became louder and louder as Wilson neared the batting crease. 'What about your lying cable?' was called as Wilson went to the end at which the bowling began. When Wilson took strike . . . there was a long babel of noise – 'Why don't you play the game?' 'Hook him on the jaw, Warwick.' 'Hit him on the head, Gregory, and wake him up.' 'Never mind the wicket, Gregory, crack him.'

This worked a charm. Wilson, clearly unsettled, smartly got out stumped, amid widespread schadenfreude. But then, as *The Herald* continued, something curious happened.

> Hobbs' name appeared on the scoring board . . . When he did appear there was a scene never before approached on the Sydney Cricket Ground. People stood and cheered frantically, the clapping was tremendous, and all round the ground three cheers for Hobbs were called for, and spontaneously given . . . and continued long after. The members and the grand stand and hill patrons were all in it.

What was this? A tacit admission that Wilson had pricked their consciences? A desire to be seen as magnanimous in their own and English eyes? Illustrative of people's innate desire to join in with the prevailing sentiment? Different spectators that day would probably have given different answers.

In those days, of course, we were most sensitive to English sensibilities, and also English condescension. Sport, like Australia, was a monoculture; it loomed large and reinforced the status quo. Times have changed, in some respects our attitudes to crowds have not kept up with their growing complexity. What transpired during the Third Test involved a dark-skinned cricketer with a poor background in a rich team from a country both stunningly rich and terribly poor.

The shame is that the incident immediately bogged down in a mindless literalism, led by the 'you-can't-say-anything-anymore' crowd who demanded a transcript featuring explicit racial epithets otherwise it's all WOKE, FAKE NEWS etc. It is not a particularly deep reading of the scenario.

For a start, the Indian objection is cumulative. It is to the long-term boorishness of Sydney crowds. They were invited to report an instance if they heard such; Siraj did. And frankly who would willingly soak up such prolonged stupidity? Any reader who thinks so is invited to forward their work address: I'll be happy to follow them all day shouting a drunken joke about their name, taking pleasure in their misfortune and discomfiture.

For another thing, racial epithets are not a precondition of racism. On the contrary, racism can be most pernicious where it is politest. The majority judgements in *Plessy v Ferguson*, the foundational documents of American segregation, are superbly eloquent; the terms of the Wannsee Protocol for the 'Preparation of the Final Solution of the European Jewish Question' are smoothly bureaucratic; the mumbo jumbo of eugenics masked itself with a tone of science and learning.

There is also such a thing as a racism of tone. A fair-skinned person addressing a dark-skinned person with a note of contempt or mockery carries an awful weight of history. The fair-skinned person is unlikely to grasp this, having never had to think otherwise, having never had to suffer being stereotyped or derided merely on the basis of their complexion. They may not intend offence – most, I suspect, would recoil at the idea. But it would cost them nothing to consider how they might be heard.

Now for some whataboutisms. What about the Barmy Army and their treatment of Steve Smith and David Warner in England in 2019? Yes, it was disgustingly stupid; it also ruined the Edgbaston Test for many fans, English as well as Australian. The Barmy Army is more sinned against than sinning, but they took this demonstration of allegiance far too far, and should have been more consistently called out on it. Good. I'm glad we had this little chat.

What about the young men whose behaviour was called out at the SCG? Were they not 'scapegoated'? This objection is not unreasonable. They may well have been held responsible for the misdeeds of others, and singled out because of the thinness of the crowd, for on other days their chants and cries might have been submerged in the general hubbub. Yet they appear to have suffered no reputational damage. No media jackals are in pursuit; no PC mob has accused them of cultural appropriation for wearing Hawaiian shirts.

We do not know who they are. We do not know where they went, although one report is that they were simply encouraged to move elsewhere. It is hard, therefore, to argue that their civil liberties were infringed. Their treatment, at least so far, appears to have been perfectly moderate and proportional.

What about Yabba? Yabba, for those who don't know, was the nickname of SH Gascoigne, a Balmain rabbitoh who through the 1920s and 1930s was the personification of Australian barracking, drawing crowds to the Hill simply for his own booming voice and acerbic wit.

In 2008, he was commemorated in a bronze cast in the Victor Trumper Stand. 'By today's juvenile standards,' erupted a heckler of this column a couple of days ago, 'it's a wonder they haven't demolished the statue of Yabba.'

This is perfectly bogus. Yabba loved cricket. He patronised Test matches and grade games alike. He drank little; he did not swear or curse. His declared enemies were boring batsmen ('Whoa! He's bolted') and inaccurate bowling ('Your length is lousy but you bowl a good width'). He ribbed everyone alike; he developed strong affinities for visiting players like Patsy Hendren, Arthur Gilligan and the aforementioned Jack Hobbs. When Hobbs played his last Test in Australia, he made a point of going to the Hill to shake Yabba's hand.

Yabba, according to Richard Cashman's canonical treatise on Australian cricket spectating, *'Ave a Go, Yer Mug!*, even liked women's cricket when introduced to it and refrained from his usual boisterousness. 'Why should I?' he asked. 'The ladies are playing all right for me. This is cricket, this is. Leave the girls alone.' Some readers will probably regard this as making him unbearably woke.

So Yabba is under no threat at all. In fact, we could all do with being a bit more like him, he who supported honest effort in good spirit by whomever caught his eye, setting an example of seeing through the cricketer to the cricket itself.

One last thing: what goes around comes around. Remember Rockley Wilson? He went on to teach at Winchester, where one of his students was none other than Douglas Jardine. When Jardine was appointed England's captain ahead of the Bodyline series, he confessed a deep foreboding. 'We shall win the Ashes,' Wilson prophesied. 'But we may lose a Dominion.' He wasn't far off.

Tim Paine

PAINE SYMPTOMS (2021)

Tim Paine is the captain of Australia's cricket team. Steve Smith is his predecessor and, some argue, his ideal successor. Both take the field at the Gabba today with some ground to make up.

'I think it's boiling away,' Paine said on the eve of the Sydney Test. 'There's some stuff starting to happen, there's a bit of chat starting to happen.' He spoke of 'tension' in India's camp about the venue for the Fourth Test, Brisbane being a venue 'they don't want to go to'. He concluded: 'I think it's starting to grind a few people. We'll see how it goes.'

Projection? Because in Sydney it was Paine who looked like a captain being boiled and ground, and we did see how that went. His keeping was flawed; his captaincy was sub-par, even if it's arguable that Australia's declaration proved well timed and well calibrated. Most of all, he was strangely truculent, with opponents, and with umpire Paul Wilson, incurring a fine for an audible obscenity.

The day after the Test, fulsomely and manfully, Paine expressed contrition: 'I want to apologise for the way I went about things yesterday. I'm someone who prides themselves on the way I lead this team and yesterday was a poor reflection of the team. I let the pressure of the game get to me. It affected my mood and my performance.' This speaks well of him: it is hard to recall an Australian captain reflecting so candidly.

For this, Paine has received a good deal of credit. The Australian Cricketers' Association even issued a press release of approbation. Yet I'm not sure what the ACA has to do with this. Paine has ample support. And his apology fell short in an important respect: it made no mention of Ravi Ashwin, whom Paine impugned gratuitously and nastily in a lengthy monologue that was eagerly transcribed and disseminated.

Ashwin had done nothing to deserve such a tirade except resist the Australians stoutly and successfully. We are told that sledging is about making opponents think too hard about what they are doing. Yet Paine's remarks referred not to a shot or the pitch or the circumstances of the game, but to Ashwin's reputation, among teammates and the Indian Premier League.

The comments were neither droll nor funny; they were spiteful; they also placed the match officials in an awkward position. Looking at the umpire, Ashwin said pointedly: 'Your guy.' The Indians are well aware they are being umpired by Australians; frankly, we have seen how that can end.

Paine admitted that he 'looked a fool' when he dropped a catch the following over; actually he already did. He is well aware of the stump mics: indeed, it was he who pioneered their use as a kind of propaganda tool in Perth two years ago. Yet on he carried, apparently wishing to be heard by the widest possible audience.

Thousands of children have now heard Australia's captain refer to an opponent as a 'dickhead', to query his status in the team, to brag about his own record. Paine, however, expressed regret only about 'the way I spoke to umpires'; the inference must be that he cares less about how he addresses opponents.

I regret having to say this. Paine has been a fine captain. He seems to be a good man. And stump mics, while great for television, are a pernicious influence on the game: a 'route to madness', as my friend Mike Atherton observed in *The Times* yesterday. So in the aftermath of the Sydney Test, Paine missed a chance to set a standard for Australian cricketers generally. And because no sanction was imposed, the Cricket Australia-approved message is that you can call a rival what you like, providing you fix it up with an apology afterwards. Then you're sweet. Then you'll be praised for being a 'great leader'.

Smith, meanwhile, has unwittingly found himself at the centre of a cricket tempest over his mucking about in Rishabh Pant's block, which has been rather wildly proposed as an instance of gamesmanship. Smith is upset at the allegation, and rightly: it was impossible to see how Pant might be misled, or even what Australian advantage might accrue. The explanation furnished was entirely plausible: the Australian was merely partaking of his obsessive shadow batting, which we know occurs even in hotel rooms, and in full whites.

I confess some fellow feeling here, being myself a compulsive shadow batsman, knowing that marking a phantom guard is part of the kinaesthetic pleasure. I have two bats in my kitchen, where I have played most of my best innings. All of them, actually. Still, there was a lesson here for Smith. It is my kitchen; it was not Smith's pitch.

A fielder, for that's what Smith was at the time, having finished his batting for the match, has no business being anywhere near a fifth-day pitch. Had Smith been batting, and a fielder walked into his crease to play shadow strokes, he would have been first to object.

If it was compulsive behaviour, it is a compulsion Smith needs to resist. It suggests an obliviousness to the world around him; it suggests, in fact, that the self-absorption which proved problematic at Cape Town in 2018 has not abated.

Perhaps because we are so invested in the idea of Smith the batting savant there has been too much pandering to his quirks and mannerisms. The Australians are so protective of Smith's much vaunted 'bubble' that there's an apprehension about pricking it.

It also sets a poor example. Much has been made, for example, of the simpatico between Smith and Marnus Labuschagne – in the main benign, even nourishing. But Labuschagne should also be being encouraged to become his own man, not a Smith manque.

There is a budding Smithesque egocentricity to Labuschagne's cricket, most noticeable in the time he can take to get off the field when dismissed. Disappointment is one thing. On occasion, Labuschagne is in danger of being timed in. The field belongs to everyone, not just to those who feel entitled to rule it.

This has been a terrific Test series: by their skills and presences, Paine, Smith and Labuschagne have played huge roles in making it so memorable. It would enhance the experience for everyone were they to sign off in the Gabba Test on a note of grace.

Brisbane Test 2021, Day 3

INDIA HOLDS THE LINE (2021)

I t takes a lot to shift established images in cricket. England will need to win a few more World Cups before its players cease to be regarded as pragmatic, professional, a little dour. A certain amount of calypso glitter still sticks to the West Indian cricketers decades after this characterised their cricket.

For Indian cricket, however, the summer of 2020–21 promises to be regarded as transformative. Over the years, Indian teams have been associated with virtuoso talent, home advantage and the occasional miraculous comeback from the brink of defeat. Yet as much as they have challenged Australia during this Border–Gavaskar Trophy, the Indians have also departed their traditional modes of success: they have battled; how they have battled, confined by COVID-19, pounded by pace, raked by injuries, riled by crowds.

Yesterday at the Gabba, it seemed, they must break, their top order swept away, their innings in the hands of two tailenders, Washington Sundar and Shardul Thakur, playing their first Test innings. They bent, but by the close were, again, unblinkingly eye to eye with Australia, having restricted their first-innings deficit to 33.

Two years ago, India beat Australia on the back of formidable individual performances: from Virat Kohli, Jasprit Bumrah and Cheteshwar Pujara. It was regarded as an epochal achievement. This summer Kohli has been largely missing, and the contributions of Bumrah and Pujara have been in a lower key. Instead, the Tests in Melbourne, Sydney and now Brisbane have testified to the visitors' resilience, depth and improvement in important degrees. In the first three Tests, most particularly, India dropped its tail like a gecko; here its tail grew like a mermaid's.

Early on there was a hint of fatigue about the Indian approach – of the toll taken by an attritional series. Every batsman played themselves carefully in; only Pujara could be genuinely said to have been prised out, being the recipient of a fine ball from Josh Hazlewood, the pick of Australia's bowlers again. None of the deliveries that had Ajinkya Rahane, Rishabh Pant and Mayank Agarwal caught in the cordon compelled strokes, while the airspace between second slip and gully was seldom quiet.

Yet it was, at least, an orderly withdrawal; Australia were unable to turn one wicket into two except gradually. And it may not have been a coincidence that the best cricket came from the visitors' freshest members, who would not be playing here but for injuries to Bumrah and Ravi Ashwin. Their stand of 123 in 217 balls extended beyond nuisance value through exasperation to vexation – from pain in the Australian neck to the head via the backside.

'Discipline is the soul of an army. It makes small numbers formidable; procures success to the weak, and esteem to all.' Washington Sundar may not actually be named for George of that ilk, but his partnership with Thakur called some of the General's wisdoms to mind.

Five years ago, Sundar batted in India's top four in an under-19 World Cup; he has since been repurposed as a T20 bowler of stump-to-stump slows, but seems to have been storing his batting rather than losing it. He left with a flourish, ducked with alacrity and defended with a big stride and full face; consecutive boundaries from Starc, off the legs and down the ground, were as good as anything played in the match; a six off Lyon soared over mid-wicket amid general rapture.

Shardul Thakur took more of a chance, getting off the mark with a pulled six from Cummins, raised his half-century by hoicking Lyon over long-on for another. But he got behind the ball robustly, and under it too. Especially with the second new ball, Australia's pace bowlers looked determined to blast their way past; the pair would not be moved.

Thakur fell only when he got a little loose, as though he suddenly remembered that he had a first-class average of 16, like a trapeze artist suddenly looking down. He played a hare-brained hook that fell safe, then was bowled through a head-in-the-air drive. Even then, the last few spun the innings out a further nine overs, adding to the general Australian irritation.

David Warner slapped three consecutive boundaries off Mohammed Siraj's second over to show how integral he will be to Australia's prospects of setting India a testing fourth-innings target, especially with rain in the offing for the last two days. India need only draw to retain the Border–Gavaskar Trophy. But whatever the outcome, Rahane's men have already gained much.

Brisbane Test 2021, Day 5

THE BUTTERFLY EFFECT (2021)

Around 2 p.m. at the Gabba yesterday, Josh Hazlewood was mid-gallop to the bowling crease when Cheteshwar Pujara held up a gloved hand. Hazlewood came, grumpily, to a stop.

Normally in such circumstances, the batsman will point out some movement in the crowd within his eyeline. Pujara cast a look around, made a vague gesture – the distraction, it turned out, was a pale butterfly that had fluttered momentarily into his airspace. It was as though cricket's great apostle of non-violence was putting in a word for nature or placing a plea for peace.

Hazlewood was unhappy; Hazlewood is seldom happy, save around wickets. His response to the butterfly was to sting like a bee. His sharp lifter dislodged Pujara's stem guard as it seamed back and cuffed the helmet firmly. 'Did ya see that one?' Hazlewood asked helpfully. Pujara picked up the guard, studied the helmet, and the game, as it did regularly yesterday, adjourned for physical attention, running repairs. Onlookers paused too, for breath, on a day where every ball seemed loaded

282

with meaning. It was perhaps the characteristic exchange of the first two sessions: pent-up Australian fury dashing itself against Pujara's full face, soft hands and yogi-like patience.

India began the last day of this extraordinary Test series needing only a draw to retain the Border–Gavaskar Trophy. So they did not chase the 324 runs they needed so much as stalk them, gradually and stealthily. The point was to bat through, to stay the distance so that the objective remained in view for long enough to be a legitimate option, to draw the sting from Australia's marauding pacemen so that a final push was possible after tea. And no batsman goes through like Pujara, not to mention round, under and over.

Pujara reminds me of that line of Harold Pinter's about Sir Leonard Hutton's forward defensive shot being 'a complete statement'. India's number three starts with that unvarying communion with his bat, setting his grip low on the handle, the 'V' of the hands in line. At the point of contact, the bat is tight into the body, its face almost withdrawing from the ball as it delays contact as long as possible – Pujara gets beaten on the outside edge from time to time, but very seldom on the inside. The ball is not simply blocked; it is neutralised; it is terminated with extreme prejudice. It drops to the ground heavily, as though it weighs a tonne.

One expects this of Pujara, of course, but he yesterday recruited the whole of his body in the act of resistance, as he was bombarded by Hazlewood and Pat Cummins with short leg and leg gully. It is a hard thing to be hit by a cricket ball; it is harder still to volunteer to let a ball hit you. One lost count of how often Pujara was struck and consented to be struck: helmet, gloves, ribs, hip. At one point the broadcasters showed a diagram of where each blow had landed, with little cricket balls superimposed on a photograph of the batsman, who was, a little incongruously, smiling. The smile, however, was not misplaced. By prolonging his resistance into the eighty-first over, and only being dislodged by the new ball, he made the games of others possible – viz Shubman Gill and Rishabh Pant.

A scary thought, for bowlers, is that Gill is twenty-one. He has time, in every respect. He has a young man's face, almost an air of innocence. He hangs back, leg side of the ball, in the modern fashion; he waits until it seems almost too late; then, and only then, does he play, right under the eyes. He has a shot all his own, a half-cut, half-drive off the back foot with a diagonal bat that is sure to be named for him, although he plays it so naturally it feels like it should always have existed.

Above all, Gill has nerve. He hooked Starc in the air despite two men back; he slashed Starc over slip despite a deep third man; Starc's twelfth over went for 20. The only regret India might harbour about Gill is having ignored him in favour of Prithvi Shaw in Adelaide.

Rishabh Pant did not play in Adelaide either, when India were bustled and bullied out in their second innings for 36 – how long ago that seems! Funnily enough, had India been dismissed for 150 that day, and Wriddhiman Saha perhaps scrounged 20 together, Pant might still be an onlooker.

As it was, the visitors felt compelled to replace the superior gloveman with the better batsman. If he felt the pressure of that, Pant never showed it, and certainly not yesterday, so relaxed at the crease that he might as well have been whistling. Far from being daunted by the approaching target, Pant played shots like wisecracks: cheeky sweeps, slogs out of the rough, a fall-over ramp, a fall-over pull. If Pujara is India's centre of gravity, Pant is its centre of levity.

The Indians also benefited by their staunch last day fight at Sydney, which left Australian legs leaden, and by another Australian pitch that did not really deteriorate – for which, it's worth noting, drop-in technology cannot be blamed. There was some variation in bounce, occasional sharp turn. But whether the prohibition on saliva was the cause, as has been the case all summer, they could conjure little from ball, orthodox or reverse. Hazlewood finished the day with a full toss, decisively driven, thwarted by multiple factors as well as his opponents. One might well have called it the butterfly effect.

Border–Gavaskar Trophy 2020–21

PHOTO CALL (2021)

At first glance, this photograph of India's cricket squad in the aftermath of their stunning victory at the Gabba on Tuesday is like myriad others, lots of big smiles and pumped fists, to be filed under 'Winning team celebrates as winning teams tend to'.

When summing up India's success in retaining the Border–Gavaskar Trophy, however, the picture is worth at least the 1000 words I'll write about it here, partly because I can think of few teams come to these shores who have depended so much on one another as Ajinkya Rahane's happy band.

For a start, look at how many of them there are, players, coaches and officials. It had to be that way, because of the business of introducing new names to the biosecure enclosure. As we know, India had to call on a score of cricketers in the four Tests as their ranks were raked by injury, and in Virat Kohli's case imminent paternity. When only eleven can play at any one time, and there are no tour games between times, that is an awful lot of players to keep fully involved.

The English footballer Rodney Marsh once said that a manager only had to keep eleven players happy: the members of the second XI; the first XI are happy because they are in the firsts. Yet you would not know here who had played what, when and with what success. For example, there is nothing sheepish about the celebrations of Prithvi Shaw and Kuldeep Yadav, who wear whites despite having barely played on tour at all.

Perhaps the injuries kept everyone on their mettle, even the supernumeraries, for there was a sense one might play at any time. Perhaps, too, that turnover did not work entirely to India's disadvantage. While the team changes were mostly compulsory, they introduced fresh faces, fresh legs and fresh challenges to an intense contest against an Australian team who favour planning, discipline and repetition.

What else? The formal team photograph is a hierarchical genre: senior players sitting, juniors standing, maybe tall guys in the centre up the back. The groupings we form for ourselves are inherently more suggestive. This image, then, accents the youth and comparative inexperience of Rahane's team by placing the youngest players at its centre. The four players closest to the Border–Gavaskar Trophy are among its most junior members: none of Mohammed Siraj, Rishabh Pant, Navdeep Saini or Mayank Agarwal played all four Tests; the three senior pros, Rohit Sharma, Cheteshwar Pujara and Ravi Ashwin are peering over the back.

The coaching staff look just as happy as the players but by composing on the flanks defer to them nonetheless. Head coach Ravi Shastri has never been so inconspicuous. The captain? Were you not familiar with his face, you would not necessarily pick Rahane as leader, except maybe by the faded shade of his cap. He's off to one side, kneeling, an elbow companionably propped on Siraj's knee. His smile lacks the wattage of his colleagues; his hands are not clenched; he radiates in triumph the same moderation he showed on the field.

For purposes of comparison, I rummaged in pic libraries for comparable images of Indian celebration after the Sydney Test two years ago. It may not surprise you to hear that Kohli, for whom the tour was a kind of personal crusade, featured at the centre of almost all of them, caressing the trophy with a proprietorial air. Rahane does not feel the same need to be centre of attention, although he was quite capable of leading by example. He scored the only Indian century of the series; his cameo of 24 off twenty-two balls on Tuesday was crucial in demonstrating Indian intent.

Nor did Rahane sense any obligation to out-Aussie the Aussies. One weird expression of Australian *amour propre* is the affectation of conferring unofficial Australianness on successful visitors. At the top of this tour, for example, Greg Chappell judged Kohli 'the most Australian non-Australian cricketer of all time', which was meant to be an approbation, but just sounded condescending. So good he's almost an Aussie, eh? Oh, pass me the sick bag . . .

Rahane calls for no such absurdities. He could hail from no other country, and he led India exactly as anyone would have expected who knew anything of him: bravely but calmly, adventurously but humbly. You can imagine his quiet team talks causing everyone to lean in so as not to miss a word. You can imagine his insistence on dignity and decorum in victory and defeat alike. On Tuesday night, rather than bask in his team's success, Rahane first invited Nathan Lyon to the microphone to present him with a shirt signed by the Indian team on the occasion of the Australian's one hundredth Test. Lyon applauded, as well he might.

Perhaps this also derives from a feeling of having Australia's measure in the Border–Gavaskar Trophy. Two years ago when

India won for the first time down under, it was regarded as a great and sudden shift in the countries' cricket relations. In fact, the change has been far more gradual, and over the course of two decades. Commencing with that phenomenal turnabout match in Kolkata in March 2001, India have won nineteen Tests to Australia's fourteen – a minus record of the kind decidedly rare in our annals.

They have fans here now to cancel out the Australian noise advantage. They're wise to our tricks: the manufactured on-field confrontations, the tired off-field bullshit (they broke the quarantine, they're afraid of Brisbane, they won't make their own beds etc.). And day-in, day-out, chasteningly, they are better than we are. So if the members of this team look confident, who can blame them?

Nagpur Test 2023, Day 2

MURPHY V ROHIT (2023)

Finger spinners making eye-catching Test debuts ten years apart: Todd Murphy and Ashton Agar have a bit in common. But two days into Murphy's career, their paths are already diverging.

Trent Bridge 2013: the memory is still fresh as day of Agar's improbable dash as last man, dragging Australia back from the brink in a tight-wound Test. The slow bowling for which Agar had actually been chosen was still unpolished, tidy but unmenacing. Still, we told ourselves, time was on his side.

Ten years, much patience and considerable investment later, maybe not. The way Murphy confirmed Australia's selection preference for him here has suggested a bowler waiting for no-one. The seeds in cricket's garden germinate and blossom at different rates: having opened on the first day here, Murphy yesterday bloomed.

You can already imagine kids imitating him: windmilling arms à la Graeme Swann, upturned collar buttoned high like Michael Clarke, circular spectacles like ... well, like Todd Murphy. They are already his look, his style, part of his owlish charisma. He has been impressing hard-to-impress judges for years already, and so far appears to have no ceiling: every step up, now including Test cricket, has been taken in his stride.

Make no mistake, this was a challenge to Murphy's precocity. A small total to defend; only three other bowlers; a phalanx of batters for whom finger spin holds few terrors. But it was not long before he looked not only the part but almost the senior spinner, allotted the preferred slow bowler's end in a spell of 14-4-40-3 broken only by lunch.

Murphy picked the plan, whirling quickly from round the wicket, endangering the stumps as Ravi Jadeja and Ravi Ashwin had the previous day: he commenced, in fact, by Ashwinning Ashwin, coaxing India's primo off-spinner into playing round a tentative front pad.

For most of the time, the twenty-two-year-old was content with a single outfielder, and manoeuvred his formations constantly, even his captain, whom at one stage in the afternoon he motioned a metre or two straighter. Cummins responded with a cheerful thumbs up.

As his Victorian skipper Peter Handscomb remarked the previous night, Murphy needs little counsel; he always appears to know exactly what he wants. Cheteshwar Pujara's miscued sweep spooned to where Scott Boland had been precisely placed, at 45 degrees.

Virat Kohli was the one gimme, giving in to temptation and following a drag-down – the feather down leg was juggled but held by Alex Carey. Spinners cherish such poles: they feel like God's apology for slogging's impertinence. Murphy disappeared into his team's embrace, welcomed like a homecoming son.

When Suryakumar Yadav's debut Test innings ended with a brief razzle-dazzle, Australia appeared to have lassoed runaway India. They were assuredly restrained, but Rohit Sharma wasn't going anywhere in a hurry. He seldom is.

Nobody in world cricket moves so economically as India's captain. You get the impression that he would, were it permissible, prefer to bat sitting down. Contrasted with the trim, taut Kohli, he is built on observably generous lines – not Inzamam generous, but maybe Warne comfortable. His resting expression, placid and herbivorous, seldom changes.

Yet, somehow, Rohit always gets there. Despite no elaborate prefatory trigger movements, he is always found in perfect position at point of contact. On a slow pitch such as this, he seems to have more spare time than a man at a bus stop. His bat, pale and broad, sends check drives zooming.

There were a few strokes of violence: from Cummins, a hooked six and a pulled four. Rohit went to his 171-ball, 263-minute hundred by hitting Murphy inside out over cover, which was in its way a tribute: it was his first such stroke. He had to hasten once only, diving for the crease after being sent back by Kohli: at lunch the dusty shirt was carried reverently from one side of the ground to the other by a BCCI minion.

Cummins got a measure of his own back by extracting Rohit's off stump after tea with the second new ball, which he also correctly intuited might suit Murphy. Five wickets on a spinner's debut is not so uncommon: it's two months since teenager Rehan Ahmed achieved the feat for England. But Murphy already has the look of one capable of holding fast to a seized opportunity.

On the field while Matthew Renshaw went for a knee scan, meanwhile, was Ashton Agar, a limber figure beneath his back-tilted sun hat running here and there, wondering perhaps if and when he might next command a place in the XI.

Nagpur Test 2023, Day 3

THE LAST ROUND-UP (2023)

When Ravi Jadeja beat Marnus Labuschagne with his first ball after lunch at VCA Stadium Jamtha yesterday, smiles and smirks broke out across the field. Even the batter turned appreciatively towards the replay on the big screen, to study the sharp turn, the telltale dust puff. It was going to be one of those days.

Make that one of those sessions, which two hours later was all over, in dusty disillusionment. We'd taken on faith that Pat Cummins's team deserved their number one Test ranking, on the basis of streeting teams on flat surfaces at home. We'd trusted that this was a new Australia, more experienced in and better equipped for what we, a little lazily, elide as 'Asian conditions'.

It had even seemed a good omen that the venue of the First Test was Nagpur, scene of perhaps the finest Australian performance in India in half a century – their series-clinching win in 2004. It will now be associated with one of their most abject: an eight-session pantsing, in challenging but far from impossible conditions, ending with their lowest total in this country.

No Australian batter made a fifty; only two faced more than a hundred balls. Spinners took 80 per cent of the wickets in the match, but Australia's senior slow bowler only one. The *soidisant* people's champion, Usman Khawaja, totalled six runs; the nation's recent favourite, Scott Boland, went wicketless, and dropped a soda. A team confident it could not only cover the convalescences of Mitchell Starc, Josh Hazlewood and Cameron Green but also leave out Travis Head experienced the rudest awakening.

It started badly and did not improve when Ravi Ashwin took the new ball from the President's End. Khawaja stroked a boundary, then drove out of the rough – a naive shot to complete an anonymous match for the world's eighth ranked Test batter. The contrast from the morning, when the Indian tail had wagged vigorously, was palpable: abruptly the field seemed bigger, the ball smaller, the bounce lower, the rough rougher.

Out of this, the ball spun inconsistently, sometimes a little, sometimes a lot, generally away, as left-handers David Warner and Matthew Renshaw saw most of Ashwin, right-handers Labuschagne and Steve Smith most of Ravi Jadeja. The sense was that India had the Australians pretty much where they wanted, right down to the ends.

From this unforgiving scenario, Warner could scratch no more than two singles in his first thirty-eight deliveries, during which a sharp chance from his edge also eluded Kohli's right hand. He had no sooner disposed of consecutive over-pitched deliveries than he was tripped up by a third that hit his padded ankle.

On the eve of the tour, Renshaw described Ashwin as a 'smart bowler', but 'you do get used to him once you've faced him for a while'. Strictly speaking this remains true, as it was to only his seventh ball that he played back fatally, leaving Australia 4/42. Had this been a ship, rats would by now have been deserting it. So much for the plans. These dissolved into such plans as survivors make on lifeboats.

Peter Handscomb played well forward; Alex Carey deployed his repertoire of sweeps. Neither saved them from lbw. Carey's reverse sweep, so formidable in Pakistan and Sri Lanka last year, here got him out twice, just as Steve Smith was beaten twice on the inside – the latter was lucky that Jadeja cut the crease the second time.

Let nothing detract from India's consummate professionalism. Before lunch, Axar Patel and Mohammed Shami had prolonged India's innings to the point of pain, worsened by their both offering chances that should have been taken.

At number nine, Axar Patel should be charged with false pretences: he is masquerading as a humble bowler in the face of overwhelming evidence that he bats well enough to be in most countries' top sixes. His defence is watertight, he hits a long ball, and with a bit more support at the other end would have reached a maiden Test century.

After play on Friday night, Mohammed Shami took three quarters of an hour of throwdowns on the outfield from a perspiring colleague – impressive commitment from one who accumulated half a dozen consecutive Test noughts four years ago. But Shami has worked hard on his batting these last couple of years, taking a couple of half-centuries off England, and here enjoyed a licence to indulge his pet slog.

Boland should have caught him off Lyon at long-on when he was 6, which would have reduced India to 9/337 and spared Todd Murphy being hit for consecutive sixes. But by now the match was, as they say in these parts, in fast forward, and only getting faster: 10×, 30×, 60× etc. At one point in the afternoon, despite the Australians' increasingly frantic recourse to the third umpire, India were fourteen overs ahead of the required rate: it was like the players had somewhere else to be.

What of the pitch? It further verified the saying about never judging a surface until both teams have batted. Any surface where one team makes 400 deserves at least one tick, no matter what else transpires. In contrasting the performances, we are also talking about the difference between batting in pursuit of a small first innings, and batting under the cosh of a 200-run arrears.

Australia's failure, then, was not yesterday, but on the first day, when 174 was a poor use of success at the toss. If the pitch was fated to break up, as the team suspected, we will now never know: the match has simply not lasted long enough. Were this a murder, we would be silently congratulating the killer on disposing of the body.

Factors slowing the pitch's deterioration included the relatively mild temperatures, and the limited involvement of heavy-booted fast bowlers – what the players now call 'traffic'. But one other factor overrode all others: Indian's overwhelming superiority.

Indore Test 2023, Day 1

THE WIDENING GYRE (2023)

Shoe? Meet other foot. At Indore, India have not prepared a pitch as bad as either at Nagpur or Delhi; they have produced something worse, a surface with a touch of Yeats about it: things are falling apart, the centres aren't holding, and the ball is turning and turning in the widening gyre.

Yesterday, however, the hosts were caught in their own snare. On a pitch they hand-picked as the driest of three options, Rohit Sharma's team indulged in batting as frenetic as Australia's in the first two Tests – an excess of enfeebling wokeness, no doubt. Australia, meanwhile, exhibited some of the resilience they developed last year in Pakistan and Sri Lanka, largely abjuring those neo-Marxist sweep shots.

By the afternoon, the world had turned topsy-turvy, Australia patiently defending, India combustibly burning reviews, Rohit arms akimbo and thinking cap tilted back. Who knows what is coming next? They talk of fast-forward cricket in these parts; this Border–Gavaskar Trophy series is hurtling along at warp speed.

For Australia, the start had actually boded ill. With Shubman Gill partaking of some rusty half-volleys from Cameron Green,

India were 0/26 after five overs, with one 145 km/h delivery from Mitchell Starc having bounced twice before reaching Alex Carey.

With the introduction of spin in the sixth over, however, batting looked an entirely different proposition, Starc's footfall having already disturbed and discoloured the pitch at the Scindia End, a little morning moisture perhaps helping the ball grip. Matthew Kuhnemann demonstrated precisely why Australia's selectors have been obsessed with equipping their team with a left-arm spinner, even if he is not the one they first chose.

Kuhnemann settled at once on a probing, fullish length, eliciting little plumes of dust as the ball landed. His sixth delivery turned sharply, and Carey executed an excellent stumping to punish Rohit's frolic down the pitch – a culpable, even slightly apathetic, shot.

Obliged to defend, Shubman Gill, finally preferred to KL Rahul, then pushed too hard and nicked to Steve Smith. But no footmarks were necessary when Nathan Lyon spun his second ball almost at right angles to beat Cheteshwar Pujara's diagonal bat and withdrawing back leg.

Ravi Jadeja, promoted to interrupt India's bunched right-handers, then showed the other peril of batting on pitches such as these, fastening overenthusiastically on some width, and picking out cover: it is not only the deviation that kills you here, but the desperation to seize such scoring opportunities as are offered.

No sooner had Shreyas Iyer impetuously dragged a ball from Kuhnemann onto his stumps that barely bounced than five members of the ground staff appeared with brooms, buckets and paintbrushes, patches of the square's red clay already resembling the surface of Mars. Flecks of green on the pitch's mid-section were at best misleading, like those imagined Martian canals.

Having found the boundary thrice early, Virat Kohli was subdued by Todd Murphy, adding seven singles in thirty-five balls of solemn defence, tested by the angle from round the wicket. Presently, beaten on the outside the previous over, Kohli was beaten on the inside and adjudged lbw – his first real error, but one is all it takes.

When KS Bharat stretched forward without quite stretching outside the line and Ashwin erred the other way either side of lunch, India was in danger of failing to reach three figures. Umesh Yadav cheered the crowd with some slogging, but Axar Patel, compact, calm-browed and easy on the eye, was let down by last man Mohammed Siraj's delinquent running.

India compounded their sloppiness with the bat with the ball, Jadeja obtaining a second wicket in the series from a no ball, leaving Labuschagne free to repent what had been a repeat of his shot in the second innings at Delhi. It all smacked of undue hurry – a gung-ho desire to finish Australia off that made no allowance for the very conditions the home team had designed. When India finally turned to pace, Yadav, in the twenty-first over of Australia's reply, and Siraj in the thirty-fourth, it felt like a significant moral victory, for they posed as little threat as Starc and Green.

With whatever early moisture long gone, the pitch proved to repay conscientious defence. Labuschagne and Khawaja, bat ahead of pad when playing forward, carefully allowing access to the ball while playing back, closely studied the bounce.

This is now varying from low to lower, trending towards the lower still – as Labuschagne found after tea, when Jadeja beat his backstroke with something flatter and faster that went on with the arm. Australia, of course, must bat last here, which looked at one stage like being today. Whatever happens, don't take your eye off that gyre.

Indore Test 2023, Day 3

ONE DAY AT HOLKAR (2023)

8 a.m. Steve Smith, cap on backwards, one pad on, shadow bats on the pitch at Holkar Cricket Stadium, where he might later be part of the Australian chase for 76. He looks absorbed. His movements are minimal. It's his mind he's tuning not his body.

8.30 a.m. Peter Handscomb does the same and Nathan Lyon follows, standing where the previous day India's batters had lined up for his delectation. The Australians look relaxed in their warm-ups, although Lyon then also takes throwdowns. If it's up to him later . . .

9 a.m. 'Can India Fight Back?' asks Star Sports 1 as its coverage resumes. Well, yes, is the message of its opening montage, which intersperses footage of anguished Australian batters reeling in confusion from Indian wiles. We see a house of cards. On fire. Then crashing to the ground. Then being crushed by an avalanche and enveloped in a mushroom cloud. Okay, I made up the last bit, but you get the idea.

9.30 a.m. Usman Khawaja takes strike. Ravi Ashwin takes the new ball, sauntering up with that approach that always looks like a man trying to unscrew a tight bottle top. He opens up Australia at once. The second ball grazes Khawaja's outside edge as he plays forward, as confirmed on review.

9.32 a.m. 'How are we feeling today?' says a text from a former Australian cricketer, who admits his hands are shaking as he sends it.

9.36 a.m. Jadeja windmills his arms at the Members End, Travis Head works his first ball to leg, and Australia now need . . . 75 to win.

9.38 a.m. Jadeja beckons his off-side sweeper and Labuschagne gets four where he might have got one. A little fillip. Then he looks penitent as his edge is beaten.

9.40 a.m. Ashwin, the first bowler in history to obtain the wickets of 200 left-handed batters, bowls to left-handed Head, Test average in Asia less than 20. He defends, flirts and misses, twice, by a lot. There is a foot of daylight between bat and ball. Crikey.

9.44 a.m. Labuschagne works a single off Jadeja. A grubber that Head digs out with a gravedigger's shovel. Gill sticks a hand out at second slip to stymie a single. Detente.

9.46 a.m. These spinners don't give you much time, eh? Ashwin has Head defending round his ankles, trying to overhit a cut, and finally bunting a single down the ground. Nobody moving on the Australian balcony. Are they even breathing?

9.49 a.m. Rohit tinkering. Wants a short mid-wicket. There's a leg-bye. Labuschagne cuts at something too full, reminding me of the Yorkshireman's admonition: 'T'cut nivver were a business stroke.' The sharp leg-side single is better.

9.53 a.m. Ashwin to Labuschagne, with men back for the sweep and the slog-sweep. Another ball tunnels beneath the bat, another balloons off the pad, and the mercurial Kohli dives for the 'catch' at leg slip. He's heard something; the stump mics have not.

9.56 a.m. Head throws his hands at Jadeja, thick edges into space. Labuschagne mimes squatting in defence. Ten runs in half an hour. On the balcony, Steve Smith's normally expressive face is a mask.

10 a.m. Ashwin again. Labuschagne won't be hurried. He watches a replay; he draws attention to the flutter of the sightscreen, to motion in the crowd. Joel Wilson has a stern word, Rohit Sharma a friendlier one. A single down the ground. A little mental win.

10.06 a.m. Jadeja appeals for lbw, but the ball has pitched outside leg. Otherwise Labuschagne bends forward, a statue of defence.

10.09 a.m. The umpires agree with Ashwin that the ten-over-old ball needs changing, which superstitious cricketers suggest can bring about a change of luck. It does. Head poaches 13 off the over, including a sweetly struck six into the Nayudu Stand. Ashwin is immediately interested in another ball. No is the answer.

10.17 a.m. Now Head pumps Jadeja back over his head and hearty applause breaks out on the Australian balcony, which continues when Labuschagne sweeps for four. Turns out he didn't need that Hayden masterclass after all. Forty-one to win.

10.21 a.m. Labuschagne comes down the wicket to defend, then to attack, stroking Ashwin through cover, causing the bowler to come over the wicket. A joke or two on the balcony, although everyone remains in their seats.

10.24 a.m. Head cuts an extra micron of width from Jadeja, then slog-sweeps for four. Rohit pushes his cap back, which he does when perplexed by the unfamiliar – like, in this case, India's first defeat in a home Test against Australia in six years.

10.26 a.m. Ashwin is getting desperate. It happens even to him. Too full in his previous over, he now drops short, and Head reduces the victory target to less than 30 through cover.

Drinks arrive after Labuschagne reverse sweeps for four. Suddenly, the pressure is escaping and there's a hint of brio about the Australians.

10.32 a.m. Finally Umesh Yadav, round the wicket to Head. Too early for the reverse he obtained in the first innings surely. Head coshes the third ball through cover and it races away over an outfield as flawless as the pitch has been lousy.

10.37 a.m. Three singles off Ashwin. Destiny beckons.

10.41 a.m. Umesh again. It's reversing, but Labuschagne pulls a bouncer meatily for four, and it's eight runs to win.

10.45 a.m. Early tremors behind him, Head pumps Ashwin straight for four. Labuschagne has a rush of blood, gets tangled in his advancing feet, miscues into the ground. Once bitten, never shy, he repeats the shot successfully and Australia has won by nine wickets.

Smith scampers down the steps in his pads to welcome the partners in. Star Sports 1 has thrown to a commercial. Ground staff starts watering the pitch. Better late than never.

11.35 a.m. Having, it turns out, had nothing to do but watch, Smith walks into the press conference. He's in his whites, cap facing forward, face unmoving, tone even, sentiments muted. Then a smile breaks through. 'It's been a good week,' he consents. It sure has.

Border–Gavaskar Trophy 2023

THE LOSING CYCLE

Steve Smith's captaincy in the Indore Test has been rightly praised for its acumen and flair, but he saved perhaps his deftest flourish for the post-match press conference.

The pitch, Steve: tell us about the pitch. 'All the wickets have spun,' Australia's locum captain began non-committally. 'We haven't gotten past three days yet so that shows that it's been spinning from day one in all the Test matches.'

Then: 'But personally I really enjoy playing on these kind of wickets. I prefer this than just a genuine flat wicket that goes five days and can be boring in stages. There's always something happening on these wickets. You've got to really work hard for your runs. But it's showed that the guys can do it.'

If Smith wasn't so ingenuous, you'd call this A-grade trolling. The Board of Control for Cricket in India provided a garbage fire: Smith has pulled up a chair and praised its cosiness. The International Cricket Council has, rightly, censured the Holkar Stadium's wretched surface. Narendra Modi's predecessor as prime minister Manmohan Singh once called India a rich country inhabited by very poor people; the BCCI appears to be a rich organisation replete with poor pitches. And abruptly, the BCCI find themselves facing a dilemma, their bluff called. Australia's spinners were as serviceable in Indore as India's. Matthew Kuhnemann even joked about moving here. And India's batters are now struggling every bit as much if not more than Australia's.

Worse, this is for India the continuation of a long-term trend. Since Australia drew in Ranchi six years ago, only three Tests in India have seen a fifth day; since the start of last year, Tests have averaged not much more than 300 overs.

Somewhere along the line, the idea that dusty, desiccated pitches were useful to India toppled over into the conviction that they were necessary, even essential. Nobody expects other than conditions friendly to spin in India; but their being inimical to batting is relatively new and frankly corrosive.

Historically, Indian batting has been a great glory. But since the last Border–Gavaskar Trophy, Kohli and Pujara average 25 and 23.2 respectively at home. The imperative of reinforcing one strength has inflicted collateral damage on another.

To watch Kohli's struggles in this series has been tortuous, like watching a great thespian reduced to farce, a mighty novelist condemned to writing jingles; it is symbolic of the overall eclipse of his influence since he surrendered the captaincy.

The motif of Kohli's leadership was the idea that India could beat anyone anywhere anytime. DRS? Bring it on. Winning on the road? Let's do it. The Kohli doctrine reached its fullest expression at the Gabba in January 2021, when India bearded Australia in its own den. An excellent newly published retelling of that series, by my colleagues Bharat Sundaresan and Gaurav Joshi, is titled *The Miracle Makers*.

But maybe India overinvested in the idea of a miracle. After all, it was not providence that won them the Border–Gavaskar Trophy but excellence in depth. How else to explain the strange drift back to old ways, the defensive frame of mind that India must have everything in its favour to win?

Perhaps it's to do with the BCCI's capture by the Bharatiya Janata Party, its harnessing to nationalist agendas: the risk of defeat, of going without a familiar psychological blanket, has become too difficult to countenance. Perhaps it's the conspiratorial cast of mind that sees everyone else as up to something, and therefore anything is justified – something of which Australia were guilty during Sandpapergate.

Whatever the case, it feels like short-term gain for long-term sacrifice. It weakens India's claims to being a top-class team; it undermines appreciation of their best players.

The Ravis, Ashwin and Jadeja, are superb bowlers – skilled, crafty and thoroughly watchable. But will there now not lurk some suspicion that their records have been padded by tailored conditions? Most spinners benefit by turning surfaces. Great spinners are distinguished by their defensive skills, their ability to bowl well on a range of pitches. What are we learning of this pair that we did not know already? Are their capacities being genuinely tested?

In Australia, Shubman Gill looked like the most gifted batter of the next generation. How is he to build the basis of the career that may await him if every pitch is a lottery, every game over in three days? In Australia, Mohammed Siraj appeared to be the most exciting Indian pace prospect since Ishant Sharma in 2007–08. In the last three Tests, he has been allocated two-dozen overs for one wicket – essentially a paid holiday. In Indore, he bowled six overs, made a pair, fielded indifferently.

Over time, furthermore, poor conditions can equalise rival teams, narrowing gaps between teams rather than widening them. The pitch becomes the opposition. Chance enters into the equation and exerts outsize influence. All very fascinating, as Smith observes. But less so if it should become the default model of Test match cricket and a disservice to the players of both sides.

Border–Gavaskar Trophy 2023
CRICKET'S MODI QUESTION

India's Gujarat being a dry state, you won't be able to avail yourself of a beer at the Fourth Test in Ahmedabad. But if you like your cricket with a side serve of fascistic ostentation, the climax of the Border–Gavaskar Trophy in Ahmedabad will be right up your alley.

The first day will begin as a cricket match within a political rally, India's Prime Minister Narendra Modi felicitating himself at the gargantuan stadium bearing his name as his Australian counterpart Anthony Albanese looks on, its first political visitor since Donald Trump, with that faintly queasy politeness that these days passes for diplomacy.

The players will be introduced by their respective prime ministers. To ensure a suitably ecstatic throng, the bulk of the tickets were 'set aside' in advance for 'local families and students' by the Board of Control for Cricket in India, in its role as propaganda wing of Modi's Bharatiya Janata Party and the Gujarat Cricket Association, where Modi was president during his long, chilling and viciously sectarian rule as the state's chief minister.

Before one of the world's great authoritarians will be paraded Steve Smith's Australians, including Usman Khawaja, whose co-religionists were slaughtered and displaced in their thousands twenty-one years ago during the pogroms following the Godhra train burning while security forces answering to Modi remained mysteriously inactive. Strange that in Australia there's all that sensitivity to Khawaja being anywhere near a can of VB, but here nobody's fussed about his being placed in uncomfortable proximity to a political leader whose whole career has been characterised by demonising and disenfranchising India's Muslims.

Hey, look, I get it: the idea of 'friendship through cricket' holds enormous appeal. When Indian and Australian teams take the field, there's something powerful and inspiriting about their heritage as representatives of colonised lands who took to and mastered an English game, in their similarities and their differences. And Modi Stadium, awe-inspiring in its Legoland brutalism, has in prospect a match worthy of its extraordinary dimensions.

This is also an area in which cricket and politics blend as a matter of course. It was a Gujarati, the off-spinner Jasu Patel, who with 14/124 engineered India's first Test win against Australia in 1960. It was a Gujarati, India's first home minister, Sardar Patel, for whom was named Ahmedabad's first stadium to host a Test.

But there's an irony to this. It was Patel, a partner of Gandhi's in the Indian freedom struggle, who temporarily banned the Rashtriya Swayamsevak Sangh – the Hindu nationalist paramilitaries from which had emerged Gandhi's assassin, and from which would emerge the BJP. Today India's home minister is the unappetising Amit Shah, who like Modi started his career in the RSS's youth wing, who became Modi's closest political confidante and successor as president of the Gujarat

Cricket Association, and whose son Jay is secretary of the BCCI and cricket's number one nepo baby.

It's all very cosy, not to say incestuous. Jay, for example, has appointed a septuagenarian Gujarati policeman to run the BCCI's anti-corruption unit, while the GCA is run by the Ambani group executive who helped organise Trump's bizarre 2020 visit (where Trump expressed pleasure at visiting 'Ahdabard' and admiration for 'Soo-chin Tendul-kerr'). Passing through the atrium of Modi Stadium, one gazes up at giant images of Modi and Shah, in their familiar double act as narcissist and enabler. They are quite the partnership, and this Test and this stadium play to their strengths in staging spectacles of power.

The pair have also honed the time-honoured repertoire of political strong men everywhere: intimidation of rivals, subversion of institutions, falsifications of history, manufacture of conspiracies, and the pretence that criticism of their rule is a wound to national pride. Thus the Modi government's frantic efforts to suppress the BBC's two-part documentary series *The Modi Question*, which screened in January, though not in India, where it was predictably decried as 'lacking objectivity' and evidencing a 'colonialist mindset'. Needless to say, Modi takes the same attitude to the media as Tommy Docherty: 'There's a place for the press but they haven't dug it yet.'

While concentrating carefully on matters of public record, *The Modi Question* is a vivid depiction of the Modi operandi and its many victims. It not only should have been available to Indians but deserves an audience in Australia – in fact, Albanese should be taxed on the question of a) whether he has seen it; and b) whether he thinks others should be able to.

One area the BBC neglected, however, is the increasing overlap of cricket with government messaging – a phenomenon first noted four years ago in the wake of the terrorist suicide bombing of a military convoy in disputed Jammu and Kashmir, after which India took to the field in an ODI against Australia wearing commemorative camouflage caps.

Modi has used India's cricket successes abroad in his political rhetoric; cricketers' social media accounts have echoed Modi causes, from voter turnout to political protests. In December, Ravi Jadeja was even part of his wife Rivaba's successful campaign for the BJP in Jamnagar North in the Gujarat assembly elections. 'Our thinking is one and [we] have [the] same ideology,' volunteered Rivaba.

Politicians have always welcomed themselves to a share in national sporting achievement; cricketers are also perfectly entitled to political beliefs. But in indulging the game's recruitment for the purposes of political symbolism, Australian cricket, and Australia, bat on a turning wicket at which their opponents are a great deal more practised and skilful. The ever-prickly BCCI is reported to be considering a challenge to the International Cricket Council's deeming Holkar Cricket Stadium's a 'poor' pitch for the Third Test. The council, of course, has a record of accommodation where India is concerned.

After all, imagine if the ICC paid serious heed to article 2.4 of its constitution, to the effect that every member of the council 'must manage its affairs autonomously and ensure that there is no government (or other public or quasi-public body) interference in its governance, regulation and/or administration of Cricket in its Cricket Playing Country'. That's cricket's Modi question.

Ahmedabad Test 2023, Day 1

USMAN OF THE YEAR (2023)

Since the start of 2011, Australia have played 124 Test matches. Usman Khawaja has played in fewer than half of these. It is an anomaly to tax future historians, that a batter whose average is now swelling towards 50 was in his time regularly overlooked in favour of rivals averaging in the mid-30s.

Least affected by this, however, seems Khawaja, who in taking each innings as it comes has recalibrated Australian batting since the beginning of last year, moving it beyond its former axes of Smith–Warner and Smith–Labuschagne. As this innings in Ahmedabad came, it loomed as one of his most important. You'd hardly have known it.

The opener has it tough at times like these. As players looked on at all the morning's diplomatic rigmarole, lining up for the delectation of their respective prime ministers, Khawaja stood in his pads, required to focus on the near future as well as the present.

As he and Travis Head emerged to commence Australia's innings after the hour's ceremony, it was almost to the sound of their own feet, as though the crowd had forgotten about the day's cricket component. Mohammed Shami started with an arthritic wide outside the tram lines, then four wides that eluded KS Bharat's clutches.

When Bharat shelled Head in the sixth over, the replay was delayed by highlights of Narendra Modi and Anthony Albanese waving from the back of their toy town chariot. Into the contest Khawaja eased himself, never beaten, barely hurried, with the aim of something lasting – something, in fact, whose influence would linger beyond its end and potentially shape the rest of the match.

Khawaja's natural rhythm suited the task. He sets a pace whereby innings can seem to occur around him. His hands are so soft against spin in defence that it's as though the ball merely rubs against the bat rather than hitting it.

There is a suavity even to Khawaja's saunter down the pitch between overs; his glove punches are perfunctory, like he's almost too cool for them. When Ashwin twice feinted a non-striker's run out, Khawaja was found motionless, a pillar of rectitude. When drinks came on, he wrapped a towel round his neck, relaxed as a beach holidaymaker.

As he reached his fourteenth Test hundred in the day's last over, there was a sense of his having hit budget: three figures and not a penny more or less. It was in keeping with a day of Test cricket as we knew it, as distinct from as we have known it in this series, on the best pitch rolled out so far: slow but sound, taking a little wear.

In the presence of Narendra Modi and Anthony Albanese, the day did not start out that way. Modi Stadium, the world's largest cricket ground, is very much in Modi's spirit: stern, joyless, heavy on the saffron. Like the measurements of Modi's Putinesque chest, reports of its capacity vary. Is it 110,000? Is it 130,000? In India's Hindu triumphalist press it's probably a million and anyone saying otherwise is guilty of treason. The views are excellent, except in the press box, distant and obstructed – the view from which Modi looks best too.

The ground was about half-full at 8.37 a.m. as festivities began, with Ravi Shastri booming greetings from the microphone he arguably hardly needs. As the teams had been confined to the nets for their warm-ups so the prime ministers could be entertained by dancers and felicitated by minions, the cricket presently went out of focus.

The captains dawdled in the middle awaiting the toss as Modi and Albanese took a laborious lap in a car that looked like Noddy's idea of a limousine; the commentators mugged as the pair inched past a 'wall of fame'. Starting time of 9.30 a.m. was beginning to look dicey, players milling about awaiting direction, when the leaders emerged, but hasty handshakes and anthems meant that no time was lost.

Head then took five crisp boundaries in ten ragged deliveries from Umesh, so that Australia surged to 0/56 after a fourteen-over first hour. As the prime ministers exited, however, the Indians composed themselves, the ball softened and runs dwindled. Head shanked to mid-on; Labuschagne contrived to play on. Eight runs accrued in the morning's last ten overs, so Khawaja's sweep for four from the second ball after lunch seemed as festive as Holi. He presently opened the blade to guide Shami to third man for four and register his third half-century of the series – the most of anyone in this series.

Smith, remarkably, remains in search of his first. He practised the same rigid self-denial as at Indore, and suffered a similar dismissal, against the run of play, defending, this time on the inside edge rather than outside. Just as remarkably, thanks to the near subterranean bounce of pitches in these parts, this was the thirtieth bowled dismissal in the series, with the thirty-first coming. Shami's bouncer forced Khawaja to genuflect, and he took a thankful single; the next delivery sent Handscomb's off stump tumbling through space like a wayward javelin.

Two velvety cover-drives from Khawaja, shots of placement not force, restored the visitors' heart, and Cameron Green notified his quality with boundaries in an over from Umesh on the eve of the second new ball. It was the day Australia had hoped for, in a Test where India must bat last. For Khawaja, these games have been worth waiting for.

Ahmedabad Test 2023, Day 3

GILL'S MARKER (2023)

In pursuit of metaphors to convey the day-to-day reality of cricket in India, Australians are apt to talk of games bursting suddenly into 'fast-forward'. The three previous Tests in this Border–Gavaskar Trophy have moved at times so rapidly you've wanted to install speed bumps; yesterday, this Test hit pause, and maybe even rewind, to an earlier time, when batters in India grandly lorded, and bowlers humbly toiled.

Shubman Gill made 128 in 263 balls, a first Test century against Australia – if it is not the first of many, nobody has ever known anything about batting. His previous best against Australia had been an underestimated innings of 90 in India's fabulous win at the Gabba just over two years ago; he may have primed himself on the same ground last month when he became the fifth Indian to achieve centuries in all three formats, hitting twelve fours and seven sixes in an innings of 126 not out in sixty-three balls. Apparently he learned his game on concrete, to which this surface is the nearest turf can come.

In the last over of the previous day, Shubman Gill had driven Lyon for six; he resumed, busy and alert, in a similar mood. Later he was restrained by three-six and even two-seven fields, and his defence punctured on 62 by a ball of Murphy's that exploded from a stray footmark. Travis Head might have run him out with a direct hit from mid-off on 77.

But runs, occasionally scarce, were seldom far away. Gill spurted through the 80s with consecutive shots off his fellow twenty-three-year-old star-in-the-making Cameron Green – a chop through cover point off the back foot and a drive through mid-off off the front foot, disposed of as cursorily as throw-downs. That chop: slightly leg side of the ball, executed with a diagonal bat, it's going to be one of the shots of the next decade.

Green got a smidgen of reverse; Alex Carey came up to the stumps; Gill paid no heed. He swept Todd Murphy to reach his century, celebrating with a decorous bow; he later reverse swept a ball that landed in roughly the same area, a gap having opened to invite him. In the dugout, the overlooked KL Rahul, lumbered with batting at Nagpur and Delhi, may have been watching his career fade in the distance.

Matthew Kuhnemann obtained the only wicket of the day's first half, although he was merely a passive presence in the event, Rohit Sharma overeagerly shovelling to short cover. The highlight of the afternoon looked like being a press box visit by BCCI secretary Jay Shah, son of India's home minister, inconspicuous except for a great circle of rubberneckers, awestruck at this descent from Olympus.

Shah has claims to being the most powerful man in world cricket. In person, only thirty-four, short, stocky and with a head looking slightly too heavy for his body, he might have passed for one of the friendly local IT staff coming to deal with an internet outage. 'Hello,' he said exclusively to *The Australian*, who didn't ask for a selfie. Look, I'm sure he's perfectly fine, fond of children, kind to animals etc. His father, on the other hand . . .

317

Did Steve Smith miss a trick by allotting Todd Murphy only three of the first fifty overs of India's innings? As it was, Murphy's distinctive approach, like a dancer sweeping into a tango, was not seen at length until after drinks in the afternoon, when he bowled a teasing, various and finally successful spell to Cheteshwar Pujara round the wicket to a two-seven field.

As Pujara awaited the review of his lbw verdict, there were heard the first stirrings of excitement at the portent of Kohli. He had been sitting visibly in the team dugout in his pads, attracting admiring glances, occasionally flashing a telegenic smile, trending on Twitter in anticipation.

With Pujara walking off, one half-expected to see Kohli glide past him in the chauffeur-driven sandal in which Narendra Modi and Anthony Albanese were feted on Thursday morning; in the end, he simply floated in on a wave of roars and chants. He had merely to defend his first ball to inspire a tumult.

In fact, just either side of tea, Kohli looked a little tentative, playing and missing twice, edging short of slip and short leg, waiting a dozen balls to get off the mark, and subdued until some boundaries from Starc set him in motion. In the pitch, he soon liked what he saw. Notwithstanding his thin returns in this series, Kohli has invested patiently, in anticipation of a market correction. Nobody should ever short sell him; he is the bluest of blue chips.

Australia plugged away. A few deliveries turned more sharply than in the morning. The new ball was taken in the ninety-fourth over, but Jadeja hit it for six to remind us of India's batting depth. And Kohli, if he was going nowhere fast, was also going nowhere: at stumps he was a vigilant 59 in 128 balls. The day will come to anoint his successor, maybe even Gill, who might be a better fit at number four than opening. But on Test days like today, it feels like all decisions can wait.

Ahmedabad Test 2023, Day 4

DIET KOHLI (2023)

No power on earth was capable of preventing Virat Kohli score his twenty-eighth Test century in Ahmedabad. Adani Group could have started digging for coal at mid-wicket, or prime ministers done donuts on the outfield in the Modimobile. Nothing was coming between India's premier batter and the 42 runs he began the day needing to reach three figures in a Test match after a forty-one-innings hiatus.

I know, I know: every Test batter of quality starts an innings with the glimmer of a hundred in the eye. And Kohli at the crease never appears other than entirely poised and possessed. But while he has looked and sounded the same these last few years, some indefinable quality has been missing, as though we have been watching a very convincing Kohli ChatBot.

It was a phase, of course, of personal change, of fatherhood, of relocation, of maturing. Kohli surrendered the captaincy of Royal Challengers Bangalore; the Indian captaincy surrendered him. The Board of Control for Cricket in India began rolling out pitches that could only have been less hospitable had they been coiled in barbed wire. Was some motivation lacking? Were bowlers maybe looking on their old nemesis with slightly less awe, at least in Test cricket? In that same period, it needs be noted, Kohli averaged 41 in one-day internationals and 57 in T20 internationals.

All we know, really, is that this time last year, Kohli's Test batting average slipped beneath 50, where it had spent the better part of five years, reaching the high-water mark of 55. He came to Ahmedabad with an average of 48.12, without a half-century in this series. Two days watching Australia pile up 480, however, must have had him biting his arm off to get started. The bowlers had their work cut out; the crowd was in his corner; the DRS was gathering cobwebs; the pitch could serve as an extra lane on the NH48 to Mumbai. All he needed was the patience of Browning's low man, who 'goes on adding one to one/His hundred's soon hit'.

Yesterday's 186 in 364 balls was not an innings laced with memorable shots: there was no equivalent of the back foot whizzbang off Chris Woakes at Pune in 2017, or last year's home run off Haris Rauf in Melbourne. At one stage, Star Sports threw to highlights of Kohli during the 2016 Indian Premier League, in case viewers failed to recognise him. The man who once called his bat 'not a toy but a weapon' beat it into ploughshares, a tool of entrenchment.

What kept your interest was the utter security and control. Kohli, a perfectionist, has never regarded defence as beneath him. He derives as much satisfaction from, and can introduce very nearly as much flourish to, a forward push. Again and again yesterday, he stretched out, striking poses of militant neutrality, working towards a kind of platonic ideal of the front foot defensive shot, giving new meaning to the vogue expression 'batting with intent'. On 69, a ball from Lyon glanced his d went down rather than up: no batter is so great that [they] can do without that tincture of luck.

Throughout, Kohli exuded an air of both superfine tuning, quivering slightly in his vigilant stance, and breezy nonchalance, cheerily chatting to his partners and opponents between overs. Tim Paine accused Kohli of loving to 'lord it over the opposition', but that volatile combatant of yore now seems like a stage he was going through. He remains an extrovert: he has, as Bernard Darwin said of WG Grace, never regarded cricket as 'a game to be played in deathless silence'. Now, however, he has the amiability of a neighbour leaning over a fence. Having jogged through for his hundredth run, he emitted no blood-curdling cry nor loosed any suppressed rage – instead he bestowed a mellow kiss on the lucky amulet round his neck.

His 42-run gap having been bridged in a methodical 116 deliveries without a single boundary, Kohli grew a little freer and the Australians a little wearier. At the non-striker's end, he began rehearsing exotic thrusts and slices; he drove Starc, searching for a yorker, down the ground, and flicked him soundlessly off the pads; he advanced on Green and smoked him through the covers; the tiring spinners offered more latitude. When a low chance off Murphy to mid-off Green went begging, the crowd settled in to enjoy the show.

Kohli had by now found another showman to go with him, Axar Patel justifying his belated promotion to number seven by belabouring the exhausted spinners in their sixth full session of bowling. His gloriously free swing made the world's biggest cricket stadium look decidedly small. Otherwise, four days after the beloved Indian festival of Holi, this was a festival of the beloved Kohli – inevitably.

Ahmedabad Test 2023, Day 5

THE BATTLE OF THE SNOOZE (2023)

In Ahmedabad yesterday, a Test match ended as absurdly as it began, completing its arc from the prime ministers' everything-is-awesome opening pantomime to the players' agreement on a nothing-is-happening conclusion.

The Fourth Test at Narendra Modi Stadium was not altogether futile: two grand old stagers, Usman Khawaja and Virat Kohli, compiled big hundreds; two twenty-three-year-olds, Shubman Gill and Cameron Green, made maiden centuries substantiating their advance claims to being players of the next generation.

Otherwise, the final day played out as a variation on the rest of the series: the players pitted less against each other than against the conditions, Travis Head and Marnus Labuschagne not so much batting with intent as batting within tent – the little enclosures of their creases, the slight deviations of the turn.

Ravi Ashwin, in pursuit of his 700th international wicket, went to work as that lovely Indian writer Rajan Bala once described Srinivas Venkataraghavan bowling, like a dentist trying to extract a stubborn tooth. But neither he nor Axar Patel, on the ground where two years ago he took twenty wickets for 198 across consecutive matches on tailor-made turners against England, could do better than a wicket each.

Fast bowlers did not add to the eighteen wickets that the pace attacks of both sides have managed across four Tests. As on a long intercontinental airline flight, every time you looked up there seemed longer to go. When the players shook hands at 3.20 p.m., the match was a suitable case for euthanasia.

Thank the Board of Control for Cricket in India's propensity for pitch-fixing. The pitches have not been altogether terrible in this series – I have seen worse, and the cricket, thanks to the quality of the players, has at times been absorbing. But neither have the pitches been as good as they should have. And as the dreary tarmac rolled out for this match has testified, the habit of designing surfaces to specifications is exceedingly hard to break. It is like sawing a bit off one table leg; no matter how you adjust the other three legs, the table is never quite level again.

In the currency of this series, New Zealand have, against first England now Sri Lanka, played two of the most exciting five-day Tests of all time, on pitches where batters made hundreds, both fast and slow bowlers took five-fors, and the result was in doubt till the last ball. This Border–Gavaskar Trophy pivoted from a Test of two and a half days to a Test that would if permitted have lasted two and a half weeks. Curators can do better and they should be allowed to.

In any event, this is not a problem of acumen so much as of ideology. It's not a coincidence that the BCCI is the only cricket board in the world that maintains the old-fashioned 'control' in its title. From its communications to its commentators, it is obsessed with orchestrating every process, managing every variable, flattening every wrinkle – ever more so given its interpenetration with the BJP.

Pitch preparation represents the continuation of such policies, invincibility at home having become an important symbol of Indian hegemony. Oh sorry, those with delicate sensibilities would prefer us to keep politics out of sport – everyone, that is, except politicians, who are just fine with it. Anyway, the BCCI got what they bargained for here yesterday. The world's largest cricket stadium became the world's emptiest, a giant vortex of uninterest, all the better to see the untenanted vistas of saffron seating, but confirmation that this arriviste's vanity project was hardly the place for a game so important.

Twenty-two years since Australia's last Test at Eden Gardens in Kolkata, nineteen years since Australia's last Test at Wankhede Stadium in Mumbai, the vagaries of Indian venue selection remain impenetrable to outsiders. Not that the BCCI's potentates will care: after all, it's only seventeen days until Gujarat Titans commence the defence of their Indian Premier League title on this same ground. They're minting it.

But you did feel for the players, going through such futile motions. By the afternoon, even Ashwin's expressive shoulders were slumping a little every so often, while Rohit Sharma looked as desperate for inspiration as a writer staring at a blinking cursor – and I use the metaphor advisedly.

Khawaja looked on, with his weirdly non-specific 'lower leg injury', which could be anything from a stubbed toe to gangrene. Shreyas Iyer again sat the day out with his bad back, a setback for an exciting player, as getting into India's top six has historically been like trying to become a fifth Beatle or an additional musketeer. It all made for a sorry conclusion to a series that, at times, lived up to the vaunts that it, and not the match starting at The Oval on 18 June, was the proper climax of the World Test Championship. We must await that rematch in England to learn the real gap between these two teams.

The ICC
THE GREAT RIP-OFF (2023)

This year marks forty years since 'the longest suicide note in history' – the socialist wet dream of UK Labour's election manifesto after which the party spent nearly a decade and a half in the wilderness. International cricket now has its capitalist equivalent: the proposed model for revenue distribution for the next four years of International Cricket Council events, to be voted on at next month's annual meeting.

It will not be instant suicide, but, then, neither was UK Labour's. It is more like a smoothing of the dying pillow. As you may have read, it will involve the Board of Control for Cricket in India, already wealthy beyond the dreams of avarice, making off with nearly four in every ten dollars of the projected $900 million. In dollar terms, because the quantum is larger than the last distribution, everyone else will get a bit more, albeit that its value will be eaten away by inflation, exogenous and endogenous – the latter including the endlessly rising cost of cricket talent, inflated by the Indian Premier League.

But the huge expansion in India's rake off can only hugely worsen the asymmetry between that country and the rest of the cricket world, speed the global game's demise in favour of franchise cricket's dominance, and further entrench the influence of Indian crony capitalism. This was, perhaps, the idea all along, once the rights were split along geographic lines, obviously favouring the world's most populous nation, and a lesser degree England and Australia – India's craven enablers in 2014's Big Three shakedown, now, deservedly, busted to a slightly superior level of mendicant status. And this, for international cricket, is a disaster in the making – or, to be more precise, it is the continuation of a disaster already unfolding, as the number of genuinely competitive teams shrink and the pretensions of the ICC to actual governance dwindle almost entirely.

Think of it this way. Why does the BCCI need hundreds of millions more when the rights to the IPL are already worth $8 billion? The answer is, of course, that it hardly needs them at all; it merely wants them, like a Caesar his tribute. The attempt to justify the distribution pays lip service to merit by factoring in 'performance in ICC events, men and women' over the last decade and a half or so. But this logic, as Mike Atherton observed last week, is perfectly circular, given how India, England and Australia have hogged hosting rights, and thus home advantage, in that period. In any event, if it is anything like nine years ago, the arithmetic will have been reverse engineered to meet a previously agreed answer anyway.

Cue India's perfervid nationalists. That's 'our money', they will insist. But even leaving aside whether a board of control can effectively 'own' its fans, the money belongs not to India, or even the BCCI, but to cricket. As is the case for every ICC member, India in international cricket is the creation of generations of tours and tournaments, of rivalries and reciprocities, fostered by the whole world. No country can accomplish anything on its own in international cricket, and every country contributes. Some, for reasons of economy and demography, cannot offer so much. The objective should always be to put a floor beneath and handholds beside the weakest because from a generally rising standard everyone benefits – I'd call it 'levelling up', had Boris Johnson not, like everything he ever touched, debased it.

The funny thing is that, on one hand, the BCCI understands this. Look at the way it runs the IPL. Everyone has the same salary cap. Everyone plays the same number of home and away matches. Thanks to this, the newest participants have been able to enjoy instant success: Gujarat Titans carried off the last IPL in their first season and lead the way in this one. The equality of resources that is integral to the IPL's competitiveness may be harder to achieve in international cricket, where the countries are so different. But the principle is the same.

What's disturbing is that, on the other hand, the BCCI chooses to ignore the evidence in front of its own eyes. Greed? Wilfulness? Or is it politics? After all, the bigger the moneybags, the greater the scope for largesse. If you were in Ahmedabad for the Fourth Test, you already know how sickeningly the BCCI truckles to India's demagogic Prime Minister Narendra Modi and acts as an extension of his Bharatiya Janata Party.

Not that Australia can talk: when Modi arrives next week, our political commentariat will be queueing to kiss the hem of his kurta. But let's just say that it would be nice, given that we're all working so hard to generate it, to know where all that ICC moolah will end up, to be sure it was to be used for the benefit of cricket.

Where should the money go? In a nutshell, where it's needed most. Not only India but England and Australia still make good money from bilateral cricket, and have well-developed domestic structures. Why should they be effectively returning to the front of the cafeteria queue when they already have full trays? And, really, how is it possible that this game with allegedly global aspirations will allot barely one dollar in ten to cricket outside the Test-playing full members? Ah, but who will argue for that?

Probably nobody at the ICC, because no board dare step out of line, while also bearing some responsibility for their own predicament through funking governance reform ten years ago. Probably not too many in the media either, so lucrative are those Indian commentary gigs. International players? C'mon. India's players? The BCCI keeps them nice and busy, so as to take their minds off that the IPL upstreams most of its money, leaving less than one dollar in five for those who actually play it.

In the absence of anyone better, fans should. Because everyone has an interest in more competitive teams and more robust global competition – even, if they could just look beyond their own immediate self-enrichment, the BCCI. Otherwise international cricket is locked in a murder-suicide pact.

World Test Championship Final 2023

GIMME HEAD (2023)

Pretty soon you will look up the word 'counterpunch' in the dictionary and find a photo of Travis Head. Since the start of the last Ashes, he has become Australia's beacon of bouncebackability, as hard to bowl to as David Warner in his pomp and nearly as reliable. His 163 from 174 balls in the World Test Championship final, the first century in that fixture, has now taken this capability to the world, where previously it had been largely for home consumption – as reflected in a Test average in Australia of 58 and abroad of 27 going into the match. By the end of the Ashes, the gap should have narrowed further.

So what goes into a game like Head's, which Ben Stokes confided a week or so ago made him as challenging a rival as anyone in Australia's top six? 'He was so hard to bowl to in Australia when we were there last time [2021–22] because he just threw counterpunches,' said England's captain – no stranger to using opponents as speed bags.

'Counterpunching' – essentially the choice to attack when the orthodox response to a scoreline might be to defend or consolidate – may be counterintuitive but it is not illogical. Attacking field settings and bowling to wicket-seeking lengths are also favourable to enterprising batsmanship. So a bit of nerve can go a long way.

Head himself has also always been a batter harder to subdue than to get out. His maiden T20 hundred took fifty-three balls; he has made two List A double hundreds. He relies on fast hands to make up for flat feet, but his attacking options are broad: he not only savages width but owns anything bowled too straight; left-handedness and sharp running enhance his value further. That makes for rapid impact, and the boundaries that Head peeled off through and over the leg side after coming in with Australia having lost three wickets in the first twenty-five overs of the innings on Wednesday seemed to turn the match in a trice.

After sixteen deliveries, Head was 27. Bowlers who had come into the match after two months of one- and two-over spells in the Indian Premier League suddenly found themselves challenged to maintain consistency for anything longer.

The Oval's outfield is as frictionless as a polished mirror: Head would eventually hit twenty-four fours, one six and only one three. But India had to keep attacking in order to justify their decisions to bowl first and to exclude Ravi Ashwin (who has dismissed Head thrice in six encounters, just saying). Rohit Sharma's struggle to contain is reflected in the balls Head took for each of his half-centuries: 60, 56 and 48.

Any prolonged innings by Head, it is also true, contains its share of miscues and misfires, and this was no exception. Between the powerful cuts, pulls and punches, he scattered some wacky wafts and ham-fisted hooks. Twice he was hit on the bonce; he nearly dragged on; he top edged into space. When the ball was hip high, Head looked like he'd been administered a shock with an electric cattle prod. But his control percentage of

69 per cent proved less significant than his intent percentage of 100 per cent.

The South Australian reminds you of the phrase 'good bad books' that Orwell popularised for 'the kind of book that has no literary pretensions but which remains readable when more serious productions have perished'. For Head is a master of good bad batting. He lays no claim to easeful style or technical precision yet has found a way to accumulate more than 10,000 first-class runs.

It is not only the moustache that lends Head a 1970s retro chic; the unselfconscious roughness of his technique has defied the homogenising influences of coached conformism and video self-scrutiny. Like Doug Walters, he can contribute useful overs also.

Stokes and Baz McCullum now have more counter-counterpunching to contemplate. With his reliance on boundaries, Head will likely find himself hemmed in with more defensive fields; with his propensity for closing off, he will cop a lot more along the body. His Head-to-heads with Moeen Ali are unlikely to last long either way. Early thought in England had been that the Labuschagne–Smith axis would prove the home team's most formidable obstacle in these Ashes. Australia's number five has now countered that too.

World Cup Final 2023

XI VERSUS XI (2023)

This is why we love sport, yes? Here we are, all set for India's coronation at the end of a forty-five-day pageant of self-celebration. The terraces are walls of blue. The skies are scored with patriotic contrails. The boxes are full of puffed-up poohbahs and lotus-eating slebs. Oh look, there's Narendra Modi, in Narendra Modi Stadium, in Narendra Modiland, with its ambitions for a Narendra Modiworld. Oh dear, it's all spoiled by eleven happy-go-lucky Australians . . .

Nobody gave them a chance. Even I didn't give them much of one. India are just so good. A five-finger exercise I set myself during the World Cup was to pick a second Indian XI from players not in the first-choice team. You'd have Ruturaj Gaikwad and Yashasvi Jaiswal, Ravichandran Ashwin and Axar Patel, Ishan Kishan and Sanju Samson. Maybe Ajinkya Rahane to skipper and Umran Malik to bowl smoke. Crikey, they'd beat most international teams; they'd certainly flog the next-best Australians. By their abundance of talent, and by the game's enjoying such precedence, India will always trade at an advantage in the multi-format world.

But, in the end, it's always XI versus XI. It's where Orwell's timeworn 'war minus the shooting' metaphor falls short, because the sporting battlefield is arbitrarily even, the forces are by consent restricted, and efforts at interference stand out – they can even be seen as slightly shameful. Prepare for the Board of Control for Cricket in India to argue that in view of their overwhelming contribution to cricket's financial health, India should be allowed to field fifteen players to everyone else's eleven . . .

Anyway, to the final. Australia's first glimmer is at the toss, affording Pat Cummins the opportunity to bat under the lights. Three of the four World Cup games, and both IPL finals, have been won by the pursuers, so the gamble seems worthwhile; nor is it so mercilessly hot that fifty overs in the field will be a punishment. Then, a tiny portent. Mitchell Starc's second ball floats wide in search of inswing. Rohit Sharma thrashes and eyes swivel to the point boundary. But Travis Head, right where the data says he needs to be, tracks speedily left and saves two runs. And even as the Indians strain to get loose, they go on feeling an Australian check. At eight an over, they exceed their Cup Powerplay average. But the Australian fielding probably saves a further 20 runs and heralds the breakthrough, Head catching Rohit, running back, diving forward, celebrating perfunctorily. This, as Head described it later, was cricket in the best Australian vein. Thought he had no chance. Had a go anyway. Was surprised to catch it. Wasn't inclined to make a fuss.

Two balls on from the Powerplay, India lose a third, and Australia are suddenly three further wickets from that invitingly elongated home tail: number eight Shami, whose highest score in a hundred ODIs is 25; number nine Bumrah, whose highest score in eighty-eight ODIs is 16. Sure, there's SKY to come, but he's unproven in ODIs and hardly a like-for-like swap with Hardik Pandya. So now it is circumstances, as well as the

Australians, bearing down on India's fourth-wicket partners. Cummins distributes the bowling load widely; the part-timers get off lightly; the fielding, a couple of overthrows aside, remains wonderfully vigilant. India find themselves in a game; it's a while since they have been.

Though the cameras dwell on Virat Kohli's handsome features as he achieves his fifth consecutive score of 50 or more, the game has commenced an arc away from the hosts. Whether Kohli and KL Rahul spent too long over their runs will long be debated; after all, people still wonder whether Mike Brearley and Geoffrey Boycott spent too long over theirs in the 1979 final. I'm more inclined to be forgiving: the design flaw of the order was always bound to catch up with India at some stage, likeliest of all in the final against the strongest opposition. Kohli, generally so decisive, seldom if ever drags on – a dismissal characteristic of conglomerated thoughts. Now he does, and Ravindra Jadeja, with so little recent batting, is all at sea against the reversing ball. It all gets very messy until last-man-picked Marnus Labuschagne ends it with his fourth run out of the tournament.

Now it's over to Australia's other selection long shot, Head, included in the squad while still convalescent, and having gone six weeks without a hit before reappearing against New Zealand in Dharamshala. Thanks to the dew, 240 is effectively 210; thanks to Head, Australia take 15 off Bumrah's first over. Australia are three down after seven overs but have already reduced the required run rate to 4.5. Shami's lethality to left-handers does not prevent Head from picking two boundaries off him in the last over of the Powerplay, affording Labuschagne time to settle the way he likes; in fact, Head has a fifty-eight-ball 50 by the time Labuschagne first finds the boundary.

You've seen all this, so further detail is probably superfluous. So let's just concentrate on that brooding atmosphere, that eddying disbelief. When cricket and crowd feed off one another in India, there can be a feeling of playing against a whole country. Quiet, such as that now pervading Modi Stadium, is oppositely telling. The crowd know it. They ache to cheer, but cannot cajole themselves to do so. As Glenn Maxwell and Labuschagne complete the winning run, the hush renders the cries from the Australian dugout audible.

Now, a realist could well argue that India won this World Cup anyway: they were able to jog around the rest of the cricket world like traffic cones for six weeks; they will rake off almost four in every ten dollars the tournament generated. The year 1983 portended great cricket change; 2023 confirms little more than that Australia is represented by an experienced, spirited, resourceful cricket team, that is even now approaching the end of its life cycle. The balance of global cricket power, politically, demographically and economically, is fundamentally undisturbed; the BCCI and BJP will remain separated by a fag paper; the international game will continue as an elite racket. Cricket's World Cup had ten teams and forty-eight matches; football's next World Cup will have forty-eight teams and 104 matches.

But there'll be a satisfaction elsewhere today at India finishing second – the same satisfaction experienced when Australia, in its pomp, was bested, every so often (2001 in India, 2005 in England etc.). Nobody now would remember the *Titanic* had it simply arrived in New York; India hitting an Australian iceberg is an infinitely superior sporting story.

India today is as much a 'birthplace of giants' as England ever was. Gandhi, Ambedkar, Nehru, Sardar Patel. Rabindranath Tagore, Amitabh Bachchan, Ravi Shankar. Narendra Modi, can you hear me? Your boys took a hell of a beating!

T20 World Cup, 2024 Super 8s
ROHIT'S REVENGE (2024)

What goes around comes around in sport and what went around at Gros Islet in the penultimate Super 8s game of this T20 World Cup was Rohit Sharma's bat. Even in repose it is a beautiful object, always spick and span, broad and deep. In action, it seems to expand to double the chunk, twice the heft.

For the last couple of years, Rohit has been leading India's white ball encounters by example, setting out to place his personal imprint on every scenario. On occasion, it has not worked: his miscue in the World Cup final was a heavy self-inflicted blow to India's prospects. But his assault on Mitchell Starc in the third over of India's innings turned the Australians back on themselves. Starc kept searching for swing; Rohit kept swinging. Twenty-nine runs was the toll and only the last six over third man carried a hint of hazard. A punitive four down the ground may have been the best shot of all.

By that stage, India had lost Kohli to a protestatious pull shot, seemingly justifying Mitchell Marsh's decision to go with the trend of the tournament rather than the trend at the ground by sending India in. Marsh did the same against Afghanistan, even if the graver Australian error was spilling six catches in a defeat that made this match unanticipatedly consequential – virtually a must-win for his team. He'll think twice before doing it again after today.

When Rohit reached 50 off nineteen deliveries, his partners had eked two singles out of thirteen deliveries, and you did get the feeling this was personal. Rohit has been the losing captain to Australia in two formats in the last year; a third would have been an affront. He has had a subdued tournament by his standards. But the slog-swept six off Pat Cummins, to whom he had had to defer at Modi Stadium and The Oval, was *mano a mano* cricket at its best. Rohit affected indifference, but must surely have cast a sideways glance at the roof from which the ball needed retrieval. Starc finally – belatedly, perhaps – went round the wicket and under Rohit's bat, arresting India's caper.

Suryakumar Yadav and Shivam Dube hit their T20 high notes and Hardik Pandya capped off his innings against Afghanistan and Bangladesh with a handy seventeen-ball cameo to push India past 200. The currency of the 200 total may have been debased in the Indian Premier League, but this tournament has reflated it. It looked daunting. It *was* daunting and grew more so when David Warner ignored a floating slip and went looking for a ball from Arshdeep Singh too short to drive and too near to cut – a stroke of strange indeterminacy for one usually so decisive, and from international cricket a muted sign off.

The crucial intervention in Australia's reply came after they had surged to 1/65 in the Powerplay thanks to some emphatic strokes from Marsh and Travis Head. A metre higher or a metre either side and Marsh's pull shot off Kuldeep Yadav would have left no change out of six; Axar Patel, loitering off the fence, timed his leap exactly. It was the kind of show-stopping catch that has eluded Australia in this tournament – the kind of catch that Marnus Labuschagne pulled off in the Vitality Blast a few days ago. Nobody seems to think Australia missed Labuschagne in this tournament, but I wonder whether fielding has not mattered more for the unexpectedly low scores of the last few weeks. There are some poor fielders in this line-up and a few less mobile units.

Australia needed something and Glenn Maxwell almost provided it, maintaining the rate with his instant energy and bizarro flair. In the IPL, he looked like he needed witness protection; to this T20 World Cup he has responded with growing buoyancy; might he have bowled today, given that the medium-pace looked samey at times? It took Kuldeep Yadav to do him in with the latest in the tournament's sequence of significant googlies, also delivered by Adam Zampa, Adil Rashid and Tabraiz Shamsi. Thanks to T20 cricket, BJT Bosanquet's original cricket innovation is 120 years young.

When Bumrah's change of pace ended Head's 76 off forty-three balls, 56 were needed from the last twenty-one deliveries, and Tim David, despite flashes, has not proved quite the finisher Australia hoped for when first he loomed. And so Australia, who a week ago were eyeing the mantelpiece where a third global trophy might sit, fail to add to their silverware. Their defeat by Afghanistan coincided with an earthquake, but this defeat might prove more seismic, with the pending departures of Warner and possibly Matthew Wade. Meanwhile, Rohit advances, swinging that always pristine bat in glorious arcs.

Border–Gavaskar Trophy 2024–25

FIVE OF THE BEST

No game is so various as cricket in its durations. It has been played for ten days without a result; it can, in the event of a T20 Super Over, be decided in ten minutes. The general direction recently has been to further and terser abbreviation – from fifty overs a side, to twenty, to ten. This summer, Australia and India will shirk that trend, extending the Border–Gavaskar Trophy to a full-dress five-Test series.

The combatants have played as many as six Tests in a series, but that was in 1979, when India was yet to partake of cricket a day at a time. Australia hosted five in 1991–92. Reverting to that length is no small thing. In an era in which there is little incentive to play series longer than three Tests, and most bilateral meetings stop at two, five almost constitutes a genre of its own: only the Ashes and India v England are played over comparable distances, with their manifold additional challenges of environment and attrition. Nobody does anything without an eye to the bottom line, so a fifth Test must be assumed a paying proposition. Yet let us say that any initiative to expand Test cricket's footprint, which in some countries has shrunk to a toehold, today stands out like a good deed in a naughty world. The big just got bigger, and the already excellent better yet.

Australia can hardly be said to hold terrors for India anymore, now that the visitors have beaten their hosts twice in six years. Rohit Sharma's team will bring considerable experience of recent success – last time even with the arduous exactions of COVID-19 biosecurity. They start with the advantage of incumbency, as it were, holding the trophy retained last year at home. Nor will either team start with many new faces. David Warner is done; Cheteshwar Pujara may be. But there will be a goodly proportion of faded caps in the field. Names don't win Tests in Australia. India came in 2011–12 with a team of galácticos, only to find them more like, as Rahul Dravid put it, 'creaking Terminators'. The crucial match-ups, however, can already be glimpsed, and they are not so different to the Border–Gavaskar Trophy in 2023: Cummins v Rohit, Lyon v Kohli, Bumrah v Usman, Ashwin v Smith. And sport is unlike movies in that sequels can be at least as good if not better than the originals.

Since the teams last met on a Test match field, they have traded white ball blows, with Australia superior at fifty overs, India at twenty. Such encounters would be easy to dismiss. Who cares at Ashes time who won the last Australia v England ODI or T20I? But maybe, with these antagonists, it matters just a little more, thanks in part to the overlap in red and white ball personnel, in part to the prestige the rivalry is now accorded. India's last win in Australia inspired two books: *Mission Domination* by Boria Majumdar and Kushan Sarkar, and *The Miracle Makers* by Bharat Sundaresan and Gaurav Joshi. In modern publishing terms, that is itself a miracle, a testament of the momentous, and a comment on change.

I started the introduction with the proposition that cricket is a deep bond between Australia and India in an otherwise shallow relationship. While true, that is shifting. Those with

Indian ancestry are a youthful and fast-growing proportion of Australia's population. Twenty years ago, Indian faces in Australian crowds were a rarity. Now the MCG brims for India v Pakistan let alone India v Australia. It is an opportunity for the diaspora population to reassert its cultural identity, and also for Australians to recognise the newcomers in their midst.

In great sports rivalries, the antagonists define themselves in contradistinction. *We* become everything *they* are not. While England and Australia have a vast common heritage, England in the Ashes still feel like the establishment and Australia the upstart – as underlined at Lord's last year. Australia v India likewise affords a contrast, of old versus new, of Australia's status as co-founder of Test cricket v India's emergent economic heft. Could Australia even be an underdog? It is not a mantle that has ever come naturally to us on a sporting field, least of all a cricket ground. Yet twenty-six million population versus 1.4 billion must count for something . . .

Predictions for this summer are at this distant worth very little, but two observations may be worth making. These are two massively experienced and garlanded teams setting out, as remarked, across the longest of cricket distances. So while it is true that on any given day it is XI versus XI, India's strength in depth is not to be underestimated as a factor. By the back end of a long series, gaps will have emerged in both first-choice XIs. By the terminus of 2020–21, India were absent Kohli, Bumrah, Ashwin, Jadeja, Hardik and Vihari, yet still handed a full-strength home team its soundest defeat in a decade after losing the toss in Brisbane. The only way the series could have been improved would have been by a Fifth Test. This summer we'll have one.